ECONOMIC MANAGEMENT AND ECONOMIC DEVELOPMENT IN PERU AND COLOMBIA

ECONOMIC CHOICES BEFORE THE DEVELOPING COUNTRIES

General Editor: Keith Griffin, Professor and Chairman, Economics
Department, University of California, Riverside

This series of volumes contains the results of a major research programme.
Its purpose is to assess the rich and varied experiences of economic
development in recent decades and to test the strengths and limitations of
the most widely advocated policy approaches or development strategies
against actual practice.

Charles Harvey and Stephen R. Lewis, Jr
POLICY CHOICE AND DEVELOPMENT PERFORMANCE IN
    BOTSWANA

Azizur Rahman Khan and Mahabub Hossain
THE STRATEGY OF DEVELOPMENT IN BANGLADESH

Rosemary Thorp
ECONOMIC MANAGEMENT AND ECONOMIC DEVELOPMENT
    IN PERU AND COLOMBIA

Economic Management and Economic Development in Peru and Colombia

Rosemary Thorp

Fellow of St Antony's College, Oxford

in association with the
OECD Development Centre

First published 1991

Published by
MACMILLAN ACADEMIC AND PROFESSIONAL LTD
Houndmills, Basingstoke, Hampshire RG21 2XS
and London
Companies and representatives
throughout the world

and

Organisation for Economic Co-operation and Development
2, rue André Pascal
75775 Paris Cedex 16

Printed in Great Britain by Billing and Sons Ltd,
Worcester

British Library Cataloguing in Publication Data
Thorp, Rosemary *1940–*
Economic management and economic development in Peru and
Colombia. — (Economic choices before the developing
countries).
1. South America. Economic conditions, history
I. Title
330.98

ISBN 0–333–54687–3 (hardcover)
ISBN 0–333–54688–1 (paperback)

For Kate

Contents

List of Tables

List of Figures and Maps

Foreword

This volume forms part of a series on economic choices before the developing countries. The experience of economic development over more than four decades is varied and rich and it is possible to learn much from it, both analytically and in terms of economic policy. Already it is clear that there are many paths to development although some no doubt are more circuitous than others. Enough time has elapsed and enough data are available to make it possible to test the strengths and limitations of the most widely advocated policy approaches or development strategies against actual practice.

This was done within a comparative framework in my own contribution to the series entitled Alternative Strategies for Economic Development. That volume as well as this one on Economic Management and Economic Development in Peru and Colombia are but a part of a much larger research programme on the economic choices or alternatives facing the Third World in the closing years of this century. The research programme and this series which reports the results of the research programme were sponsored by the OECD Development Centre in Paris and received the personal and unstinting support of the President of the Development Centre, Louis Emmerij.

This comparative study of economic policy-making in Peru and Colombia by Rosemary Thorp is fascinating because it enables us to assess two very different styles of management in countries which in many other respects are rather similar. Peru and Colombia share a common history, culture and language; they are similar in that the geography of both is dominated by the Andes; and by the middle of the 1960s both countries were searching for a new development strategy, the experience with import substituting industrialisation having been broadly comparable.

Apart from its comparative focus, three features distinguish this book from the other country studies in the series. First, Rosemary Thorp situates her analysis within an historical context stretching back to the nineteenth century. This is highly appropriate since unlike most Third World countries in Asia and Africa, Peru and Colombia have enjoyed political independence for more than a century-and-a-half. Secondly, the economic analysis is embedded within an institutional framework and this enables the author to highlight the peculiar characteristics of each country. That is, the structural features of the two countries are shown to be an integral part of the explanation of policy and performance. Finally, the author supplements the material obtained from more conventional sources with information obtained from interviews with senior politicians, high ranking civil servants and prominent businessmen. The reader thus is able to learn not only what in fact was done but what some of the major actors at the time thought was being done.

Peru's economy has experienced boom and bust and its economic policy has moved in parallel, swinging violently from the radical populism of Velasco to ultra-orthodoxy under Bermúdez and Belaunde back to heterodox populism under García. Colombia's economy, in contrast, has exhibited unspectacular but steady progress and its economic policy on the whole has been subtle and conservative with a judicious addition of heterodox measures. Policy-making in Peru has been very highly centralised whereas in Colombia regional interests have exercised more influence. Foreign involvement in the economy has been substantial in Peru whereas Colombia has been careful to preserve its national autonomy and until recently foreign participation has been modest.

A central question is what accounts for these differences in policy and performance. Rosemary Thorp argues that the contrast between the two countries is due in part to differences in the character of the export sector and to differences in the strength of regional interests. In Colombia exports historically were dominated by coffee. Indeed by 1925 coffee exports accounted for 78 per cent of the total. Foreign participation was absent, production was on small- and medium-sized farms and the need for internal transport, processing, banking and shipping encouraged diversification in the rest of the economy and local industrialisation. Exports from Peru, on the other hand, were based either on a plantation crop (sugar) where land ownership was highly concentrated or on the extraction of raw materials (copper, oil). Foreign influences were strong from the beginning and the expansion of Peruvian exports contributed little to the general development of the economy.

Despite its centralising tendencies – under Velasco the state accounted for more than half of total investment and half of output in the modern sector – the capacity of the state and public administration in Peru to manage the economy is limited and hence it is difficult to implement any set of economic policies, be they orthodox or heterodox. The relationship between the state and private sector is one of distrust and consequently it is difficult to create and then sustain a partnership in development between the two sectors. In Colombia, the characteristics of the predominant coffee export sector, in combination with the play of competing regional interests, helped to create a relationship between the state and the private sector based on mutual confidence and respect. This in turn helped to shape a political and economic system capable of formulating and implementing workable, coherent development policies.

Colombia's record of macroeconomic management, in periods of crisis and in booms, is superior to Peru's. The populist experiments in Peru have turned out to be less successful in the long run than the incrementalist and more consistent policies adopted in Colombia. But there is a nasty sting in the tail! Both countries have a very unequal distribution of income, the improvements in indicators of basic needs satisfaction are similar in both countries and 'neither country has yet gone very far in attacking its poverty problems'. The one big difference is that in Colombia many more women receive an education and this has contributed to a lower fertility rate, a more rapid decline in the infant mortality rate and a slower rate of growth of the population.

Clearly, competence in macroeconomic management is not enough. Contemporary Colombia, like Peru, suffers from serious social violence and if anything, the crises in public order in both countries are becoming worse. Indeed in Peru the state is weak, has lost control of the polity as well as the economy and is even in danger of disintegration. Events in Colombia have not gone so far, but there too the state as a political and economic entity has been gravely weakened. Both countries are experiencing a boom in the illegal export of drugs which they are unable to control. In Peru the production of coca on small plots in impoverished regions has helped the poor, reduced income inequality and contributed much desperately needed foreign exchange. One could thus imagine coca in Peru playing a role analogous to coffee in Colombia. Yet in Colombia the processing and exporting of cocaine, while contributing significant amounts to gross domestic product and export receipts, have increased economic instability and accentuated inequalities in the distribution of income. Thus cocaine is playing a role in Colombia not so different from that once played in Peru by exports of minerals and oil. The analogy can be pushed further: Colombia today appears to be shifting away from its older pattern of development in favour of a natural resource-led growth strategy based on oil and coal and relying on large-scale foreign participation. One is thus left wondering whether the contrasts between Colombia and Peru will tend to diminish in future or whether they will continue to pursue distinctive approaches to economic development.

Keith Griffin, Series Editor

Paris

March 1990

Preface

'We have a project for consuming food we produce here in Peru, not imported food.' 'We took it to the Palace – we marched in a big group.' 'The police didn't like it – my arm is still sore where they hit me.' 'We haven't heard anything.'

Gladis and Carmen,
Directors of 'People's Kitchens'
in the slums of Lima.

This book has been written out of intense curiosity and frustration, though neither has been substantially assuaged in the writing. It is a book that poses far more questions than it answers, for which I make no apology at all. The project began with a single frustration: how could one country – Colombia – so consistently handle short-term economic management rather well and another – Peru – so poorly? The search for an answer sent me back into the history of the two countries, and opened up questions concerning class structure and interest group formation which a mere economist is ill-equipped to handle. But, as if this was not enough, as the project developed a 'second level' of frustration was added: how could such different records of efficiency and coherence in economic management permit such similar stories of growing violence, inequality and threat to the fabric of society? How could 'good behaviour' in economic management terms make so little difference in regard to all our deepest concerns about poverty, violence and inequality?

In the last eighteen months, the media have made us all aware of the 'down' side of the Colombian story. The assassination by narcotics interests not only of major figures in the judicial and legal system but also of the only Presidential candidate prepared to challenge such interests, has forced tough measures against drugs which in the short term have escalated violence. The sense that the legitimacy of the political and legal system is under threat is strong, as members of the judiciary resign and leave the country. Meanwhile Peru likewise faces growing violence, as the terrorist acts of right-wing para-military groups escalate on top of the steady spread of the Maoist-style Sendero Luminoso. Left-wing parties in particular found it understandably difficult to field candidates in the elections of April 1990 given the rate of assassination of left-wing mayors and other civic figures.

Yet despite the blackness of this picture, anyone deeply involved in either country cannot fail to have some sense of optimism, too, and this is the third 'level' of frustration and curiosity, since the grounds for optimism are hard to pin down and rationalise, and it is harder still to know what conclusions to draw. The issue is particularly important, since a controversial study of Peru by Hernando de Soto[1] has recently stressed the grounds for optimism as lying in the informal sector, if only it can be freed from the deadening weight of government restrictions which has created it, and so be able to grow and blend into the formal sector. My own perspective is different, coming out of my study of Peruvian economic history. While government restrictions are indeed deadening, the existence of the informal sector is principally due to the form of development followed, and its adequate evolution requires a more positive and 'enabling' role from the state than De Soto allows. Nevertheless it is at the grassroots that I also find a source of optimism: in the strength and coherence of groups such as the one quoted at the start of this chapter. The popular organisations received a strong (unintended) impulse, as we shall see, under the radical-national military regime of the 1970s: their growth in twenty years has been dramatic and the self-help and community solidarity which they represent are today a central means of defence against both economic crisis and growing violence. Their very success means that they are also fragile, since they are increasingly recognised as a target by the guerrilla movement. The frustration of course is that such energy is not channelled, either by the state or by the political parties. The project produced by Gladis and Carmen and the rest of their group was not taken up, as we hear in the quotation (despite the fact that it corresponds to a favourite idea of President García when he first took office). Instead the government turned to foreign food aid, which will endanger all that such groups as this have worked for, in developing supply lines from peasant producers and autonomous community groups to run the kitchens.[2] It remains to be seen how the new Government of President Fujimori will respond to such challenges.

In Colombia the source of optimism is completely different and perhaps more obvious, though not necessarily any stronger. The vitality and coherence to be found in movements such as the 'popular kitchens' of Peru is less in evidence in Colombia – perhaps precisely because the state, the elite groups and the political parties have always been more in evidence. The optimism derives from the relative sophistication and health of the entire management system, which is undoubtedly facing a severe challenge but is also well-equipped, and backed by impressive resources in terms of academic and technical skills.

Needless to say, the book does not even tackle, let alone deal adequately, with all these questions. In particular, what 'superior economic management' reflects and originates in is left an open question, hopefully sufficiently provoking to the political scientists that answers will be forthcoming. It seems obvious that the answer has to do with the comparatively harmonious and cohesive class structure of Colombia, plus its regional elements necessitating sophisticated trading mechanisms with the centre. This *permits* the 'learning by doing' which successive chapters emphasize, and perhaps provides a security which makes possible the relative pragmatism which is also a repeated comparative theme.

The focus and plan of the book are as follows. The core initial hypothesis, that Colombia's short-term economic management is superior to Peru's, is explored in Chapters 4–9, which cover the two decades since 1967. 1967 is taken as a significant date, since for different reasons in the two cases it represented a discontinuity, a point of re-evaluation, as the relatively easy boom years of the 1960s gave way to more unsettled conditions. For Peru this in fact represented a deep crisis in the former model of export-led development, as Chapter 2 explains. The governments of Juan Velasco and Carlos Lleras redefined the rules in both cases, though in totally different ways. In the two decades that followed, the analysis gives especial attention to the management of external shocks, both positive and negative. Chapters 1 to 3 provide what I hope will be seen as vital historical ingredients to explain the rather remarkable differences identified in the two 'management stories'. Chapter 3 attempts to 'take stock' of the two countries as the relatively easy period of post-war expansion comes to an end with the decade of the 1960s. As I have indicated, however, we are left with the question 'so what'? Chapter 3 begins to explore the vital questions of poverty, distribution and basic needs, but these are taken up more fully in Chapter 10, which looks at the quality of economic management in relation to longer-run development issues, as opposed to those addressed in the middle chapters of the book, and reaches conclusions which radically shift the balance of the appraisal of the two countries. No reader should omit this final chapter, which draws together the various themes of the book, reassesses the different strands of evidence, and forms the conclusion.

The sources used are largely government data and documents. The Memorias of different Ministries were an excellent source, particularly for Colombia. In addition I carried out interviews in 1987 and 1988 with businessmen and public sector figures, exploring the relationship between the public and private sectors and the nature of public investment planning. I was also able to gain insight into Colombian economic management by talking to most of those who played a central role in economic policy in the Lleras administration and many from later governments.

My first debt is therefore to all those who gave me time – often large amounts of it – to talk about these topics. I have tried to acknowledge where I could and preserve confidentiality where that was required.

Next, many people have read and commented, always helpfully. Alan Angell has been throughout a careful and encouraging reader. Jorge Chávez and Felipe Portocarrero gave a great deal of time to reading and commenting, though I fear I have not been able to follow up the themes they would have had me develop. I received helpful comments on some chapters from Eduardo Lora, Victor Bulmer Thomas, José Antonio Ocampo, Alicia Puyana, Nohra Marulanda, Sven Winder and Gabriel Turbay. Conversations with Gustav Ranis were helpful in making me think about policy-making.

Malcolm Deas immensely illuminated my understanding of Colombia, while Adolfo Figueroa, Javier Iguiñiz and Richard Webb have done the same for Peru over many years. Richard generously shared with me much unpublished material. I owe too much to too many good friends in both countries to be able even to start naming them. One exception however is essential: the 'home base' I have always had in each country has been an essential part of my work: Carmen and Esteban Kisic and Carlos and Nohra Marulanda have taken me into their families with extraordinary generosity. Claudia Rodriguez, Bishnupriya Gupta, Martha Delgado, Catalina Crane and Carlos Londoño worked as research assistants at different stages of the project. Martha deserves especial mention for surviving the struggle with my chaotic bibliography. Caroline Wise was as always an endlessly willing and expert typist. The Institute of Economics and Statistics provided superb facilities. The Leverhulme Foundation provided partial funding, as did the Development Research Centre of the OECD. It was Keith Griffin's presence there, and unrelenting insistence that I must finish, that are responsible for the fact though not the content of the book.

Notes

1. *The Other Path*, by Hernando De Soto. We return to the issues raised by this book in Chapter 6. The book focuses on individual, small-scale endeavour, rather than the communal action I find impressive.
2. The awareness of the group of such dangers is however impressive. This is based on a meeting with six such directors of 'comedores populares', or people's kitchens, Lima, September 1989. As they said, 'What's important about us is that we're independent, of the people.' They could see that outside aid could mean interference that would sap that independence.

1 Colombian Coffee, Entrepreneurship and the State

AN HISTORICAL PERSPECTIVE

Had anyone attempted to predict in 1900 the outcome of a comparative assessment of Peru and Colombia, he or she would have been far sighted indeed to get it right. Colombia was enmeshed in civil war and an inflation that was to scar the memories of policy makers for decades. Industry was virtually non-existent, while as we shall see Peru had experienced a significant and locally-led decade of industrialisation in the 1890s.

What was to change radically this relative position was the surge in coffee production in Colombia, as order was restored and settlers moved west, opening up new lands and producing the remarkable rise in coffee as a percentage of exports from 31 per cent in 1910 to 69 per cent by 1919 and 78 per cent by 1925 (Table 1.1). As is well-known, the hilly terrain of the coffee belt resulted in a predominant pattern of small-scale farms. Large farms also existed, with the mix varying regionally, but in most areas small producers constituted the greater part of the land area.[1] With the surge of settlement, coffee revealed itself as a crop unique in many ways in its capacity to generate development – at least at that time and in that place.

Take first the question of infrastructure. In the early twentieth century, Colombia's transport system still turned on rivers, with the Rio Magdalena as the main artery connecting the coffee-growing regions to the port of Barranquilla and bringing imports to the main internal centres of population (see Map 1.1). But the Magdalena was vulnerable to drought, which paralysed the transport system every few years. And with time erosion was making the rivers even less dependable.[2] A patchy but useful railway network did exist, as the map shows. However, as of the early 1920s there were a number of obvious and crucial needs. First, the Magdalena route itself needed improvement, in the form of canals and the major port works of Bocas de Ceniza to clear the river entrance.

Second, with the opening of the Panama Canal in the 1910s the Pacific had begun to assume a new importance; the new coffee areas in Caldas and Antioquia needed an efficient and reliable route linking them by rail to the Pacific coast, and a new port needed building at Buenaventura.

Table 1.1
Colombia: Composition of Exports by Value[a] 1877–1960
(percentage shares)

	Coffee	Bananas	Petroleum	Gold[b]	Tobacco	Hides
1877[c]	16	–	–	35	6	9
1905	39	3[d]	–	14	3	6
1910	31	9	–	19	2	10
1915	52	6	–	17	1	12
1919[e]	69	3	–	1	2	11
1925	78	7	8[f]	2	–	4
1930	54	8	23	8	–	3
1935	55	6	20	13	–	2
1940	44	3	24	25	–	1
1945	74	1	16	–	–	1
1950	78	2	16	–	1	–
1955	82	3	11	2	–	–
1960	71	3	17	–	–	–

Source: Urrutia and Arrubla (1970).
   Revista del Banco de la República.

Notes:
[a]Components do not sum to 100, as only principal exports are included.
[b]Non-monetary exports only.
[c]1900 figures are not given.
[d]1906 figure.
[e]1920 figures are not given.
[f]1926 figures.

It was remarkably fortunate that this strong demand coincided with a flood of money into Latin America that is only paralleled in the 1970s. As the First World War came to an end, the United States found itself abruptly a net creditor to the tune of US$3 billion – having begun the war a net debtor to the same amount – and the 1920s found a flood of salesmen descending on Latin America offering both products and cash.[3] Only countries already suffering an export crisis, such as Ecuador, did not share in the bonanza. We shall see that in the 1970s Colombia was wise enough to resist such offers; in the 1920s the strong demands from productive sectors at least saw to it that a relatively high percentage of the cash went through to productive needs.

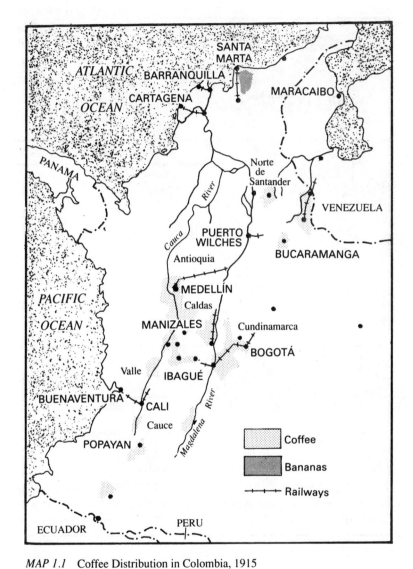

MAP 1.1 Coffee Distribution in Colombia, 1915

SOURCES: Garcia (1937), McGreevy (1971), Beyer (1947), *Colombian Review, Commerce Reports, Diaro Oficial.*

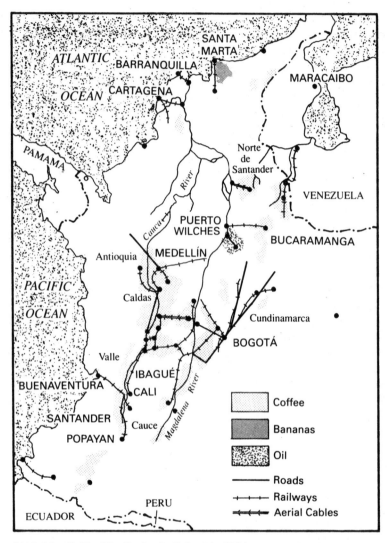

MAP 1.2   Coffee Distribution in Colombia, 1934

SOURCES : as Map 1.1, plus *Memoria de Obras Públicas* (1926), *Revista de Ministerio de Obras Públicas* (enero–abril 1925), *Anuario General de Estadística*, Federación Nacional de Cafeteros (1933)

A vivid visual demonstration of this comes from Maps 1.1 and 1.2, which show how in the course of only 19 years national and departmental governments used foreign finance to integrate and transform the production and trading patterns of the country.

The key national project was the extension of the Pacific railway, from Cali to Popayán and from Cali to Ibagué. Regionally for Antioquia it was the finishing of the Amaga railway up to the Cauca river, opening the Amaga coalfields and linking coffee growers to the Pacific railway. Caldas, which by the 1930s was to displace Antioquia as the leading coffee department, was busy building its own links to the Pacific railway, as well as completing a cable link up to the Magdalena. Cundinamarca improved the links between Bogotá and the Magdalena. The coffee and commerce sectors in Norte de Santander pushed to shift exports from a route through Venezuela to the Magdalena. Roads played a role too, but were of less importance.

This is the background to the figures on transport investment: we find that transport represented nearly 80 per cent of public investment 1925–30 – an incredible sum of about $280 million compared with some $30 million in Peru.[4]

There was an obvious political element in the investment: the motive of national unity. The lack of a national transport system diminished the power of the central government while increasing the 'caciquismo' of distant regions and towns.[5] But it also clearly responded to coffee and wider commercial interests[6] and opened up the internal trade in food-stuffs. The Pacific railway connected the sugar producing area of Valle with the home market, the Canal de Dique opened up the interior to purchasing meat, rice and sugar. The North and Northeast railway opened the wheat and fruit regions of Boyacá and Santander.[7]

But coffee not only led to such indirect stimulus to other agriculture: it also had a number of quite direct and rather unusual links to other activities. We will see how sugar and cotton competed directly with food for domestic consumption in Peru and this is the typical situation we would expect. In Colombia, however, the countless small coffee farms virtually all produced some food – some interplanted for shade in a direct complementarity, such as bananas. A contemporary British description speaks of the small planter who accounts for 75 per cent of the crop 'and whose needs from the outside world are small, his subsidiary crops of maize, sugar, yucca, etc, and his fowls and pigs, being sufficient to sustain him'.[8] Between the increasing internal trade in food-stuffs and this degree of self sufficiency, food imports were less than half of their level in Peru.

The relationship between coffee and industry has been a fascinating and controversial theme in Colombian economic history. Every author has felt that it was positive, but the analysis has differed sharply. For some, such as McGreevey and Hugo López, the small-scale labour-intensive nature of coffee production represented a mass market at an early stage.[9] Others (Arango, Palacios) have stressed the poverty and miserable work conditions in coffee production, which combined with self sufficiency could hardly have comprised a stimulus to industry.[10]

While the evidence for the second view is clear,[11] it is still the case that the wide spread of incomes at the intermediary stage, via money lenders and the thousands of agents buying coffee and conducting the simple processing required, reflected a spread of income which was a stimulus to regional consumption. The commercial side of coffee activity happened – and still happens – in the coffee regions: the major export houses all had their bases in Antioquia, Caldas, etc. This is the opposite of the Peruvian situation: here the merchants such as Duncan Fox were based in the ports. The accumulation in the commerce sector which resulted from coffee took place in the coffee regions, and in addition incipient industrial activities in these interior regions benefited from considerable natural protection. Thus we can begin to make sense of one of the most striking facts about industry in Colombia: that there are at least four substantial regional industrial centres. This arose from the availability of surplus, from natural protection, and from the existence of a market, though not the mass market postulated by McGreevey.[12]

How far capital and initiative from coffee was actually the initial stimulus to industry has also been much debated. Our own research on industry in Medellín, Antioquia, in the 1920s yields convincing evidence: of the 75 firms we could trace, a remarkable 65 could be linked by ownership data to some part of the coffee sector – exporting, processing or producing.[13] There were one or two instances of immigrants playing a role, and one foreign firm. A stronger contrast with Peruvian industry at the same date is hard to imagine. In textiles, the leading sector, we continued to trace the large number of new firms appearing in the 1930s and 1940s: of 17, 14 were linked in some way to coffee – as well as to existing textiles firms.[14] The process was aided by the fact that after the initial investment coffee tended to need little reinvestment of surplus. This meant a surplus available in local hands, ripe for investment in other sectors.

A further and very specific linkage from coffee was to capital goods. From the early days of coffee production, there was a demand for simple coffee pulpers and roasting and cleaning machinery (Bell, 1921, p. 234). From the nineteenth century small foundries in Antioquia and Cundinamarca were turning out simple agricultural machinery. With the development of a manual depulper in the early twentieth century the technology became accessible to very small farmers (Palacios, 1979, p. 222). The foundries also made machinery for cleaning the jute used for coffee sacks. The same firms also made machinery for the chocolate, sugar and tobacco sectors.

What is interesting is again the contrast with Peru. We will see how by the early twentieth century such enterprises in Peru had been eliminated by international competition and the purchasing policies of the multinationals involved in the export sectors. In Colombia it is clear that these enterprises continue to thrive, protected again by natural factors,[15] by the national character of the coffee industry, and by the nature of technology in the small-scale coffee sector. Both the nature of the terrain and the nature of the crops in Colombia made technological advance implausible.[16]

An element supporting and supported by the continued regional spread of these activities was the regional base of banking. Typically, banking in Latin America had concentrated in size and centralised in the capital city by the turn of the century, and certainly this was the Peruvian pattern. In Colombia this process occurred only in the 1920s.[17]

Colombia was thus clearly not immune to the processes of concentration. But what is unusual is that the two characteristics of coffee we are stressing here as having favourable developmental characteristics, the small-scale nature of production and the absence of foreign participation, both actually became more evident with time. The former is the result of geography, technology and infrastructure. The direct characteristics of production always favoured the small family enterprise, given Colombia's hilly terrain and high quality coffee. Family labour could provide the intensive care needed for good harvesting. But initially the large haciendas played a certain infrastructural role, roasting and transporting coffee. As, on the one hand, simple pulpers and, on the other, centralised roasting and better transport became available, so the one role for size diminished.[18] By the 1930s and 1940s population pressure led to the parcelization of estates, a fall in the average size of holding and a vast growth in the number of owners.[19]

The reasons why foreigners did not buy into coffee need more clarification, but, as with cotton in Peru, appear to be the result of three factors: the lack of economies of scale, the shortage of labour and the resulting need to operate within the local labour system (difficult for foreigners), and the fact that it was more profitable to concentrate in commerce, given the bargaining power of the large export house versus a fragmented and small-scale production system. The foreign presence in coffee commerce did increase initially: with the collapse of the brief world-wide boom in primary commodities in 1915-21, several US houses bought into the sector.[20] To understand how this process was reversed, and to understand also the various elements of support to small-scale production, we need to explore the role both of the state and of a unique Colombian institution, the Federación Nacional de Cafeteros.

The two themes, the State and the Federación, have to be treated together, for their relationship has always been close and subtle. By the 1920s, it was clear that a producers' organisation was needed. Brazil had been working hard since the 1900s to introduce some measure of control into the supply side; numerous schemes had been tried and the need to articulate and defend Colombian interests itself required an organisation. But also as those interests became defined, it became clear that Colombia's future lay in differentiating her product and promoting her higher quality carefully selected beans. This in turn required organisation, classification schemes and, above all, control to prevent Colombian producers of inferior coffee trying to hide behind her growing reputation.[21] The small-scale nature of the sector, however, led the organisers to feel that the usual voluntary contribution scheme would never work;[22] by 1927 a most unusual organisation had been set up, the Federación Nacional de Cafeteros Colombianos, a private organisation but empowered to collect and spend an export tax on coffee.

Initially, the tax was small, and indeed only paid for the first time in 1930.[23] But the tax was increased twice in the 1930s, and the institution grew rapidly, in membership, activities and prestige, if always in the midst of conflict.

The conflicts occurred at (at least) four levels.[24] First was the inevitable party conflict. Second was the fight to reduce the level of foreign control. Third was the sense of exclusion on the part of small producers. And fourth was the issue of how best to regulate the industry: whether to go in with Brazil and curb production (the liberal line) or assert Colombian confidence in the uniqueness of her coffee and reject any such scheme (the Ospina Pérez line – the manager from 1930 to 1934).

Liberal–Conservative infighting for its own sake was bitter and constant. It had been the dominant theme of Colombian politics throughout the nineteenth century, and the cause of the greater part of the violence which was prevalent in most regions, and continued to be so through the twentieth century. The Constitution of the Federación was meant to preserve it from such infighting but of course it failed.

The conflict with foreign interests began very early in the 1930s. The story is so vividly told in a British Embassy report of 1935 that it is worth a lengthy quotation. 'First and foremost, they [the Board of Managers of the FNCC] attempted to free the industry from foreign control. With the exception of England, which is a secondary market, the consumers of Colombian coffees had always maintained their own buying organisation in Colombia, so that it was entirely a "buyer's market", in which the great New York and Hamburg houses ruled conditions. The Colombian Federation of Coffee Planters set to work to break down the buyers' control, by establishing bonded warehouses throughout the coffee areas, where small producers could deposit their crop against negotiable warrants, thus acquiring enough independence to withstand the blandishments or threats of the international buyer. In 1931, the large buying firms had attempted to obtain admission to membership of the Federation on the same terms as the producers. Their failure had made them resentful, the more so when, from 1932 onwards, the Federation developed an organisation for the sale of coffee consigned to it direct to the consumer in Germany, Sweden, France and other lesser European markets. The great United States buyers felt that their position of control was being threatened and that the next attack would be launched in New York itself.'[25]

This was the beginning: as the web of FNCC activities extended further, gradually the foreign houses found themselves more constrained and without a role. The FNCC built warehouses, instituted monitoring and controls on quality, and extended credit and extension services to build themselves a clientele, so leaving less and less space to the private exporter. By the 1950s foreign export houses were handling only 20 per cent of export sales.[26]

The conflict over whose interests were represented in the Federación was not to be resolved easily, though Ospina Pérez launched a membership drive which increased members from 4 000 to 5 000 in four years: this represented one-third of the total number of coffee growers in 1934.[27] And as activities were developed which were genuinely available to the small producer, so the tension lessened. This was particularly true of credit.[28]

The conflict over output regulation was the most violent and the most public, involving as it did much public debate between two very prominent figures, Ospina Pérez and Alfonso López.[29] There were many peripheral but important issues, such as the need for Brazilian support in the dispute with Peru in 1933.[30] Also involved was each side's view of the nature of social relations and how to solve them: the Ospina position was that to resolve social tension it was essential not to restrict production but to extend it, whereas the Liberal position considered that a serious agrarian reform was anyway necessary to deal with the social problem, making the restriction of production a subsidiary issue. In 1936 Colombia did eventually join with Brazil in an attempt to restrict sales, but the effort rapidly collapsed.

As part of this struggle, in the meantime the Liberal Government of Alfonso López (1934–38) took a much firmer control of the Federación, changing the constitution to introduce a majority of government members in the Board. Paradoxically, this paved the way for a strengthening of the Federación, since when the Second World War came and the Coffee Pact was introduced, it was somehow acceptable to introduce the Fondo Nacional de Café, with initial capital from the government, to finance the management of the quota scheme.[31]

Once the Fund came into existence, the financial position and capacity of the Federación seems to have gone from strength to strength, aided by a period of prosperity for coffee internationally from 1948 to 1956, and by the long period as manager of Manuel Mejía, whose prestige and experience were greatly respected by each government in turn during his long period in office from 1937 to 1958. When the wartime pact ended in 1946 there was no question of abolishing the Fund, which by then had ample resources. By 1946 the Fund was able to invest in shipping in the form of the Flota Mercante Grancolombiana, and subsequently in other business. In the 1950s the government in fact reduced its participation in the Board of Directors; the genuine autonomy and solidity of the institution seems to have been thoroughly established by this point. The range of activities by now had also broadened to include the building of schools and hospitals as well as technical services and credit.[32]

This rather lengthy discussion has been necessary, since we consider that it holds the key to the continued national character of the industry as well as showing the extent of support to the small producer. A further and intangible aspect is the degree to which it actually generated a whole chain of involvement, by creating departmental and municipal committees and requiring that wherever possible meetings of members be convened to elect such committees. The benefits to be achieved through the system were such that there was every incentive to participate. And sometimes there was a requirement to participate, e.g. in the building of a primary school.[33]

Remarkably, the system also appears to have remained relatively free from corruption;[34] this is said to be due in part to the fact that officers of the Federación cannot also hold political office.[35] The prestige of the very small number of managers over thirty years has undoubtedly also helped. So have the facts that salaries are relatively good and posts are stable.

A further level of activity of the Federación began to develop once the International Coffee Organisation was formed in 1962. With the turnaround in prices in the mid-1950s, Colombia abandoned all her earlier hesitations and became a founder member. The prior existence and solidity of the Federación meant that Colombia was soon fielding a team in the annual round of negotiations whose expertise and experience far outshone the rest. In the 1980s, of the team of seven key negotiators, three had been there since the beginning in 1962. In contrast, the negotiators for Brazil and the African countries constantly changed.[36]

We have told the Colombian story as if coffee was the only export. Of course, as Table 1.1 makes clear, this was not the case. Gold had a brief boom in the 1930s, and bananas and oil continued to play a role right through the period, though together they never formed more than a quarter of exports after the 1930s. Both these sectors had characteristics completely opposed to coffee: they were enclaves, geographically rather separate and foreign controlled.[37] Their chief incidence in the Colombian scene was via the intense labour conflicts which developed from the 1920s on,[38] and the way in which they fed a low-key distrust of foreign capital which characterised Colombian policy-making through this period. The relevance of this will become clearer as we look more closely at economic management in the early phase.

Economic management in the early stages

It is no part of this study to evaluate in depth the political economy of these early years; our task here is merely to set the scene for the detailed study of the period which begins in 1967. But the tendencies are so striking that a few comments are worth making, to indicate the roots of the sharp contrasts which make up our story over the two decades which form the core of our study.

This contrast begins with the first debt crisis of the century. As we have made clear, for reasons which had to do with structure, not management skill, Colombia made rather better use of the inflow of foreign money in the 1920s. Although corruption abounded in both countries, the pressures from productive forces to achieve economic goals did produce even then somewhat more efficiency in management in the Colombian case. Fascinating documents appearing in the *Boletin de la Contraloria* in Colombia show a degree of sensitivity to the need for control over expenditure which we were not able to find in the case of Peru. In one case the accounts of Ulen & Co., working on the Bocas de Ceniza project, were examined with a fine-tooth comb.[39] In another the corruption and inefficiency in the Ferrocarril del Carare project was exposed.[40] Such items, of course, bear eloquent witness to corrupt practices – but the care taken to prevent them contrasts rather strongly with Peru in the 1920s .

When the Depression hit, all of Latin America of course reacted passively, allowing the outflow of gold to create a liquidity crisis, in line with gold standard rules. The collapse of exports fed through to demand and employment. The interesting issue throughout the continent is why and at what point orthodox behaviour patterns were rejected and recovery became possible. The trigger was the British abandonment of the gold standard in September 1931: with that, it became suddenly acceptable to abandon gold and allow exchange rates to depreciate. Once that happened, default on debt was more or less inevitable, since the depreciating exchange rate made the burden of debt on the government budget completely unmanageable. Most countries also resorted to the full range of instruments – import controls, tariffs and controls on capital – to try to reduce the payments deficit. The pressure of exporting interests also explains the fascinating further step into unorthodoxy, observed clearly for instance in Brazil, where government policy became 'Keynesian before Keynes' with expenditures responding to the need of the coffee sector.

The structures we are identifying from the 1920s influenced our two countries' response within this panorama. In Colombia, public works expenditure was by the 1930s intertwined with important domestic regional interests whose new importance had not a little to do with the new liberal government. We shall see the consequences below. As far as possible a development programme had to be maintained, and for this the government was aware of the importance of foreign capital. It was also acutely aware of people's fear of currency depreciation, given memories of the inflation of the '1 000 Days' War'.[41] It therefore fought against default and to maintain the exchange rate, even when almost every other Latin American country had defaulted. In this it was able to benefit from its 'federal structure'; departmental and municipal governments went into default at an early stage, but the national government was able to point to national virtue, conveniently ignoring the fact that the non-national debt was actually the larger of the two. As default became more of a necessity, the government resorted to the issuing of 'scrip' bonds, in lieu of the greater proportion of interest due. The exchange rate was maintained for two years at considerable cost to the reserves. But the 'reward' was that the USA and other creditors were apparently prepared to take a tolerant view of the alternative measures – exchange controls, multiple exchange rates and tariffs – seeing these as preferable to default and abandonment of the gold standard.

The strength of the regional interests behind public works programmes meant that while of course many had to be abruptly suspended, there were strong efforts made to maintain others. Departmental and municipal governments fought particularly hard, and were able to succeed partly because of the weakness of central control. The legal position was apparently that departments could embark on public works and *tell* the national government what subsidy it now owed them; by 1931 of course such subsidies were simply not being paid – but in the meantime local governments had raised loans on the basis of such anticipated subsidies. By 1931 the national government owed the departments 11 million pesos on account of such subsidies – more than the total of actual departmental expenditure on public works in that year. The municipalities were even less willing to cut and were assisted by private money: in October 1930, for example, the municipality of Cartagena raised a loan from Canadian sources to begin work on an aqueduct. Local initiatives were also important, as the following rather remarkable description suggests:

> Bajo la iniciativa de las respectivas gobernaciones, se agruparon los principales capitalistas de las grandes ciudades, los cuales a través de préstamos permitían al departamento o a los municipios emprender obras que a su vez necesitaban de brazos para llevarse a cabo; así fue como en Cali se adelantaron toda una serie de mejoras ... en Antioquía esos fondos iba a ayudar a impulsar la construcción de la Carretera al Mar y a la colonización de Urabá y en Barranquilla igualmente hubo iniciativa similar.[42]

At national level too, while there was stricter adherence to orthodox economics, there were some surprising initiatives. The *Memoria* of the Ministry of Industry records in 1931 its endeavours to reduce unemployment. A system of free railway passes for the unemployed in

Bogotá willing to return to agriculture had been made use of by 1 699 persons in its first year of operation. But the more specialised workers were the problem; here the Ministry had made contacts with firms in the private sector, offering them public sector contracts preferentially, 'even when their products could not compete in price with the imported good', if they would take on extra workers.

Another story of developing producer co-operation and pressure resulting in an increased role of the State, occurred at this period in the sugar sector, where the Depression is described by López as 'obliging' the producers to associate and count on state help.[43] This echoes the claim made by Palacios, that the Depression wedded the coffee bourgeoisie to the State – with the solidity of a traditional Catholic marriage.[44]

How far reflationary pressures actually led to state spending itself leading the recovery is hard to analyse precisely given the data problems. CEPAL's claim that the Colombian government played a strong reflationary role from 1929 on is clearly based on incorrect statistics: in fact expenditure did fall more rapidly than prices at both national and departmental levels in 1929 and 1930, leading to a fall in real terms of some 20 per cent compared to 1926–28. Very early, however, pressures from the coffee sector and other quarters pushed the government into unorthodoxy: as Ocampo and Montenegro have shown, the monetary data indicate that by 1931 (and well in advance of the Leticia 'War') the government was indeed using deficit financing to expand activity quite strongly. We can conclude that Colombia even in 1929 and 1930 probably avoided a total collapse, partly by borrowing from and promoting the private sector, possibly partly by lack of control over regional spending, while from 1931 on policies were decidedly Keynesian – a characteristic accentuated by the Leticia 'War', a border incident between Peru and Colombia which led to a real fear of invasion by Peru. The unorthodox spending pattern continued, spurred by the fact that the coffee price did not recover early.

We have seen that the government sector played a countercyclical role in the early years of the Depression. What is particularly remarkable is the rise in real terms in government spending in the absence of any recovery in exports at this stage. Then came Leticia: while the Peruvians were relatively unaffected, the incident provoked a strong nationalistic response and patriotic effort in Colombia, with defence loans being oversubscribed and jewellery and ornaments being donated to the effort. Real revenue does not appear to have risen: internal loans financed the gap, in part drawing on private wealth. Once Leticia was over, however,

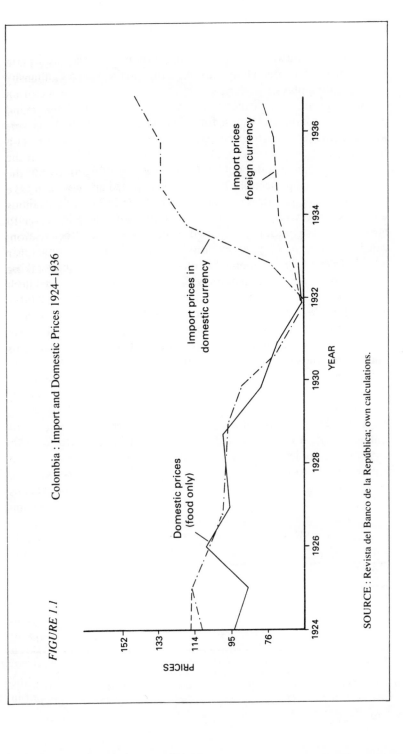

FIGURE 1.1   Colombia : Import and Domestic Prices 1924–1936

Import prices
foreign currency

Import prices in
domestic currency

Domestic prices
(food only)

PRICES

152
133
114
95
76

1924   1926   1928   1930   1932   1934   1936

YEAR

SOURCE : Revista del Banco de la República; own calculations.

the role of the state was not expansionary. Its importance lay more in the development of its role relative to coffee, than in the macro significance of its spending plans.

But the greater significance of the 'War' was probably that it at last provided an honourable excuse for default and devaluation. Much care was taken in the public relations associated with the default to make the connection clear.

Once the exchange rate could move, then we see in Figure 1.1 how far industry received protection. The gap which opened up between import prices and domestic prices can be seen to be large and we will see that it was considerably larger than in the case of Peru. More importantly, tariff reforms significantly increased protection on a number of items which led the way in the acceleration of industrial growth which now occurred. The level of nominal protection for non-traditional manufactures rose from 25 per cent in 1927 to 76 per cent in 1936 (weighting by pre-Depression market size) while in Peru, in textiles for example, nominal tariffs rose only from 19 to 20 per cent, and tariffs fell on many other consumer goods. Certain important sectors received a significantly larger increase in effective protection in Colombia than in Peru, notably all kinds of yarn, wool and rayon cloth, and cement.

We can now turn to the indicators of recovery shown in Table 1.2. What Colombia experienced was at least in relative terms an autonomous recovery, in advance of the upturn in export prices, and owing much to the countercyclical effect of government spending. What followed thereafter represented a distinct shift in structure, with the industrial sector leading the recovery and much progress being made in import substitution. The policies which aided this formed a logical continuum with the trends of the 1920s, and reinforced those trends.

Table 1.2
Colombia and Peru:
Measures of Medium-term Recovery by 1937
(1926–28 = 100)

	Colombia	Peru
Volume of industrial production	205	n.a.
Volume of cotton textile production	449	126
Export quantum	150	132
Terms of trade	78	106

Sources: Industrial production – CEPAL (1957). Textiles – Colombia: Chu (1972); Peru: estimate made by Thorp and Bertram (1978). Trade data – Colombia: CEPAL (1957); Peru: Hunt (1973) and import price index estimated by Thorp and Bertram (1978).

Once the Second World War broke out, the big challenge to short-term management was the influx of reserves. Peru had the problem resolved for her: North American influence in Peru was extremely strong during the war and the USA was able to win Peru's acceptance of price controls on her raw materials. Thus by the end of the war Peru's foreign exchange reserves had risen a mere 55 per cent, whereas Colombia's rose 540 per cent in the same period.[45] Inflation in the two countries was rather similar, and typical of Latin America in World War II: prices rose 64 per cent in Colombia and 70 per cent in Peru 1940–45.[46] The fact that the rates were so similar, despite the influx of resources into Colombia, owes much to Colombian inventiveness in macro management: experience which was to stand her in good stead in subsequent coffee booms. On this we have an unusual testimony. Robert Triffin[47] visited Colombia in 1944, and wrote a brief history of Colombian banking which was published as a supplement to the *Revista del Banco de la República*. In it he detailed the measures taken to sterilize the effect of the inflow of foreign exchange from 1941 to 1943, all directed at increasing savings. They were a combination of increased direct taxation and forced savings through various kinds of bond issues, to be forcibly taken up by banks, the Federación and importers of capital. Further, 20 per cent of profits of all enterprises had to be invested in a new 'certificate', non-negotiable, of two years life with interest at 3 or 4 per cent. Capital controls were strengthened at the same time. Triffin concludes: 'The anti-inflation measures taken in Colombia comprise perhaps the most complete and balanced system introduced to date to deal with inflation in Latin America' (p. 27). He considers at least half the inflow of foreign exchange was effectively sterilized by these means. He contrasts this with the relatively passive monetary management of the 1920s and 1930s.

Once the War was over Latin America entered a 'transition' period which we have characterised elsewhere as one of 'transition to full-blown ISI', or 'import-substituting industrialisation'. This pattern or model was to be the core of the rapid growth of all but the smallest Latin American economies from the mid-1950s through the 1960s. It was based on protection plus a large role for foreign capital. As the continent emerged from the War, the typical situation was one of extensive controls and distortions combined with heavily overvalued exchange rates. The story of the decade or so immediately after the War is typically one of learning to moderate controls, rationalise exchange rates and introduce reforms that created a secure environment for foreign capital. The way in which our two case-studies fit into this general pattern is again revealing. Colombia's working out of the situation was yet again rather *avant garde* for its time. The problem dominating the country and relegating the economy to a secondary issue was that of violence: the wave of 'La Violencia' which swept the country in the late 1940s and resulted in large numbers of deaths.[48] Yet policy was still unusually coherent. In regard to imports and protection, there was a clear perception of the need for reforms, since the specific tariffs dating from 1931 had been eroded by inflation. Tariffs as a percent of imports were 22 per cent in 1936 and only 10 per cent by 1947. There was also a perception that the structure of tariffs and the needs of industry had been allowed to damage agriculture, in particular cotton production. The concept pushed by the Ospina government was 'integral protection': protection which stimulated both agriculture and industry. Purchasing local materials was, needless to say, unpopular with industry – but a solution was worked out: in 1948 import quotas began to be allocated *conditional* on purchase of local raw materials, and other measures of support to agriculture. Meanwhile, for example, the government strengthened the Instituto de Fomento Algodonero, itself an initiative of Antioqueñan textile producers. What is still more fascinating is the account of how the Minister of Economy, Hernán Jaramillo Ocampo, on introducing more severe import restrictions in 1949, went himself to Medellín to reassure producers that there was actually ample exchange available for their real needs and 'took the opportunity' to remind them of the virtues of purchasing local raw materials.[49]

The initial obstacle to tariff reform was the treaty signed with the US in 1936 freezing tariffs on 161 items. The initial solution in 1948 was a 'sales tax' with rates from 10 to 26 per cent. When the political crisis of 1948–49 permitted, a full tariff reform was in any case introduced.

Control of credit seems to have continued and strengthened the practices admired by Triffin, but by the end of the decade a new sophistication appeared to be entering in: in 1949 the plan of the Minister of Hacienda was to 'apparently sterilize' this inflow of reserves, while in fact allowing a very selective supply of credit through to important productive projects.[50]

What Colombia did not do, any better than anywhere else, and which was to await the Lleras administration, was avoid the typical pressures to overvaluation of the exchange rate, with the resulting discontinuous changes and inflationary pressures. The only 'Colombian nuance' here is that this mismanagement was possibly rather less damaging to the supply of exports than in most other cases: from 1962 on coffee's external sales were predetermined through the International Coffee

Organisation, and the internal price was a product of government policy. As the issue of other non-traditional exports became more crucial in the 1960s, so that exchange rate management became central, the way was prepared for the innovations in exchange rate management which we discuss in Chapter 7.

There is one important omission in the economic legislation of the 1940s and 1950s. We have described how generally in Latin America in the immediate post-war period there had to be an evolution from the controlled and interventionist regimes of the 1940s through to a system with clearer signals and more coherence such as would allow the ISI boom of the 1950s and 1960s, typically with large-scale foreign investment. We have identified the focal point of this transition in most countries as exchange reform and foreign capital laws, usually coming rather close together. What is significant about Colombia is that while it broke with the overvalued exchange rate of the 1940s with a devaluation in 1951, there was never a foreign capital law of the kind we find elsewhere. Colombia continued in the attitude of lack of enthusiasm for private foreign investment which had characterised the whole century. Capital could come in, but no one was going to make it particularly easy. Yet again, the Peruvian story was different, and the historical pattern makes it clear why.

Notes

1. For the best introduction to the early history of the coffee sector, see an unpublished thesis: Beyer (1947).
2. Beyer (1947), p. 193.
3. Thorp (1984), ch. 4.
4. Very rough estimates. The source for Colombia is CEPAL, *Anexo* (1957), for Peru Garland Duponte (n.d.). See Thorp and Londoño (1984) for more detail.
5. Ospinah Vásquez (1955), ch. 5–8.
6. Reading for example, the *Revista Nacional de Agricultura*, the mouthpiece of the *Sociedad de Agricultores de Colombia*, one finds endless examples of pressure and interest in transport expansion – of course not only in the context of coffee expansion, but many products.
7. *Boletín de Comercio e Industria, Boletín de Agricultura*, many issues.
8. Foreign Office 371/16570, p. 37, London.
9. McGreevey (1971), p. 196; López (1973), pp. 10–11.
10. Arango (1977), p. 124; Palacios (1979), p. 103.
11. E.g. García (1937); Palacios (1979).
12. The relevance of transport costs, natural protection and the flow of income from coffee is indicated as late as the 1950s by a fascinating study of industry in Barranquilla on the Coast, by José Raimundo Sojo. There are many pages of lament on how in Barranquilla industry has not grown faster because it cannot sell in the interior because of poor transport, and the advantage the interior has because of coffee (Sojo 1955).

13. This figure is no doubt too high, since we have often only been able to rely on the same name, which could reflect a rather distant link, or even none. But as far as possible we have confirmed it with qualitative information. The basic research was done by Carlos Londoño, using a wide range of business journals, newspapers, interviews, etc. The results confirm the conclusions of Arango (1977).

14. One puzzle this leaves us with is why industry developed so late in Caldas compared with Antioquia, both major and expanding coffee-growing areas. Our own suggestion would be the number of exporting houses in Pereira which had their parent house in Medellín, thus tending to emphasize the importance of the existence of a surplus among the three elements in debate. In this case at least for some time the commerce sector opted for channelling its surplus into its already existing activities in Medellín.

15. Safford (1977) stresses the fragmentation of Colombia's economic structure.

16. The quality of Colombia's mild coffee depends on picking the berries as they ripen, which happens unevenly over a long period and thus depends on hand picking.

17. Ospina Vásquez (1974), 2nd edition, p. 419.

18. Beyer (1947), p. 291.

19. The data, needless to say, are not clear because of non-comparability between Censuses. They are well discussed in Bergquist (1986), p. 35. See also Beyer (1947), p. 292.

20. Beyer (1947), p. 224.

21. *Ibid.*, p. 262.

22. Koffman (1969), ch. 1

23. *Ibid.*, p. 84

24. The information for the following discussion comes from the *informes* of the Manager of the Federación, as well as the numerous articles written by Ospina Pérez and Alfonso López.

25. FO 371/19778.

26. Palacios (1979), p. 404. The percentage was 47 per cent in 1933.

27. Koffman (1969), p. 188.

28. *Ibid.*, p. 151.

29. Ospina Pérez was Conservative, manager of the Federación 1930–34 and President of the country 1944–50. López was President 1934–38 and 1943–45 and a key Liberal political leader.

30. Ocampo (1984), p. 123.

31. This is the interpretation of Mariano Arango: the government's intervention 'Oficializó una estructura institucional de la Federación Nacional de Cafeteros, con alta injerencia del Ejecutivo con el fin de legitimar el manejo por un gremio privado de recursos tributivos masivos, a raíz de la formación del Fondo Nacional del Café, a fines de 1940' (quoted in FNCC (1987), p. 221).

32. In both cases, the state participates by paying running costs. On education, see Rodrigo Parra (1980). In 1938 Caldas had the highest percentage literate in the country. In 1951 the coffee departments had the highest rural literacy figures.

33. The local producers petition for a school through their municipal committee to Departmental level. The Departmental Committee sends an engineer to check out the need. If agreed, the local community must participate with money or labour. Interview with Alvaro Rodríguez, Gonzalo Paredes, Alvaro Rojas, FNCC, Bogotá September 1987.

34. This is yet another topic worth exploring: this view is based only on interviews with public sector employees as well as *cafeteros*.

35. Interview, Jorge Valencia and Eduardo Melo, FNCC, 1–9 1988. In their view, this tradition owes much to the first man to be manager for a substantial number of years and at the formative moment: Ospina Pérez.

36. Based on a discussion in September 1983 with Palacio Rudas, a lawyer and University professor, a member of the Central Committee of the FNCC since 1962, and former Minister of Economy. Bogotá , September 1983.

37. See Ocampo (1987) for an excellent account, important to balance our emphasis here on coffee.
38. Bergquist (1986), p. 330.
39. A gentleman travelling from New York to Puerto Colombia made two unauthorized stopovers and had his hotels and taxis disallowed, many wages were challenged as above the minimum, expenses were disallowed because the travel costs were too high. See *Boletín*, June–July 1927.
40. *Boletín de la Contraloría*, February–March 1930.
41. A civil war at the turn of the century which led to a hyperinflation and a degree of economic chaos that coloured people's attitudes to inflation for several decades.
42. *Boletín Mensual de Estadística*, June 1976, p. 126.
43. López (1973).
44. Palacios (1979), p. 307.
45. Ferrero (1946).
46. Banco de la República, *Informe a la Junta Directiva*, June 1949, INP, *Boletín de Estadística Peruana*, 1962.
47. Celebrated US economist and expert in monetary matters.
48. The sources of violence are much debated. The tensions were characteristically between the Parties at local level, but the causes were deeper than simply political rivalry. See Oquist (1980).
49. Jaramillo Ocampo, H. (1980), p. 270, citing a report in *Semana*.
50. *Ibid.*, p. 347.

2 Peruvian Export-led Underdevelopment

AN HISTORICAL PERSPECTIVE

Peru has always been known as a country of paradoxes: a 'beggar on a pile of gold', in the famous phrase. The 'gold' was in evidence much earlier than Colombia's 'brown gold',[1] and took many forms. During the mid-nineteenth century it took the form of bird-dung: the economy rode high on a wave of prosperity generated by exports of guano to fertilize European agriculture. The industry touched the rest of the economy quite substantially, but principally through the sizeable government revenues which went largely to create a Lima-based bureaucracy. When the railway-building fever hit Peru in the 1870s she had to borrow abroad on the basis of fast-dwindling guano proceeds, and a debt crisis followed as the international economy moved into recession.

There followed an unusual and rather instructive period for the potential it shows Peru had: this is important in view of what was to come in the twentieth century. The guano boom had had the usual effect of an export boom on industry: with abundant foreign exchange its price was cheap so imports easily competed with local products and artisan industry was seriously undermined. Come the 1890s, an export boom was led now by sugar and cotton, based on the coast, and increasingly by copper.

The expected results of any primary export boom are to discourage, rather than promote, economic diversification, for three main reasons. First, because rising profitability and expectations of producers tend to encourage reinvestment of profits in the export sectors themselves (with diversification more likely to occur during periods when expectation of profits in export production are lower); second, because abundant foreign exchange earnings lead to an exchange rate which favours imports against local production; and third, because buoyant exports lead to increased tax revenue and foreign-borrowing options for government, thus reducing the revenue motive for raising tariffs on imports. Where such conditions hold, the expected pattern of economic growth may be summarised as a concentration of investment in export sectors, a strong exchange rate supported both by export earnings and by

MAP 2.1

Peru : Physical and Administrative Structure

SOURCE : Bourricaut, F. (1970), *Power and Society in Contemporary Peru*, Faber and Faber, London

the capital inflow which they encourage, and relatively low tariffs which fail to compensate local import-competing industry for the economy's high import capacity. In so far as surplus is generated in excess of the investment needs of export sectors, it tends to be invested abroad (especially when foreign firms are significant among export producers) or spent on capitalists' consumption.

As we probe Colombia's more recent experiences, we are going to find many instances of exceptions to this general pattern. It is therefore of considerable relevance to our comparative theme that Peru also at least in the 1890s diverged from this pattern: export growth went hand in hand with economic diversification and industrialisation. An examination of the circumstances in which this occurred reveals an unusual conjuncture: successful export sectors with high returned value, generating large demand effects in the local economy and leaving surplus in the hands of local capitalists over and above that required for re-investment in further export expansion; yet, at the same time, a relative-price situation which made urban manufacturing sufficiently profitable to attract investment capital.

Around the turn of the century, most of the major Peruvian export sectors were returning a high proportion of their foreign-exchange earnings to Peru. Despite tendencies towards increasing concentration and capital intensity (especially in the sugar industry), techniques of production were still relatively labour intensive. In addition to the stimulus to local demand from the wage bill of the export sectors, both sugar production and mining generated linkage effects of some importance, especially by their purchases of capital goods from local foundries. These foundries had long been supplying equipment for sugar mills (even in some cases complete mills), while in the 1890s the building of smelters to process silver and copper ores created a new demand for equipment since many of the smelters erected during the 1890s and early 1900s were of local manufacture. The engineering workshops attached to the railways also constituted important centres of capital goods production.

Local ownership was the rule in the leading export sectors, and the profitability of those sectors provided local capitalists with surplus funds over and above their re-investment needs. Once confidence was re-established after the War of the Pacific (fought with Chile 1879–83), large sums were available for investment in any activity which promised to return a good profit; by 1899 President Pierola was remarking on the mobilisation and investment of 'capital previously concealed, unproductive, or diverted to foreign countries'.[2]

Strong local demand and large supplies of funds for investment, however, do not suffice to generate a diversification process in an open economy. Demand can be met by imports as well as by local production, funds can be invested in export sectors or abroad, or used for luxury consumption, rather than invested in non-export activities. Only sectors which are protected from import competition by their very nature (utilities, for example, and products with very high weight-to-value ratios) can expect to benefit automatically from such a situation. In Peru during the 1890s, however, relative prices shifted sharply in favour of import-substituting industry, which as a result became profitable enough to attract investment capital. Both a depreciating exchange rate and large increases in tariffs accompanied the expansion of demand fuelled by the export sectors. The falling exchange rate (a result of world developments rather than domestic price movements) created a price advantage for local industry which was amplified by an increase in effective tariff protection.

The depreciation of the exchange rate was substantial. Between 1890 and 1897 the fall was nearly 40 per cent,[3] a result simply of the effect on a silver-based currency of the fall in world silver prices which occurred once the US ceased to support the price in 1892. Domestic price data for this period are non-existent, but the qualitative evidence indicates that it was only by 1898 that the problem of inflation had become serious. Wages in the meantime rose more slowly, widening the margin of profitability for local industry.[4]

The increase in tariff rates was a result of the Government's need for revenues. An export boom might have been expected to relieve any revenue constraint, by increasing the yield from export taxes and the Government's ability to borrow abroad. In Peru, however, export taxes did not exist in the 1890s, as during the high prosperity of the guano era these and various other taxes (notably the poll tax on the Indian population) had been allowed to lapse. After 1880 the political strength of the export producers enabled them to resist the imposition of export taxes. Foreign borrowing was impossible, given Peru's reputation as a recent defaulter, combined with the effects of the Baring Crisis on the London financial market. Inflationary financing of the government sector had been ruled out by the monetary reform of 1887. To cap all this, the transfer of guano export earnings from the Government to the Peruvian Corporation as part of the 1890 Grace Contract abruptly cut fiscal income by about half. Of the few tax options which remained open to maintain solvency, tariffs on imports were the easiest to apply, and encountered the least resistance.

In the 1860s, the highest rate of import duty had been 30 per cent *ad valorem*, and the average was about 20 per cent. The first increases were introduced in 1874–75: by 1891 the average incidence of duties on the 80 per cent of import items subject to duty was 39 per cent, giving an overall incidence of 31 per cent. After long debate a new customs schedule was introduced in 1889–90, and an 8 per cent surcharge on all import duties was added in January 1893. Further increases followed in the course of the 1890s.

For those consumer-goods industries which could be quickly established or expanded, the combined effects of high effective protection and exchange depreciation made local production profitable in competition with imports, at a time when the expansion of export earnings was providing a strong and sustained boost to local demand. Capital poured into industry, to the alarm of local defenders of the theory of free trade and comparative advantage, and in the closing years of the century debate over the merits or otherwise of protectionism raged in the press and in Congress.[5]

The heat of the debate owed much to the fact that among the promoters of non-export ventures were many of the country's leading export producers and merchants. Sugar planters were particularly prominent: José Pardo, for example, established the Fábrica de Tejidos La Victoria in 1897, and was manager of the factory until he became President of Peru in 1903. The Pardo family were also involved in a series of banks and insurance companies in Lima, as were the Aspillaga family (like the Pardos, planters from Lambayeque). Investments by the Aspillagas reported in the contemporary business press included two insurance companies, two banks, a tax-collecting company, an electricity-generating plant, a tramways company in Lima, the Salaverry wharf company, a mining company, and an unsuccessful venture into jute sack manufacturing. Various other leading planters and mine owners appear on the directorates of companies listed in Yepes (1972). Export capitalists who were not themselves directly involved in the promotion of new projects could contribute funds to the ˙process through the rapidly-expanding system of financial intermediaries which emerged at this time, particularly the new banks. The principal organising genius of the financial network was the Cuban immigrant, banker and businessman, José Payán.

We have seen, therefore, how the favourable situation for industry had arisen not out of deliberate government strategy, nor from determined pressure applied by any politically powerful group, but out of a chance combination of circumstances. By the end of the 1890s circumstances were changing. Peru went on the gold standard in 1897, thus halting exchange depreciation, and the establishment of efficient tax-collecting companies made possible a switch to excise taxes on sugar, alcohol and tobacco as a major new source of government revenues after 1900, thus reducing the role of import tariffs. The preservation of protection for local industry would have required, at the very least, the existence of a large and politically powerful industrialist class. Instead, the new industrial sector was controlled by exporters, merchants, financiers, and relatively recent immigrants.

The strong export growth of the 1890s continued for three decades – but its composition and its nature now changed sharply, and in ways important for our story. Within certain sectors, there was increased concentration and foreign penetration, while the weight of those sectors within the whole also rose. Table 2.1 shows the changing composition of exports. It can be seen how first sugar and copper, and finally oil, increased their share, all three subject to the phenomena we have mentioned. The decline of the Sierra-based products – wool and rubber

Table 2.1
Peru: Composition of Exports by Value[a] 1890–1960
(percentage shares)

	Sugar	Cotton	Wool[b]	Silver	Rubber	Copper	Petroleum	Fishmeal
1890	28	9	15	33	13	1	–	–
1895	35	7	15	26	14	1	–	–
1900	32	7	7	22	13	18	–	–
1905	32	7	8	6	16	10	–	–
1910	20	14	7	10	18	18	2	–
1915	26	11	5	5	5	17	10	
1920	42	30	2	5	1	7	5	–
1925	11	32	4	10	1	8	24	–
1930	11	18	3	4	–	10	30	–
1935	15	33	6	7	–	10	22	–
1940	16	25	5	9	1	14	14	–
1945	19	28	5	5	2	10	13	1
1950	14	31	7	6	–	9	13	4
1955	16	26	3	6	–	9	9	5
1960	7	19	2	5	–	21	2	13

Source: Thorp and Bertram (1978), p. 40 and Boloña (1979), Table 5A.

Notes:
[a]The percentage shares are only very approximate, since some exports were valued fob, some cif – it often being unclear what the practice was. The rows sum to less than 100 per cent owing to the exclusion of minor export items.
[b]Includes alpaca.

– also strengthened the geographical concentration on Lima and the Coast which is such a marked feature of Peru.

Sugar

Like cotton, sugar was a coastal crop, and in the 1890s was grown in irrigated valleys scattered throughout the length of the country. In contrast to cotton, sugar was a sector in which economies of scale and the greater efficiency of mechanised processes dictated a trend towards large-scale enterprises organised on entirely capitalist lines and employing wage labour on a regular basis. The chief characteristic which distinguished the Peruvian sugar industry from its counterparts elsewhere in the world, and which strongly reinforced the trend towards large-scale units, was the absence of seasonality in production: sugar in Peru can be harvested all the year round, and favourable ecological conditions result in exceptionally high yields. The labour force is therefore relatively constant throughout the year, with little need for seasonal hiring of temporary workers. This has tended to favour the typical Peruvian production system, that of the large wage-labour plantation.

Consequently, one of the main features of the period was a steady increase in the concentration of ownership of sugar land. This had begun in the 1860s, and in the period following the War of the Pacific most areas experienced further concentration. The best-known case is that of the Chicama Valley in La Libertad, where the dominant families of the pre-war era were bought out by three expanding enterprises. These were the Larco family (Italian immigrants of the 1850s, who had bought their first sugar plantation in the area in 1872); the Gildemeister family (immigrant German merchants, who bought the *hacienda* Casagrande from another German, Luis Albrecht, in 1889); and the merchant house W.R. Grace and Co., which acquired the *hacienda* Cartavio from the Alzamora family in 1882 by foreclosure on a loan. All three enterprises enjoyed an advantage over the other landowners of the valley in their access to adequate capital or credit facilities, which enabled them to survive the difficult times up to 1894 and after 1900, and to finance the purchase of the estates of others less well-placed. The Gildemeister and Larco families had between them bought up at least sixteen properties by the mid-1890s, and during the depressed years of the early twentieth century they added another fourteen.

It will be seen then that in this case increased concentration occurred with the continuation of local control, albeit with a strong immigrant element. The result was dynamic growth and major technical progress in the first decades of the twentieth century, with increased capital intensity and virtually no increase in employment, thus rendering the sector an increasingly less efficient stimulator of development via the demand side. The sector was a good generator of surplus while sugar prices were high, but what is interesting to note is that local ownership was not a sufficient condition for the local re-investment of that surplus. In the 1890s the sugar planters were leaders in the diversification of the economy, as we have seen, but while they were happy thus to take advantage of profit opportunities created by largely exogenous circumstances, they did not use their considerable political power to press for policies designed to perpetuate that process of diversification. On the contrary, three Presidents who were actual or former sugar planters governed Peru for most of the period 1900–30 without taking any serious steps to sustain the growth model of the 1890s, or to check the decay of non-export sectors (and several export sectors) after 1900. When local opportunities ceased to provide attractive investment options, and when their political influence waned, sugar planters were well enough integrated into the international economy to think in terms of holding their funds abroad to be spent on the education of children, on frequent overseas trips, and no doubt in investments in the industrialised countries.

Mining

The history of metal mining in Peru is complicated by the variety of products: at different times since 1890 the list has been headed by gold, silver, copper, lead, zinc and iron, with many other secondary metals bringing up the rear. Peruvian ores tend to be complex and it is common for a number of metals to be found in the same mine.

Up to 1900, mining comprised a large number of small-scale operations, spread throughout the Sierra and concentrating on the production of precious metals. At the turn of the century, however, these metals were displaced by copper (hitherto a little-valued by-product) and it was copper which dominated the history of the thirty years up to 1930. With the expansion of copper production came also US capital, which in a short period totally dominated mining in Peru. Incidental to these trends in product markets and in ownership was also a pronounced regional concentration of mining activity.

The invasion of foreign capital was not due to lack of skill in the Peruvian mining sector: the growth and technological development in the 1880s and 1890s is impressive in silver, gold and copper, with a local School of Mines and much building of infrastructure. By the turn of the century, however, a bottle-neck existed in the form of a need for an expensive drainage tunnel at Cerro de Pasco. A Peruvian venture was ready to be launched in 1901 to solve the problem when short-term financial problems hit the industry and the offers made by US interests were too good to refuse.

The new 'Cerro de Pasco Copper Corporation' did not succeed in buying up all the mines, which meant that while returned value from copper fell below what it would have been had the sector remained in Peruvian hands,[6] it was still substantial at 50–60 per cent of gross earnings in the 1920s. The story was quite different for the remaining sector we have still to discuss.

Petroleum

The development of the oil industry in Peru began in the 1860s, but for the first sixty years growth was slow. A British company, London and Pacific Petroleum, bought the largest oil-field in 1889; the second largest was also owned by British capital. US capital entered in 1913, in the shape of Standard Oil of New Jersey, though the third largest venture in the country remained in Peruvian hands.

It is this early entry of foreign capital, years before the country became a significant exporter, that is significant. The Peruvian oil industry was dominated by foreign firms principally because foreign oil speculators developed an interest in Peru twenty years before the country became a significant exporter, and bought control of the largest oil-field very cheaply at that time. The sole remaining large field in the north, at Lobitos, was staked out by a British interest – whether by superior energies, or by pure chance, remains unclear. Thereafter, the fact that no large new fields remained to be found constituted an effective barrier to entry, and assured the oligopolistic position of the three main successful firms. The key to this situation was the London and Pacific Company's control over the entire 640 square miles of the Negritos oil-field.

The presence of foreigners in this sector led to rather startling results. Given its capital-intensive nature and small local expenditures, the sector was actually able to generate enough revenue from local sales to cover those expenses. The net amount of foreign exchange contributed to the local economy from the leading firm in the sector, the IPC, was virtually zero! So strong was this effect, that by the 1920s apparently booming export proceeds for the economy as a whole were actually generating zero growth in returned value.[7]

The fading out of the industrial boom

What happened meanwhile to the 1890s boom in industry? Unfortunately, from 1897, when Peru went on to the gold standard, more conventional forces determined the exchange rate, and the boom in export earnings plus the inflow of foreign investment caused an appreciation. Meanwhile rising world prices, particularly during the first world war, meant an erosion of the protective effect of the specific tariffs introduced and raised in the 1890s. By the 1920s their protective effect had fallen to roughly half their previous level. Why was it that such an erosion of tariff protection could be allowed to pass almost without protest from any of the groups affected? In large part, the answer lies in the extremely successful performance of export sectors during the 1910s; these sectors attracted capital and entrepreneurs away from manufacturing, and displayed such high capital absorptive capacity during the wartime period that surplus funds were held for re-investment and not used to finance diversification. The well-developed banking system provided a channel through which resources from one sector could be readily transferred to others when opportunity arose. By the 1910s, therefore, there were no longer many manufacturing ventures in which the ruling class had a direct interest; elite figures had withdrawn from manufacturing, or relegated their industrial interests to secondary importance. Entrepreneurs who remained in manufacturing did not constitute a social group either powerful or cohesive enough to influence policy.

A further element of decline concerns the incipient capital goods sector stimulated by the 1890s boom. It appears that as early as the 1900s, falling international freight rates and determined penetration of the local market by US firms combined to squeeze out this promising sector.[8]

We see, therefore, that although up to 1920 much of the boom in export earnings did feed through to domestic demand (the first requirement for a process of diversified export-led growth), this surge in demand was not a sufficient condition for the expansion of non-export industries. In fact, export expansion was itself an important reason why the depreciating exchange rate and rising tariffs of the 1890s gave way after 1900 to a stable and even appreciating exchange rate, falling protection from tariffs, and rapid domestic inflation. Local manufacturing became less competitive with imported goods, and demand was increasingly channelled towards the latter.

In the 1920s, stagnation on the demand side was added to these factors, as the increasing foreign ownership and expansion of foreign-dominated and capital-intensive sectors affected the mechanisms of export-led growth.

We see then that in the early stages Peru's export products favoured industry every bit as much as did coffee in Colombia and at an earlier date. What was totally lacking was the element of natural protection we have stressed for Colombia – the stimulus in Peru occurred on the coast and the results were heavily concentrated in Lima. (Those who do not know Peru may need telling that as Figure 2.1 shows the three great ridges of the Andes run parallel down the length of the country, so that 60 per cent of the land area is high-Sierra. The narrow coastal strip is fertile desert and the amazon jungle largely unexplored.) The bizarre currency situation substituted for geography, to provide at least for a brief time relative price protection against the natural course of events. With and around this there developed elite groups that were entrepreneurial and strongly interested in industry.[9]

As so often, the importance of the lack of natural protection and the concentration on Lima can be illuminated by the exception to the rule provided by a fascinating study of one of the very rare instances of industrial development outside of Lima: the textile industry of Huancayo, at 12 000 feet in the Peruvian Sierra. A study by Roberts shows that while from the 1930s on there was significant development of the industry, yet it was never really locally based. The capital and the entrepreneurship came from Lima and were tightly tied into the banks and the foreign merchant houses of the coast. There were good trade links with Lima. All of this meant that the surplus was reinvested not in Huancayo but in Lima, and as the competitive strength of Lima grew there was no resistance to the sucking off of surplus and eventually to the running down of the Huancayo plant. No other industry had developed around it, other needs being supplied from Lima, and there was no local bourgeoisie to oppose the forces of concentration.[10] The factory finally closed in 1972.[11]

A theme that we made much of in relation to Colombia was the extent of the complementarity between food and coffee, and the relatively low level of food imports. When we look at the relation between Peru's principal export crops and production for the domestic market, we find direct competition, in particular in regard to cotton but also in some measure in regard to both rice and sugar. As the expansion of exports occurred, all new land went preferentially to exports, and at certain times there was actually substitution of food for cotton. Food imports rose to an average of around 20 per cent of imports by the 1920s.

This did not on the whole produce a food supply bottle-neck and classic structuralist inflationary pressure: the results might almost have been healthier if it had. Instead, the problem was resolved in two directions: first by the tendency to worsening income distribution associated with the increased concentration which went with the export model; this reduced the size of the increase in demand for food as GDP rose. Second, the concentration of population on the coast and the geographical ease of resolving the problem by food imports, led to unhealthy developments in consumption patterns, as migrants from the Sierra acquired a taste for white bread and pasta products which have only been made in Peru from imported flour and have substituted for the potato and maize products which proliferate in Peru.[12] Today the import content of Lima's food consumption is around 40 per cent.[13] From the first decades of the twentieth century tariff policy favoured imports of food, and this remained a marked characteristic of policy right through the century. Out of this has come the very weak relationship between the city and the countryside which has conditioned Peru's macro management: reactivation has always led to imports and the supply response of domestic agriculture has been very slight. Typically, rice and to some extent beans have responded, but other products have not,[14] and this has simply reinforced the tendency to resort to imports.

The role of the state

We have seen, then, how the nature of the export boom had both positive and negative effects for Peru, but with the balance shifting over time. One of the most positive effects in the short run was the provision of infrastructure: this however had a paradoxical result as the boom in foreign lending occurred in the 1920s, with strong implications for one of our central themes: the role of the state.

We have seen how the multinationals who were anxious to develop copper and oil were both prepared and able to provide their own infrastructure; indeed, the major investments underlying the expansion of the 1920s – in port works, refineries and railways – had already been completed. Transport was not a problem, and marketing was carried out within the companies' multinational network. There was a need for order and regulation, particularly of oil claims, which would become serious by the 1940s, but did not affect this period. What the companies did need from the State was negative: an absence of interference and in particular of taxation. It is in this way principally that they fit into our story: the 'price' for absurdly low taxation, and a favourable settlement of the La Brea-Parinas dispute, was paid in part in direct financing of the government, and in part, in IPC's services in the negotiation of international loans.

By contrast, the sectors which had greater need in principle of government support were either not in political favour or were facing serious economic decline. The industries of the Selva and the more remote Sierra – rubber and wool – gave no motivation whatsoever for an opening up of the country. Sugar also faced adverse conditions and a number of the most prominent producers spent the 1920s in political exile during the Leguía dictatorship. Cotton clearly needed the State, for irrigation, but was composed for the most part of fairly small producers, who did not carry much weight at the national level. (The spending of local governments was tiny). In fact it would seem that irrigation needs did meet with some response, and that the investments were in part genuinely productive (largely owing to the efforts of Charles Sutton, consultant engineer in the Dirección de Aguas e Irrigación). However, a closer examination is revealing. Irrigation expenditure was made up as follows:

Expenditure on Chief Irrigation Schemes, 1919–29	
	Thousand libras (Lps)
Imperial	922
Olmos	3 453
Esperanza	612
Chira	60
Total	5 047

Source: Labarthe (1933).

The imperial scheme was in Cañete, Leguía's home ground: the list of beneficiaries makes revealing reading. Esperanza and Chira represented state takeovers of private enterprise ventures by the Graña and Checa families respectively. Olmos was perhaps the greatest scandal of the Leguía projects, with Lp 170 000 being spent on fraudulent 'expropriations' of land owned by political favourites, with the son of the President and his friends deeply involved. So also was the Lima merchant house of Ayulo & Co., which sold the machinery to the government. The project was apparently opposed by local landowners, who feared it would create a labour shortage and interfere with their comfortable monopoly of water rights. In all cases disbursement lagged badly.[15] What is really noticeable is how little was done that bore any relation to the real needs of the sector.The real beneficiaries of the schemes, therefore, tended to be based in Lima, and this was even more true of the extensive urban improvements carried out. Heavily involved were a number of foreign construction companies – notably the Foundation Co, and Frederick Snare & Co., and construction and real-estate interests. Political favouritism, corruption, speculation, luxury importing and capital flight were all commonly observable. The loans which in Colombia provided the lifeblood of the crucial productive sector, in Peru were in a real sense not 'needed'.

Given this analysis it is hardly surprising that when we compare the countries, as in Table 2.2, we find marked contrasts. Peru gave a larger place to private foreign investment - this fits with the picture we have painted. Colombia relied more heavily on borrowing than did Peru; the consequence was an expansion of the State, seen in the higher ratio of public expenditure to exports, and a far higher use of that expenditure in public works, producing the remarkable difference in the ratio of public works expenditure to exports. Whatever the sense in Colombia that there too there was waste and disorganisation in the 1920s, in relative terms we see surely a higher proportion of a larger sum going through to answer real development needs. In Peru the relative lack of such needs in relation to the points of expansion in the 1920s, meant that the pattern of corruption and extravagance which developed was not in fundamental contradiction with the economic model.

The same reasons that led to a lack of need for the state also meant a lack of incentive to develop producer organisations on the lines of the Federación. There were associations, but their role was limited, they had no state funding, and they were not offered the central role in policy-making which the Federación had to have. Nor did they play the same role in the marketing of all the main commodities: this was done either directly by the multinationals involved in producing, or by foreign-owned commercial houses, which typically were also import houses.

This 'conditions' the political economy of the management of the short term: it is time to consider briefly how Peru dealt with the various shocks of the middle years of the century.

The political economy of economic management

We have painted a surprising picture of Colombia's Keynesian management of the first such shock in the Depression of 1929. It hardly

Table 2.2
**Peru and Colombia: The Significance of Foreign Finance, Government
Spending and Public Works 1925–30**

	Colombia	Peru
Ratio of stock of US and UK investments and loans to exports, 1929	2.4	2.2
Ratio of debt only to exports, 1929	2.6[a]	0.9
Ratio of public expenditure (national and local) to exports, 1925–30	1.1	0.71
Ratio of public works expenditure to exports, 1925–30	0.49	0.12
Ratio of public works to total government expenditure, 1925–30	0.43	0.18[b]
Ratio of debt servicing to exports, 1930	0.21	0.16
Ratio of debt servicing to total government revenue (national and local), 1930	0.19	0.25

Sources: US and UK investment and loans – Normano (1931). Public spending: CEPAL, Anexo for Colombia (1957), *Extracto Estadístico* for Peru. Peruvian public works: see note [b]. Exports in local currency: Urrutia and Arrubla (1970), *Extracto Estadístico*. Exports in dollars: Wilkie (1974). Colombian debt: Echavarría (1981).

Notes:
[a]Colombian debt includes national, departmental and municipal borrowing, and that of the banks. It is possible that more has been included in this figure than in the estimate for investments plus loans from the South American Journal. Excluding banks gives a ratio of 1.6 – still significantly higher than the Peruvian figure.
[b]The total value of public works in Peru in the 1920s probably amounted to about Lp 25 million. The estimates vary according to the pro- or anti-Leguía bias of the author, ranging from Lp 19 million (Labarthe, 1933) to Lp 32 million (Capuñay, 1951) for 1919–30, the latter being inflated by the inclusion of an imputed value for forced labour used in road-building. The estimates used here are those of Garland Duponte (n.d.), which take a middle value.

needs saying that by contrast Peru was not in a position to implement such a set of measures. What we see instead is initially wholesale cuts in public sector programmes, resulting in 1929 in the beginning of the total political chaos we have already described. Once defaulting is legitimated the opportunity is grabbed: Peru is the second country in the continent to default, followed at once by abandonment of the gold standard and abrupt devaluation. Meanwhile, though the public spending pattern of the 1920s implied the need for political change, it also implied its efficacy: at least with the abrupt downfall of all political favourites public spending could be cut overnight, as it were, by wholesale abandoning of projects and above all by the cessation of payoffs and bribes which had comprised so large a part. (Not that the new political system would prove free of such things: but at least in the first instance major economies were possible). In the first years, 1929 and 1930, real expenditure fell 27 per cent from its 1926-28 level, compared with 20 per cent in Colombia; more importantly, it continued to fall heavily in the following two years.

However, these measures were certainly effective in gaining room for manoeuvre: the default alone in 1931 increased import capacity by some 20 per cent. There was thus less need for other measures: exchange controls were not used and although there were some increases in tariffs they did not compare with Colombia.

In the medium term we find a similar pattern. Peru simply waited upon the turnaround in export prices, which came early, as cotton recovered relatively soon in the international market. There was some supply response, particularly in small and medium mining where favourable prices of zinc and lead brought increased production, and in gold, exports of which rose by 162 per cent in value by 1938, compared with 1925-9. But the overall recovery to 80 per cent of the 1929 peak was achieved principally via prices, with an increase in the aggregate quantum index of exports of only 12 per cent.

Government spending recovered with exports in 1933 and continued to rise, though less rapidly than export revenue. The Leticia 'War' may have somewhat increased spending, but not by much. As to relative prices, the exchange rate movement gave some additional protection to the industrial sector, but it was slight compared with Colombia. There was rather little pressure for protection; an invasion of Japanese cotton textiles did result in import quotas in 1934, but the new tariff schedule introduced in 1936 had a minimal effect on the overall level of protection.

We can now understand only too well the comparative experience of recovery shown in Table 1.2 above. Peru experienced far slower growth, with little sign of progress in the sectors which elsewhere were leading import substitution. It must be stressed that some of the contrast with Peru is explained by Colombia's prior underdevelopment of industry rather than by policy. However, if there is a 'learning-by-doing' process in policy-making and economic management, then surely Colombia's path was more rewarding in its elements of unorthodoxy than Peru's instant-default, gaining of room for manoeuvre, and move back into a pattern of following exports. The state sector might actually have grown more than Colombia's if measured by money spent, but in terms of more qualitative and meaningful measures it certainly did not.

Peru's tendency to lag behind in promotion of industry continues through into the 1940s. We have explained how the challenge of the 1940s in general was to learn how to moderate controls in order to follow a protectionist route, but not too disastrously and typically in a manner compatible with foreign capital. In Peru, this period is extremely important, precisely because the failure to manage a policy of controls led to a great strengthening of the tendency to economic liberalism and bred such a resistance to controls that as late as the 1960s it was still being claimed, that Peruvians 'would never again' attempt such interventionism.

The failure is clear: our assessment elsewhere ran as follows: '...for the first two years the system [of import controls] appears to have operated entirely without criteria for its application. Only in mid-1947 did the Minister of Finance for the first time propose a detailed set of regulations, at a time when the processing of applications was running six months behind demand. Even with this administrative delay, the number of licences granted consistently outran the available supply of foreign exchange. These delays and shortages converted a policy which was presumably intended to help local industries, into a serious constraint on their expansion. Simultaneously, severe and increasing labour unrest (sparked off both by the increasing power of APRA and by the rising cost of living) led to reduced production and an atmosphere of uncertainty and political tension. Even orthodox elements in the policy proved impossible to implement. The combination of a frozen exchange rate, rapidly-rising internal wages and prices, import duties falling in real terms, and an import control system utterly without priorities or organisation, sufficed to deter the local elite from developing new industries, and to persuade them of the need to protect their more substantial interests elsewhere in the economy (eventually by open opposition to the Bustamante Government). Meantime, price controls had a strongly negative effect on agricultural production, while the squeeze on the export sectors, severe as it was, served no useful purpose beyond that of subsidising urban middle-class consumption.'[16]

The reasons lie partly in the complete inexperience of Peru with such policies (which was now to prove a self-reinforcing situation) and in the incoherence and weakness of the government of Bustamante, 1945–48. It was in principle an expression of new more popular forces, and initially formed a coalition with the APRA, founded in the 1920s and at that time still a genuine progressive and even radical party, but it was at the same time deeply tied into and in debt to traditional conservative interests. By 1947 the resulting political difficulties led to a situation described as constitutional deadlock. Congress was suspended in 1948 and the right-wing military coup of October of that year was greeted on many sides with a sense of relief.

While these contradictions were in evidence, foreign investors, mindful of Peru's pro-foreign investment attitude and her rich resources, were described as 'sniffing around like bird dogs'.[17] With the military coup of Odría the necessary resolution followed swiftly: Peru was one of the first countries of the continent to introduce an extremely favourable foreign capital legislation for mining, oil, and electricity. This legislation was combined with unification and devaluation of the exchange rate and the end of most controls.

Peru's process of moving away from controls and preparing for the expansion of the 1950s and 1960s differed from that in other medium and large Latin American countries in a way we can now understand in the light of the history we have described. It involved an almost exclusive return to and focus on primary sectors, which responded and led the country in a substantial renewed primary export boom for two decades, based on a strong expansion of supply.

Circumstances began to change, however, during the 1950s, as population pressure began to be felt, rural unrest grew, a constraint on land resources began to be obvious and pressure grew for some kind of land reform. All this combined to make the Peruvian economic elite, for the first time perhaps since the 1890s, seriously interested in industry, particularly since the search for oil was not yielding much and the crucial mining claims were in foreign hands. This explains Peru's belated move at the end of the decade of the 1950s to tariff reform and an Industrial Promotion Law.

The nature of the new incentives are very telling, however. This law gave lavish incentives for investment in industry, principally by means of exemptions from import duties on equipment and intermediate goods, and provision for tax-free reinvestment of profits. Laws of this type were appearing throughout Latin America at that time, but usually with the intention of stimulating the growth of selected industries and/or regions. The Peruvian law was exceptional in its generosity and lack of selectivity. Most countries restricted incentives to new activities, or activities with high percentages of local inputs and/or local ownership. The Peruvian law however offered benefits to all sectors, to established firms as well as new ones; these benefits included complete exemption from import duties for all 'basic'[18] industries, including established firms, and the right to invest tax free 30–100 per cent of profits, depending on the region. The incentives were explicitly made available to export processing activities, and their non-discriminatory nature made them more or less a straightforward subsidy to private enterprise. The most serious modification to the bill on its way through Congress was the elimination of a State agency, 'Corporación Nacional de Fomento Industrial', which was in the original proposal. The Law was deliberately intended to encourage foreign investment, and its unselective nature reflected the prevailing pro-private-enterprise, pro-foreign-capital ethos in Peru. The main argument advanced for the measure in the Congress debates was that it was 'unfair' for industry not to have a special law promoting it as other sectors did, and that, since promotional laws in other sectors had so successfully stimulated both foreign investment and rapid growth, the same recipe should now be tried for industry. Such an attitude precluded the discrimination among sectors which would have been essential for a rationally-planned industrialisation policy.

At the same time, tariff policy began to be modified to promote industry, more through the increases in effective protection resulting from exemptions granted under the new Law than through a systematic reform of the tariff for this end. We have seen that Peru had had a low level of tariffs;[19] beginning with the balance-of-payments crisis of 1958 tariffs were increased on several occasions, and in 1964 and 1967 entire new tariff systems were introduced. These tariff changes consisted largely of the raising of duties on consumer-goods imports. Higher duties on final goods, combined with exemptions under the Industrial Promotion Law, naturally brought massive increases in effective protection for import-substituting industries. Vehicles, for example, had 13 per cent effective protection in 1963 and 214 per cent in 1965; pharmaceutical products 18 per cent and 164 per cent for the same years.

This interest in industry, however, was the interest of elite groups which by this time had undergone a serious weakening of their entrepreneurial role, after decades of limited and symbiotic participation with foreign capital in the various export sectors. The atmosphere of the 1960s is perhaps most vividly illustrated in the remark made by Augusto Weise, distinguished member of Peru's business elite, as he decided in 1964 to move into fishmeal in partnership with Mecom, a Texan oilman: 'This whole fishmeal business has always smelled highly to me. But if Mr. Mecom is interested, why then, it smells like a rose.'[20]

The character of this new interest is consistent with a further very marked development at this time: a sharp increase in the dynamism of the banking sector, associated with a wave of foreign takeovers. The concomitant increase in financial savings reflected no increase in the savings effort, but the infrastructural development reflecting and facilitating the changing nature of the private sector in Peru in the 1960s.

First, it facilitated the shift of funds by the elite out of export sectors, while allowing this to be compatible with the weakening of their entrepreneurial role which we have already observed in certain export sectors. Second, by the increase in provision of specialised financial institutions for housing it aided the expansion of their real-estate interests. Third, by the provision of finance for consumption purchases it greatly facilitated the switch to an import-substitution boom centred on consumer durables. And last, it facilitated the entry of foreign investment into manufacturing, by enabling foreign firms to borrow locally, usually at negative real rates of interest, so further enhancing their profitability.

The result of these developments and of the policies we have already described was a massive wave of direct foreign investment in manufacturing, trebling between 1960 and 1966.

The weak role played by the obvious candidates for the part of the 'industrial bourgeoisie' lay behind the continued incoherence of government policy. We have seen that the Industrial Promotion Law approximated a generalised subsidy to manufacturing industry. While it incorporated certain inadequate incentives to regional decentralisation, the granting of exemptions and privileges was left to the discretion of the Government. In practice, the Government played a passive role, granting tariff exemptions to the sectors which mounted the most effective pressure campaigns. No consideration was given to the selection of industries on the basis of their real growth prospects, nor to the problem of avoiding diseconomies of scale in the limited Peruvian markets. (By 1966, for example, there were no fewer than thirteen automobile assembly plants in a country with an effective market of, say, one million families).

The result was an exaggerated version of the typical industrial growth associated with ISI: inefficient, inappropriately diversified, far too dependent on foreign inputs and foreign technology.

But the shift of elite interest from agriculture and the distorted character of the resulting industrial growth were only elements in a much wider and very alarming situation which was evolving in Peru, one which forms an essential backdrop to the policy management story we are about to tell, which begins in Peru's case with 1968. It is also one that simply has no parallel in the Colombian case. This situation is one which I have described elsewhere as a 'structural crisis', involving complex interrelationships between elements of the social, political and economic structure.

The political dimension concerns the discontent which was growing with the years of elite rule, reflected at one level in peasant unrest, but at quite another in growing middle class dissatisfaction with the slowing of benefits from growth. Unfortunately Peru's never-well-developed political structures did not succeed in articulating this discontent into a coherent alternative. With the government of Belaunde, 1963–68, the result was the growth in nationalistic and aggressive attitudes, particularly towards foreign investment, without the kind of clear and balanced redefinitions of the rules which might have allowed a new *modus vivendi*. This produced the worst of all worlds, for foreign mining companies simply withheld investments and no national alternative was forthcoming.

This political development was added to a number of more technical supply constraints, such as the reaching of the biological limit on fishing. The supply of relatively easily irrigable land also came to an end: the next projects required a degree of enterpreneurship from either state or private sector or both which was not readily forthcoming. These facts lie behind the figures on investment and export quantum which we must analyse comparatively in the following chapter in the light of our two histories.

Notes

1. From the title of Uribe Campuzano's book (Uribe Campuzano (1954)).
2. *South American Journal*, 23rd September 1899.
3. Data from *Extracto Estadístico*.
4. Sources for this and the following paragraphs are given in detail in Chapter 3 of Thorp and Bertram (1978) of which this section is a summary.
5. For documentation of the solid nature of this early industrial development, and its antecedents in still earlier developments, see Chapter 3 of Thorp and Bertram (1978), pp. 32–36.
6. This is based on the counterfactual analysis reported in detail in Thorp and Bertram (1978) and in Bertram (1974).
7. Based on the sources cited in the previous footnote.
8. The story is told in Bollinger (1971), p. 33. This unpublished thesis is an important source on this early period.
9. An interesting documentation of this is a recent history of the Prado family (Portocarrero, 1986).
10. Roberts (1978).
11. Jacobsen's documentation of Lima factory products invading the south of Peru in the 1920s and 1930s is a further interesting demonstration of our point. (Love and Jacobsen (1988), pp. 164–5).
12. Peruvian wheat has always been of poor quality, and extremely vulnerable to rust.
13. Data from the ENCA survey (1984).
14. Hopkins (1988) shows that peasants react to natural conditions not to prices. An evocative word for the nature of the supply response in Peru is 'viscosa' – Figueroa (1981).
15. For sources and more detail, see Thorp and Londoño (1984).

16.   Thorp and Bertram (1978), p. 188.
17.   *Wall Street Journal*, quoted in *West Coast Leader*, 27th June 1947.
18.   A term whose coverage was continually increased in subsequent decrees. Further, the law was almost immediately extended to consumer durables and even to the consumption goods sector.
19.   Macario (1964) gives a comparative table for Latin America. Peru has by far the lowest level.
20.   *Peruvian Times*, 5th March 1965, back cover. For an illuminating analysis of the role of the elite, see Fitzgerald (1976) and Ferner (1975). The change in character of the elite is vividly captured in the study of the Prado Empire by Portocarrero (1986).

3 The End of the Golden Age of Import-Substituting Industrialisation

The historical analysis of the two preceding chapters now allows us to characterise our two economies during the boom period of the 1960s. As the boom approached its end ISI was generally considered to be 'running out' as a development strategy.

One of the key contrasts between the two countries is given by Figures 3.1 and 3.2. Peru continued to be 'led' by primary exports throughout the 1950s and into the 1960s, based as we have seen on a massive supply expansion, aided by slightly more favourable terms of trade. But the major explanation lies on the supply side, with foreign capital playing the main role in mining, aided by favourable government policies, while domestic capital played a larger role in fishmeal. As a result the economy grew, but exports grew faster: the relationship between GDP and the capacity to import is shown in Table 3.1. Colombia meanwhile experienced steady but moderate growth of her export quantum: coffee growth slowed down as a result of lower prices since 1956, and problems of violence persisted.[1] Nevertheless the country succeeded in growing despite export trends as much as because of them: as Table 3.1 shows, GDP growth was actually able to *exceed* the growth of the current capacity to import. This is partly explained by positive capital flows – which Peru also benefited from – but also represents success in import substitution. The growth of industry is shown in Table 3.2: in Peru's case it was still dominated even in the 1960s by the expansion of export-processing, which accounts for the otherwise surprisingly large share of 'industry' in GDP in the 1950s. In Colombia's case we have seen how the structure and character of the coffee sector led to a healthier regional base for industry and to an interest in industrialization on the part of coffee interests from an early date. All this is behind the earlier and more rational development of protectionist policies in Colombia than in Peru. We have seen how the policy measures to implement ISI in Peru came very late, and in a form which implied not selective stimulus of certain activities but an across-the-board subsidy to the whole sector.

45

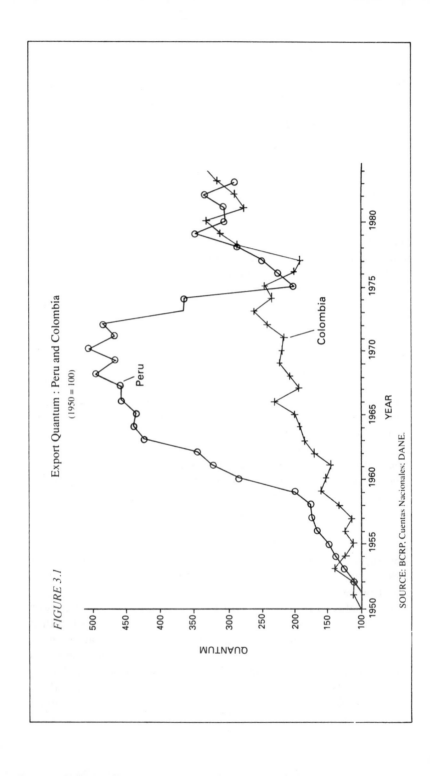

FIGURE 3.1

Export Quantum : Peru and Colombia

(1950 = 100)

SOURCE: BCRP, Cuentas Nacionales; DANE.

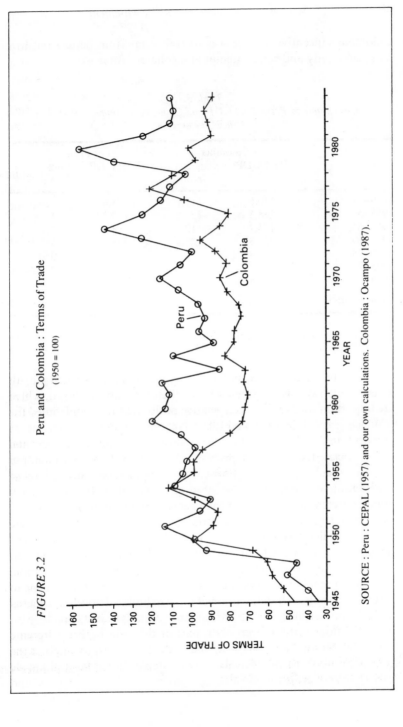

FIGURE 3.2

Peru and Colombia : Terms of Trade

(1950 = 100)

SOURCE : Peru : CEPAL (1957) and our own calculations. Colombia : Ocampo (1987).

Colombia's incentive scheme was of course far from perfect but had more selectivity and some attempt at a coherent framework.

Table 3.1
Colombia and Peru: Real GDP and Capacity to Import[a] 1950–83
Indices, 1950 = 100

	Colombia		Peru	
	Real GDP	Capacity to import	Real GDP	Capacity to import
1950–54	110.6	117.1	113.6	120.8
1955–59	138.5	125.7	142.2	127.2
1960–64	173.7	112.8	188.4	228.3
1965–69	220.3	125.4	245.0	311.5
1970–74	306.3	171.5	312.8	350.9
1975–79	393.4	260.8	369.8	377.3
1980–83	479.5	315.0*	387.3	467.2

*This figure refers to 1980 only.

Note:
[a]This is a *current* account concept only: i.e. the dollar value of exports deflated by import prices. The import price data were constructed as indicated in the notes to Figure 3.2.

As we have described the 'political economy' of the export-led growth phase in the two cases, some striking differences have emerged, which are important to assessing their relative position as they confronted the troubled years of the 1970s and 1980s. Not only did Peru's strong export growth lead to relatively little industrialization for her size (other than that associated with export processing), it also led to discrimination against agriculture for domestic use, with as we have seen strong income distribution consequences but also growing vulnerability as food imports became more important as a per cent of food consumption. This was in part a consequence of her permissive attitude to foreign firms: the policies of a firm like Leche Gloria in gradually substituting imports of powdered milk for the local product were allowed to proceed without restriction (Lajo 1983). Unfortunately, strong changes in consumption patterns were allowed to occur, which would now be very difficult to reverse. Not only is the population of Lima habituated now to powdered milk: more seriously, white bread and pasta products made with imported flour form an important part of the food basket. Migrants from the Sierra have adapted and reduced correspondingly their consumption of the traditional Peruvian staples (potatoes and a wide variety of root crops).

Table 3.2
Colombia and Peru: Growth and Structure of Manufacturing Production from the 1950s to the 1970s

Colombia	1950	1955	1960	1972
Index of industrial growth	100.0	140.6	189.5	371.0
% share industry in GDP	17.8	17.0	18.5	18.3
% share excluding export processing	n.a.	(15.4)	(17.5)	(17.7)
Composition of industrial growth:				
Export processing	n.a.	9.2	5.8	3.7
Other consumer goods	n.a.	64.6	54.3	53.7
Other intermediate goods	n.a.	19.5	28.0	31.3
Capital goods	n.a.	6.4	11.9	11.4

Peru	1950	1955	1960	1965	1968
Index of industrial growth	100.0	154	216	304	346
% share industry in GDP	17	21	23	24	25
% share excluding export processing	(14.8)	(17)	(17)	(19)	(19)
Composition of industrial growth:					
Export processing	18.0	19.1	25.8	21.5	22.8
Other consumer goods	50.7	49.4	42.4	40.8	39.3
Other intermediate goods	19.0	19.6	19.0	21.8	25.1
Capital goods and consumer durables[a]	6.7	8.6	9.9	10.8	12.9

Source: DANE, INE, BCRP.

Note:
[a]The classification of capital goods and consumer durables is very poor in the Peruvian data. We felt it was less misleading to combine them.

Colombia's record is most unusual in this respect: perhaps in part because of the complementarity between coffee and food production, non-coffee agricultural production actually rose even in the 'classic' period of ISI, in the 1950s and 1960s. Table 3.3 shows the weight of food imports in the total import bill. Peru's imports of food comprise largely products which she can produce. In Colombia's case, maize and the flat bread made from it have remained central to the urban diet. There are some imports which in principle compete with domestic supplies (wheat, barley) but their importance in the basic diet is much less.

But we have also identified wider consequences of the political economy of export-led growth. In the case of Peru, the whole model was approaching crisis by the late 1960s. This took time to become evident in the figures, but by the early 1970s was indicated not just by the export figures but by the decline in the investment coefficient, shown in Table 3.4 Behind the startling export quantum data shown in Figure 3.1 lay an

Table 3.3
Colombia and Peru: Food Imports as Per Cent of Total Imports 1950–70
(five year averages)

Colombia	1950–54	1955–59	1960–64	1965–69
Total	6.3	6.6	4.7	5.3
Meat	0.5	0.4	0.2	0.1
Milk and Cream	0.2	0.1	0.2	0.1
Cereals and Preparations	2.9	3.1	3.3	3.2
Fruits and Vegetables	0.6	0.6	0.6	0.3
Peru	1950–54	1955–59	1960–64	1965–69
Total	14.0	13.0	14.3	13.7
Meat	2.2	2.0	2.6	3.8
Milk and Cream	0.8	0.9	0.6	1.1
Butter	0.4	0.7	1.0	0.9
Cereals and Preparations	9.2	8.6	8.6	8.0
Vegetables and Fruits	0.3	0.7	1.0	1.0

Source: UN, *Foreign Trade Yearbooks.*

Table 3.4
Colombia and Peru: Investment as a Percentage of GDP 1955–84

Percent of GDP	Colombia			Peru		
	Private	Public	Total	Private	Public	Total
1955–58	15.3	3.4	18.7	17.5	4.8	22.3
1959–63	15.8	3.4	19.2	15.3	3.3	18.6
1964–68	14.9	4.4	19.3	10.8	4.6	15.4
1969–73	12.5	6.3[a]	18.8[a]	7.9	4.8	12.7
1974–76	13.0	5.3	18.3	6.5	8.8	15.3
1977–79	11.4	7.0	18.4	8.4	5.8	14.2
1980–82[b]	11.7	8.5	20.2	8.5	4.5	13.0
1983–84	10.2	9.0	19.2	7.4	9.6	17.0

Source: E. V. K. Fitzgerald, *The Political Economy of Peru, 1956–78: Economic Development and the Restructuring of Capital* (Cambridge: Cambridge University Press, 1979); Banco Central, *Memoria;* DANE, *El Sector Público Colombiano 1970–81;* Banco de la República, *Memoria.*

Notes:
[a]Excludes 1969
[b]For 1980–1982, this corrects Fitzgerald's figures using data from the Instituto Nacional de Estadística. The Banco Central estimates for these two years are implausibly high. See Thorne (1986), Appendix 3.

export supply crisis of dramatic proportions. This would not show up in the export volume series until the early 1970s, but the relevant decisions were being taken – or not – in the 1960s. As we have seen, up to this time a succession of fast-expanding products had permitted a relatively easy supply-side response to international demand; the crises had come via the faltering on the demand side. Investment had been necessary, of course, but the infrastructure – chiefly railways – had been built in time, by foreigners. Incorporation of new land – or the sea – had been possible in a relatively simple process of 'horizontal' extension. By the 1960s, incorporating new land meant huge irrigation projects, of a new order of complexity. The anchovies had been overfished and a biological limit reached. Launching new mineral projects again required a jump in the level of complexity.

By contrast, Colombia's export quantum was growing steadily through the whole three decades, as coffee increased in area and yield. The prospects were never brilliant, but usually reasonable: our emphasis on the distorting effects of Peru's booms on policy and on structure lead us to underline that paradoxically this was yet another favourable aspect of Colombian development. At the same time, there was no impending supply crisis, also unlike Peru. What helped was the very backwardness of coffee: yields were low in international terms, and the improvements that produced the figures shown in Table 3.5 were very simple. What also helped were the promotion policies of the Coffee Federation,[2] while

Table 3.5
Colombia: Coffee Area and Production 1945–84
(five-year averages)[a]

	Area (thousands of hectares)	Volume of production (millions of bags of 60kg each)
1945–49	569	6.1[b]
1950–54	669	6.3
1955–59	799	6.5
1960–64	877	7.4
1965–69	919	7.8
1970–74	953	7.7
1975–79	975	9.3
1980–84	1009	13.0

Source: Ocampo (1987a).

Notes:
[a] Refers to year ending in September
[b] Excludes 1945.

new land was also still available, as Table 3.5 shows. The second contributing factor up to 1974 was the growth of non-traditional exports, as shown in Table 3.6, which demonstrates one of the most remarkable differences between the case studies.

Table 3.6
Colombia and Peru: Non-Traditional and Manufactured Exports
as Per Cent of Total Exports 1959–71

Colombia	1959–61	1965	1969–71
Total Non-Traditional	4.5	11.7	19.8
Meat	0.0	1.6	1.0
Sugar	1.2	1.4	2.3
Cotton	1.7	1.5	4.8
Cut Flowers	0.0	0.0	0.2
Manufactures	1.7	6.9	10.8
Chemicals	0.2	1.1	1.6
Paper, Containers, etc.	0.0	0.0	0.2
Textiles and Clothing	0.1	1.9	2.2
Machinery and Transport Equipment	0.4	0.4	1.3
Printed Material	0.0	0.0	0.4
Peru	**1959–61**	**1965**	**1969–71**
Total Non-Traditional	1.5	1.3	2.3
Manufactures[a]	1.4	1.5	1.9
Chemicals	0.4	0.3	0.3
Textiles and Clothing	0.1	0.0	0.0
Machinery and Transport Equipment	0.0	0.2	0.0

Source: UN, *Foreign Trade Yearbooks.*

Note:
[a] Excludes exports of non-ferrous metals which are considered to be traditional in Peru's exports.

These facts raise many questions for the following chapters. What was cause and what was effect? What institutional and/or policy conditions permitted non-traditional exports to do relatively well in the one case, very poorly in the other? The variable that comes immediately to mind, of course, is the exchange rate. Figure 3.3 shows the strikingly different development of the real exchange rate both before and after 1965. It will be an important part of the political economy story of Colombia in Chapters 7–9 to explain how there was such success in achieving real devaluation without inflation. As to Peru, our argument is controversial: we see the overvalued exchange rate of the 1960s as *consequence*, not cause, of the export stagnation, in contrast to standard interpretations

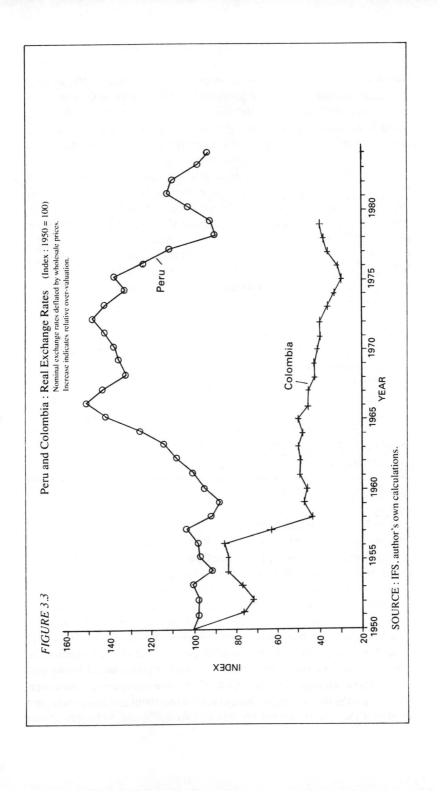

FIGURE 3.3   Peru and Colombia : Real Exchange Rates   (Index : 1950 = 100)

Nominal exchange rates deflated by wholesale prices.
Increase indicates relative over-valuation.

Peru

Colombia

INDEX

160
140
120
100
80
60
40
20

1950   1955   1960   1965   1970   1975   1980

YEAR

SOURCE : IFS, author's own calculations.

which suggest that in various ways policies failed to give the private sector an adequate margin of profitability. Such an analysis lays stress on controlled food prices, exchange rate policy, and penalisation of foreign capital, or at least the failure to create a secure and welcoming environment. Chapter 1 has made it clear that at least some of these were indeed important aspects of policy by the first Belaunde period, and were in no way positive. The point is, not that this analysis is wrong, but that it is inadequate – and so inadequate as to be quite unhelpful. Improved food prices *alone* would have only partially reduced import dependency, given what was (and is) required to raise productivity in the traditional rural sector, in terms of supply inputs, the gradual changing of practices, tenure systems and attitudes and the creation of infrastructure.[3] Given all this, better prices would in the short run have simply swollen middlemen's profits.

That exchange rate policy was a *result* of lack of interest in the export sector, rather than its cause, is evidenced by a study of elite interests in policy-making in the post-war period in Peru. The overvalued exchange rate was only the symptom of the problems with the whole export-led model: the Peruvian elite had always confidently managed exchange rate policy[4] but by the 1960s they were losing interest in so doing, precisely because of the problems we have outlined. As sector after sector ran into trouble, the economy was *becoming* for the first time since guano a mono-export economy – and in the mining sector the resource base was monopolised by foreign capital, which lacked the necessary influence on the exchange rate, given that the traditional elite groups were now moving at least at second remove into industry, where the overvalued rate plus tariffs suited them well. Consequently, for foreign capital to expand its base in mining required far more than the right exchange rate: it meant coming to terms with a history of extremely unevenly divided benefits and the development of legislation to provide and protect a more satisfactory division. The difficulty of such an evolution conditions the story of the troubled political economy of the next twenty years.

In Colombia, by contrast, coffee interests both had to and could reasonably believe in coffee – and at the same time develop activities elsewhere. These groups were not foreigners, or increasingly attacked small elite groups, but the core of the body politic, linking small and large farmers, represented in virtually every region, and articulated amazingly well at the national level. The system was built on inherited leadership at all levels, and a long-lived dominance of party oligarchies – but at the same time did not alienate but successfully co-opted interests at 'lower' levels. This gave exceptional strength and influence to the coffee sector. An exchange rate favourable to exporting was central to the country's political economy, throughout the period, though as we shall see the coffee sector often did not support large devaluations. Chapter 7 explores how a peculiarly favourable exchange regime in fact evolved.

This takes us to the wider level of analysis springing from our historical story: the very different history of the role of the state and policy-making in the two cases. In Peru the supply crisis could perfectly well have been overcome – by a sufficiently dynamic state and/or private sector. But it is precisely the conclusion of our historical analysis that the preconditions necessary to develop a state or private sector adequate for the next stage, never existed. Thus, in regard to the private sector, the weak industrial base was accompanied by a weak development of entrepreneurial groups in industry. Those that existed were accustomed to a symbiotic relationship with foreign capital and identified their interests closely with those of the foreigner. This had implications for the kind of state produced by the export-led growth experience. The groups leading the growth process were typically a small number of elite families working in happy partnership with foreign capital (instances of competition are rare). Foreign capital provided the infrastructure: what these groups needed from the state was the maintenance of order and the *absence* of things such as taxation of their profits or restrictions on profit outflow. The groups in a position to make money had up to now been able to do so in the export sector: on the whole they had no incentive to press for the creation of profit opportunities elsewhere in the economy – for example by protection of the industrial sector. Until the 1960s, the army was an effective instrument by which the elite maintained the order and control necessary to the relatively smooth functioning of their model.

In Colombia, we have shown how the needs of coffee were special, and rather fruitfully so, in that coherent mechanisms of intervention and ways of relating to the state had to be patiently built up. Thus, although the state itself was relatively small in terms of its weight in the economy (see Table 3.7), there was much accumulated experience of interventions and management by the 1960s – in the public administration, amongst the political classes and in the Coffee Federation. Perhaps more important, there was a whole tradition of participation in local politics, related to the importance of coffee and coffee's relation to the state at the local level, which we would suggest fed through not simply into the life of local politics, reflected in things such as education expenditure, but must have acted as an energising force at the national level too.[5]

Table 3.7
Colombia and Peru: The Relative Weight of the State 1965

	Colombia	Peru
Share of public sector in total investment	17	32
Public investment as percentage GDP	3.1	5.5
Public consumption as percentage GDP	8.2	17.3
Share of public sector in total employment	4.0	6.0

Source: DANE: *Cuentas nacionales*, ECLA: *Statistical Yearbook for Latin America and the Caribbean*; Ocampo et al. (ed.) (1987b) *El Problema Laboral Colombiano*; BCRP: *Cuentas Nacionales del Perú 1950–65*.

Reinforcing this and in turn reinforced by it, is the relatively small role for foreign capital in the economy.

How far did this contrasting structure result in contrasting distributional characteristics? Our story has been that up to the 1960s the Peruvian version of export-led growth functioned reasonably well as a growth model, bringing a modest but not negligible rate of growth of a little over one per cent a year in per capita terms over the long run.[6] It also 'functioned' in the sense that it did not lead to a demand for imports that outstripped the growth of exports, or to much inflation. The powerful groups in the economy experienced satisfactory participation in growth and were able on the whole to co-opt or repress emerging populist movements (notably the APRA party). But to understand the period to which we turn in detail in the next three chapters, it is important to understand that it *never* functioned as a 'development' model, in two senses. First, crucial elements of resilience which would be badly needed in this next period had not developed: we have seen the weakness of the state machinery and of both the industrial base and industrial groups, and the vulnerability of the economy via its dependence on food imports, as the export engine ran out of steam. Second, large portions of the population did not benefit from growth, or even actively lost out. The narrow distribution of benefits was rooted initially in the geographical fragmentation: what grew out of this and then reinforced it was the division between 'modern' and 'traditional' sectors: the modern, often foreign-owned, capital-using mines, sugar plantations, banks etc. against the small-scale, low-productivity peasant or artisan enterprises. The coexistence of the different sectors involved both fragmentation and interaction: they existed in part because there were obstacles to markets functioning – to the free flow of labour, to the spread of know how. Yet it was also true that the terms on which they traded led to one growing at the expense of the other. Thus the urban informal sector sold to the formal sector – but on terms which gave more possibility of accumulation and so growth to the already-stronger partner.

This is not to say, of course, that the growth of the informal sector was entirely negative: it provided a means of survival in a situation where the most likely counterfactual in urban areas would be open unemployment. The point is that the model generated worsening income distribution with time.[7] The worsening income distribution was the main reason why the expansion of export crops rather than food for the domestic market led to little inflation: the *poor* did not demand more food.

In Colombia's case, we have seen how paradoxically acute geographical fragmentation actually had beneficial effects. The early industrialisation stimulated by coffee was less vulnerable, because of geography, as international transport costs fell. Local elites retained their autonomy, in part because of the geographical remoteness of Bogotá. We have also seen the very special characteristics of Colombian coffee, not only in respect of the State and policy-making, as described above, but also in relation to the wide spread of a labour-intensive and prosperous export crop, providing locally accumulated surplus. We have emphasized the lack of a foreign presence in that sector which might have influenced the allocation of that surplus. The result by the 1960s was a most unusual *regional* income distribution: as Table 3.8 shows, the lack of industrial concentration was unique in Latin America, while only Uruguay had a comparable lack of regional dispersion of GDP per capita. These facts were reflected in and consolidated by a regional fiscal structure which was also unique. We have

Table 3.8
Latin America: Percentage of Industrial Production Accounted for by Most Industrialised Province c.1970

Argentina	(1970)	43
Brazil	(1970)	57
Colombia	(1970)	23
Chile	(1970)	56
Ecuador	(1965)	40
Mexico	(1970)	37
Panama	(1968)	64
Peru	(1970)	45
Uruguay	(1961)	78

Source: UN, ECLA (1981).

shown how resulting regional interests generated the infrastructure needed to ameliorate the fragmentation – without the foreign involvement which characterised the Peruvian case.[8]

The elements of vulnerability and lack of resilience which we have identified in the Peruvian case were therefore in a striking degree *not* characteristics of Colombia. *Personal* income distribution, however, is another story: however good the regional distribution may have been, the personal income distribution generated by the pattern of growth was still very unequal as of the mid-1960s. The remainder of this chapter takes up this issue in some detail.

Issues of welfare and distribution

When one tries to assemble global measures of distribution, the most rewarding type of material is generally that provided by household surveys. Needless to say, there are problems, since the coverage tends to vary greatly, and it can usually be assumed that the variation biases the result. The extent to which different surveys pick up non-labour income varies, again affecting the evolution of inequality rather seriously, and there is variation also in the coverage of income in kind, which likewise is non-neutral in regard to distribution. Using household data means also of course that we need to take account of changes in family size in moving to any comparative statement about individuals.

A careful study for Colombia bearing all this in mind is the work of Urrutia (1985) for the early 1970s. He estimates a Gini coefficient of 0.58 for the economically active population for 1972, with 0.63 in rural areas and 0.54 in urban.[9] Remarkably, we have a national household survey for the *same* date, 1971/2, for Peru. The Gini coefficients show less inequality both for rural and urban areas in Peru: 0.56 for rural areas compared with 0.63, and 0.46 for urban compared with 0.54.

However, when we evaluate all the probable biases of the variations in methodology, coverage and concept, we can see that such a finding is rather easily accounted for purely by such factors. Thus, omitting income in kind increases measured inequality: this is omitted in the Colombian work,[10] included, at least in principle, in the Peruvian.[11] The greater the under-reporting, the greater the apparent equality compared with the truth, it is usually assumed – and the Peruvian coverage is 60 per cent[12] compared with 78 per cent in Colombia.[13] Income from capital is in principle included in both – but the Urrutia methodology assumed underestimates in rural areas,[14] while the Peruvian work accepted the ENCA survey data.[15] Hence the Peruvian figures *may* under-report capital income more seriously. Finally, the Colombian data are for the economically active population, and while it is not clear that the poor have fewer economically active members per family, it is a possibility.[16]

Nevertheless, while we cannot conclude firmly that Colombian income distribution was any worse than Peru's in the early 1970s, we certainly also cannot conclude that it was any better. This is consistent with an entirely different approach, which estimates the income needed to satisfy minimum consumption needs. It has been developed on a comparative basis by CEPAL (see Molina, 1982). The results are again striking. As shown in Table 3.9, in 1970 Colombia has 45 per cent of the population unable to satisfy minimum consumption needs, while Peru has more – 50 per cent – but *both* are well below the continental average. And Colombian *urban* poverty appears worse than Peru's at this date.

Table 3.9
Latin America: Estimates of the Incidence of Poverty Around 1970

	Percentage of households below the poverty line[a]			Percentage of households below the destitution line[b]		
	Urban	Rural	National	Urban	Rural	National
Argentina	5	19	8	1	1	1
Brazil	35	73	49	15	42	25
Colombia	38	54	45	14	23	18
Costa Rica	15	30	24	5	7	6
Chile	12	25	17	3	11	6
Honduras	40	75	65	15	57	45
Mexico	20	49	34	6	18	12
Peru	28	68	50	8	39	25
Uruguay	10	–	–	4	–	–
Venezuela	20	36	25	6	19	10
Latin America	26	62	40	10	34	19

Source: Molina (1982).

Note:
[a] Poverty line = twice the income needed to buy a basket of food which satisfies minimum calorie needs (i.e. assumes poor spend 50 per cent of their income on food).
[b] Destitution line = the income needed to buy a basket of food to satisfy minimum calorie needs.

Because such aggregate data are so difficult to interpret, economists increasingly prefer to look at indicators of 'basic needs' or living conditions. A selection of such indicators is given in Table 3.10. Much literature now exists on the problem of measurement and valid proxies for 'quality of life': the overwhelming consensus seems to be that infant mortality, life expectancy at birth, and literacy function most reliably as welfare indicators. (Of course they cannot be interpreted in isolation: they are inter-related with other variables. Literacy, for example, is in part a proxy for skills which enable a person to take advantage of health facilities which in their turn raise the quality of life.)

Looking at Table 3.10, if we consider first the data on education, we immediately encounter problems of interpretation. Colombia's rate of illiteracy is lower than Peru's around 1970, while Peru has a higher proportion of children in school. It is not simply a time lag problem either, since Peru's enrollment rates were consistently higher through the 1950s and 1960s. One obvious hypothesis is that Peru's schools are less 'effective' – literacy measures the *result* – and/or that initial enrollment in Peru is undermined by high dropout rates. In fact dropout rates for both countries are high, but Colombia's are actually worse: in Colombia in recent years, less than 50 per cent of those entering primary school have completed the final years of primary education, while in Peru the figure is nearly 60 per cent.[17]

Table 3.10
Colombia and Peru: Basic Needs Situation, c. 1965[a]

	Peru	Colombia
Illiteracy rate[b] (1961, 1964)	38.9	27.1
Infant mortality (years 0–1) (1970) per 1 000	152.2	83.5
Child mortality (years 1–4) (1970) per 1 000	12.5	6.8
Life Expectancy at birth (1960/5)	49.1	56.2
Calories available (1964, 1966)	2 261	2 154
Calorie availability as per cent of requirement (1964, 1966)[c]	96	93
Percentage of children 6–11 receiving education (1965)	68.7	52.4
Gross enrolment rates primary (1965)[d]	101.9	84.7
Population with access to piped water (1969)		
Urban	69.1	97.5
Rural	8.4	47.6
Percentage urban population served by sewer system (1969)	61.9	71.7

Source: ECLA, *Statistical Yearbook for Latin America and the Caribbean.*

Note:
[a] Dates following each heading give Peru, then Colombia. A single date is for both countries.
[b] Using FAO norms.
[c] Percentage of population aged 15 years and over.
[d] Those of *any* age receiving primary education, as per cent of the population aged 6–11.

The *average* number of years of primary education in Colombia in the mid-1970s was 3.1 in urban areas and 1.6 in rural areas.[18] *Functional* literacy is therefore much lower than (self-assessed) census data[19] – and the slightly higher dropout rate suggests the gap may be even larger in Colombia than in Peru.

Table 3.11
Colombia and Peru: Percentage Illiterate Among Population Aged 15+

	Total	Male	Female
Colombia 1973			
Total	19.2	18.0	20.2
Urban	11.2	9.0	13.0
Rural	34.7	32.8	36.8
Peru 1972			
Total	27.5	16.7	38.2
Urban	12.4	5.9	18.9
Rural	51.1	33.9	68.0

Source: National Census data.

More insight comes from Table 3.11, which breaks illiteracy down according to gender. Peruvian urban men were actually more literate than their Colombian counterparts in the early 1970s: it is the amazingly high illiteracy figures for Peruvian women that explains the overall record. The gap was only somewhat narrowed by the 1980s. Although fewer girls were going to school than boys in 1972, the difference was not great, and data for earlier decades give a similar picture.[20] The difference appears to reside at least in part in culture, expectations and self-concept – the latter in part because census data require a person to define him/herself as able or unable to read and write. The issue is perhaps more straightforward when we look at infant mortality and life expectancy at birth (see Table 3.10). Colombia's record in 1970 is better – but not that much better in regard to life expectancy. The figure for infant mortality is much better, but still high by international standards.[21]

Nutritional data produce their own problems of comparability. There are two main approaches. First, anthropometric studies measure children's physical development compared with international standards: the 'correct' standards can be disputed and different studies use different norms. Second, the calorie, protein and vitamin requirements of the population can be compared with availability. This tends to be done either for national averages, which conceal much, or for subgroups which are not directly comparable across our countries. The most readily available data concern calories, and there is controversy over how far this measure adequately captures nutrition standards.[22] Specifically, for Peru it seems to be accepted that people consuming adequate calories probably have adequate diets, while this is contested for Colombia: Ochoa argues the reverse (on the basis of fieldwork in the Cauca).[23] In both countries, the experts are agreed that in economic crisis, calories substitute for proteins and vitamins.

Looking at the first approach, one can conclude no more than that in the 1960s the countries were 'not dissimilar'. A study for Colombia of children under 5 years for 1965-6 gives 24 per cent malnourished by one norm, that of WHO, 52 per cent by another, the Gómez criterion.[24] A study also using Gómez for Peru gives 44 per cent for 1974, but this is for children under 6: the addition of an extra year would typically reduce the level.[25] This plus the difference in data would suggest fairly comparable levels.

In both cases, the degree of regional disparity is probably great. In Peru this is clear in 1972, the figures ranging from 19 per cent in Lima to 68 per cent for the Sierra Baja.[26] Unfortunately the regional classification used in Colombia is not helpful as the five regions used in the DANE study do not reveal much variation.[27]

Turning to the adequacy of calories and other aspects of diet, again we find similarity around the beginning of the 1970s. The WHO index give 96 per cent global adequacy for Peru, 92 per cent for Colombia for 1969–71. This of course implies a huge deficiency for some groups: in Peru in 1972, 52 per cent of the population consumed less than the recommended number of calories. In Colombia the estimate is 40 per cent but this is challenged on the grounds that it used too low a level of 'requirements' and ignored serious protein and vitamin deficiency (Ochoa, (1986) pp. 80–81).

Whichever way we come at the problem, then – via distribution or via basic needs – we find a remarkable degree of similarity in the plight of the poor in our two cases. What was different, though, was the extent to which distributional tensions were beginning to affect the whole functioning of the model. In Peru, rural discontent was clearly rising in the 1960s and new social and political pressures were developing, as population growth interacted with rural stagnation.

This situation was affecting investment in agriculture. The growing middle class was feeling increasing discontent at oligarchic rule and the large share of the benefits from growth going to the foreigner. This as we have seen was finding expression in the increasingly nationalistic and aggressive attitude to foreign capital expressed in the Belaunde period. Thus political pressures and tensions were related to and expressed in the stagnation in investment and increasingly in the volume of exports. Colombia, as we have seen, had come through an extraordinary episode of violence which appeared to be in some measure contained by the 1960s. The National Front was providing a stable framework for politics and policy-making – though of course hardly a genuinely representative or democratic one. In retrospect the land reform of 1961 would seem a very weak measure but in terms of *perceptions* of the needs of the moment, land reform had been carried out and was being continued. When Lleras Restrepo came to power, he confronted rural unrest, which as we shall see he had to move strongly to defuse with the creation of ANUC and further land reform measures. Nevertheless the increasing sense of alienation of politically and economically important groups in Peru found no echo in the Colombian situation, prone to violence as it was. In *comparative* terms, there was a stability and sense of continuity in Colombia as Lleras Restrepo came to power, radically distinct from the environment in which General Velasco took control.

If we turn now to look ahead, at the years 1967-87, the macro data show us some impressive differences. As Figure 3.1 showed above, the export stagnation after the 1960s was sufficient to bring Peru back down to Colombia's level by the end of the period. Despite Peru's much faster rate of growth in the early part, the overall growth experience comes out worse (Table 3.12). Table 3.1 above shows how Peru's growth was subsequently drastically limited by import capacity – and this does not take into account debt servicing. Colombia avoided both heavy debt and rapid inflation: Peru suffered increasingly from both as her structural crisis deepened.

Clearly Colombia 'succeeds' much better than Peru in surviving the rough seas of the 1970s and 1980s. The remainder of our study is devoted to the important questions raised by this. What is the role of ISI-style policy distortions in Peru's export stagnation? Is her collapse into debt crisis a direct result of the limitations of ISI itself, as some have suggested?[28] Is Colombia's 'better' performance a result of greater respect for the free play of the market and the 'rules of the game'? Perhaps most importantly of all, what does 'better' actually mean for the poor? What does Colombia's basic needs record look like compared with Peru after such success?

The following chapters attempt to cast light on these questions, first by looking in some detail at the chronology of macroeconomic policy management in the two cases, paying particular attention to the

Table 3.12
Colombia, Peru and the Rest of the World: Real GDP
(annual growth rates)

	All	Developing Countries			World
		Latin America			
		All	Colombia	Peru	
Long run					
1960–85	4.9	4.6	4.7	3.5	3.9
Short run					
1960–64	4.4	4.2	4.0	6.0	4.2
1965–69	4.8	4.4	4.4	2.9	4.2
1970–74	5.1	5.9	5.2	4.8	3.5
1975–79	4.3	4.4	4.5	1.1	3.6
1980–84	1.5	0.1	1.6	–0.8	1.8

Source: World Bank.

moments when the international system is in some degree challenged. Thus we look particularly closely at the Velasco and García periods in Peru and at Lleras Restrepo and Betancur in Colombia. But it also turns out to be very important to look at the distorting effects of *booms*, and this leads us to look at the Colombian coffee bonanzas of 1975–77 and 1985–6, and at drugs bonanzas as well as at the copper price bonanza in the Belaunde period. We then turn to some general themes in chapter 10. We try to probe what lies behind relative success in 'management', as well as its limitations, as reflected in basic needs variables and in issues of development policy that go beyond exchange rate and monetary and fiscal policy.

Notes

1.   Ocampo and Montenegro (1988).
2.   Ocampo (1987).
3.   See Cotlear (1986), for a thorough documentation of this point.
4.   See for insight into this the correspondence between two key members of the elite, Pedro Beltrán and Augusto Gildermeister, over the period 1944–1955. This is preserved in the Agrarian Archive in Lima.
5.   What belies this is the low level of electoral participation in Colombia – which is no higher than in other Latin American countries. This theme needs further exploration, clearly.
6.   Thorp and Bertram (1978), p. 205.
7.   See Webb (1974). Chapter 10 takes up distributional issues in more detail.
8.   This is not to say of course that there were not still strong regional differences in income level, only that they were less extreme than in Peru.
9.   Urrutia (1985), p. 77. He uses the household survey data of 1971, but whereas this latter shows rural areas as *more* equal, he estimates capital income and comes out with an estimate showing greater inequality in rural areas. See also Aguilar and Perfetti.

10. Urrutia (1985), p. 77.
11. Amat y Leon (1983), p. 66 ff, Amat y Leon (1981), p. 150.
12. Amat y Leon (1981), p. 150.
13. Urrutia (1985), p. 75. His estimates for 1972 are principally based on the DANE survey of July 1971.
14. Urrutia (1985), p. 77.
15. Amat y Leon (1983), p. 76. Income from capital is given as 3 per cent of family income on average.
16. It depends crucially on the definition of 'economically active' of course. The poor are normally considered to have more family members (though that is not always true) but that is a different issue.
17. Dropout rates calculated from data in the UNESCO *Statistical Digest* and from DANE, *Boletin Mensual de Estadistica*.
18. *Revista de Planeación y Desarrollo*, July–December 1981. Both countries also have a higher figure for children repeating years in primary education – 15 per cent for Peru in 1980, 17 per cent for Colombia. The figure for total public spending on education is also rather similar: 2.9 per cent and 2.8 per cent of GDP in 1978 for Colombia and Peru respectively.
19. Census data are collected on the basis of the oral question 'can you read and write?' 'Functional' literacy is estimated to require 3–4 years of completed primary education. A study for Colombia for 1964 used only two years of primary education as the criterion, and estimated functional illiteracy as 48.5 per cent, where self-declared illiteracy from Census data was 27 per cent. (DANE, *Boletin Mensual de Estadistica*, AMIDEP, Lima, July 1985).
20. In 1972 the percentage of those in school was 82 per cent for boys, 75 per cent for girls. (Fernandez, (1985)).
21. In 1970–75 infant mortality (0 to 1 years per thousand live births) for Colombia was 60.4. Twelve among the 27 Latin American and Caribbean countries show lower levels of infant mortality. For example, the corresponding figure for Panama was 92.8, Venezuela 48.6, Uruguay 46.3 and Costa Rica 36.2. The corresponding figure for Peru for the same period was 110.3. See *Statistical Yearbook for Latin America and the Caribbean*, ECLA, 1988, p. 45.
22. Pavillon *et al.* (1983).
23. Ochoa (1986).
24. These criteria refer to estimates of nutritional requirements for children of different age groups based on weight and height.
25. The figures are reviewed in Pavillon *et al.* (1983).
26. INP (1988), p. 34.
27. Dane 1988, p. 77.
28. See Sunkel and Griffith-Jones (1986).

4 The Velasco Years in Peru: Discontinuity with Some Change?

The first attempt at dealing with the problems which the preceding chapter has outlined took a surprising form in Peru: a 'Revolutionary Government of the Armed Forces', led by General Velasco: an apparently left-wing nationalist military government of a type rarely seen in Latin America. The coup that ousted Belaunde in October 1968 was led by a group of young officers who had trained together in CAEM[1] and whose views had a strong 'developmental' content. The immediate catalyst of the coup was the concern over Belaunde's dealing with the International Petroleum Corporation (IPC) – but the deeper reasons lay in strong dissatisfaction with the kind of development Peru had been experiencing.

The challenge to orthodoxy that now resulted took place in an unusual context: that of relative affluence. Primary product prices recovered just as the military took over, and this, combined with the effects of the tax reform that the Belaunde Administration at last implemented, too late for its own good, gave the new government room for manoeuvre. Short-term economic management was effectively left to one side – without immediate disastrous consequences. This had important implications for the nature of the challenge: it did not concern, as our other cases do, the usual targets of the IMF and the World Bank – most directly the IMF. Rather, it focussed on the terms of the presence of private foreign capital in the economy alongside domestic ownership reforms.

The persistence in radical reform despite the shift in terms of trade ran against all historical precedent in Peru and represented in principle an important breakthrough (unfortunately, as we shall see, it was not to prevent a total relapse next time prices recovered in 1979). There was thus a quite unusual opening, with initially also considerable political room for manoeuvre: the Military had swept away Congress and left the political parties in disarray.

Looking back on this episode, from the perspective of the late 1980s, there are so many resonances with the García period that it is worth recounting again in some detail the form of the conceptualisation and implementation of the Military's policies, despite the abundance of literature on the period. The rhetoric focussed on the assertion of Peru's dignity and autonomy and the creation of a society where all might participate. The real content emerged only gradually, and the initial coherence is easily exaggerated.[2]

Referring back to the analysis of the previous chapter, the Military did perceive the incipient export supply crisis, and many of their ownership reforms had that in mind, as we shall see. They failed perhaps to understand its urgency, misled by export prices and overoptimistic both as to the gestation period of exports and to the ease of continuing to mobilise foreign resources on new terms. This links directly to the problem which they completely failed to understand: that of the nature of the mechanism of capital accumulation in Peru and its fragile conditions, indicated in the falling coefficient of private investment. They failed to understand both the fragility and complexity of the relationship with international capital, and the insecurity felt by local groups in response to the ownership reforms. They also had, as we shall see, a curious static concept of 'surplus'. As for the problems of ISI, here there was some understanding of the limitations of pushing too hard an extremely import-dependent industrial sector.

The details of the policies

Curiously, in some sense the policies involved a move back to the traditional focus on exports, but in a manner totally distinct from 'new export-led models' elsewhere in the continent. The key was to be the rational use of natural resources. The dynamism of the economy was perceived as related not peculiarly to industry, as under ISI, but to 'agriculture, fishing, industry and mining'.[3] And industrialisation was to be based 'on the establishment of plants which permit the incorporation of greater value added in traditional exports'.[4] Rather than an autonomous stimulus coming from protection against imports, it was to be the impulse given to mining, agriculture and fishing which would lead, via derived demand[5] and via income redistribution in agriculture,[6] to a solidly-based industrialization.

Accordingly, top priority was given to the major projects necessary to restore and sustain export expansion and increase backward linkages. Eventually, non-traditional exports based on integrated industries on an Andean basis could be sought. A more rational import policy, rational management of foreign investment[7] and expansion of domestic food production should also help the balance of payments.

The potential role of the Andean Pact was important in the Military's thinking, as with Lleras in Colombia; in turn the military's preoccupation with changing the terms of the presence of foreign capital in the economy was important in the early development of the form of the Pact and Decision 24.

Many of the targets of the strategy, therefore, amounted to the deliberate undoing of problems stemming from traditional ISI. This was supposed to include employment too – first among the targets of the plan, and the principal benefit of an increased rate of industrial expansion plus technological development was stated to be its contribution towards absorbing the growing labour force.[8] Of the new jobs to be created between 1970 and 1975, one-quarter were to come from industry, despite the fact that industry occupied less than 15 per cent of the economically active population. Industrial output was to rise annually at 12 per cent and employment at 10 per cent. An 11 per cent annual rate of growth of output 1960-66 had been accompanied by an increase in employment of 4 per cent a year, so the plan implied a considerable improvement in industry's employment-generating capacity – *despite* the new emphasis on large capital-intensive projects in basic industry.

The difference with the old model was to be that the new dynamic traditional export sector was to be made to 'contribute to the process of internal transformation'.[9] How this was to be achieved comprised the core of the 'revolution'. The key reason why such a contribution had not previously been made was seen to be the concentration of resources and decision-making in the hands of the domestic elite and foreign firms. With ownership reforms could come greater *access* to the economic surplus – by nationalization, by the freedom which would thereby be achieved to put through tax reform – and thereby the possibility of the *reallocation* of the surplus to uses which would contribute more directly to the growth of the economy. Implicit in this was a large role for the State, but central to the early thinking of the government was the idea that once the monopoly grip of elite and foreign groups was broken, there would occur rapid privately-financed growth based on middle-strata Peruvian entrepreneurship.[10]

The following three years saw a remarkable degree of success in implementing reforms that radically changed the system of ownership and control.

Expropriation without compensation of the International Petroleum Company assets in Peru,[11] the first major act of the new regime, was followed by reorganisation of the old state oil company EPF into the giant new Petroperu, which took over the north coastal oilfields and the Talara refinery, and subsequently pressed ahead with oil exploration in the jungle region, both on its own account and by means of production-sharing contracts with a series of large international oil firms. The new Agrarian Reform Law, decreed in June 1969, was followed by immediate expropriation of the sugar estates of the north Coast – a direct blow at the country's most powerful agrarian interest group, who had previously been successful in obtaining explicit exemption for their properties in the half-hearted reform proposals and legislation of the Prado and Belaunde Governments. The reform was then steadily extended to other areas of the country, and by 1975 virtually all large private landholdings had been affected. The foreign mining companies, having again refused (after prolonged negotiations) to proceed with the rapid development of new large-scale copper mines, were deprived of their undeveloped concessions in late 1970, and the new state company Mineroperu was given a monopoly of mineral-export marketing, control of future projects in the area of metal refining and the task of developing the mineral deposits recovered from foreign control. In July 1970 the Industrial Reform Law decreed the establishment within modern-sector manufacturing enterprises of 'industrial communities' which, as representatives of the workers, would have a progressively-increasing share in the ownership, management and profits of the enterprise. This law also required foreign capital in manufacturing companies to fade out to a minority ownership position, and foreshadowed the establishment of a new type of joint venture by the government and worker co-operatives, to be known as 'social property'.

Subsequent legislation extended the idea of 'labour communities' to the fishing and mining sectors. In March 1971 the Fisheries Law established state control over the marketing of fisheries exports, required a fade-out of foreign capital from the sector, and laid the basis for worker participation. (Later, following the collapse of fishmeal production, the entire sector was taken over by the State in 1973.) In June 1971 the General Mining Law established labour communities in that sector also.

Finally, in March 1972 the General Education Law appeared, with the declared objective of extending educational opportunities to all Peruvians.

This is by any criterion an impressive list. The effect was heightened by a series of *ad hoc* expropriations of large foreign firms active in the economy: ITT in 1969, Chase Manhattan Bank in 1970, Cerro Corporation in 1974, Marcona Mining Company in 1975. At the same time, as in Colombia with the Lleras Administration, the Peruvian Government played a leading role in the formation of Andean Group policies to present a strong united front to foreign capital; while in the case of the automobile industry tough new regulations and the auctioning-off of concessions resulted in a dramatic reduction in the number of foreign car firms operating in Peru.

By the mid-1970s the State had assumed the role previously held by foreign capital in mining, oil, electricity and railways; had taken over much of the banking system, virtually all export marketing, and the entire fishing sector; and had pushed through reforms designed to benefit the employees of enterprises in the modern sector of the economy. The result was the major transformation of the ownership structure depicted in Table 4.1; according to Fitzgerald's calculations the weight of foreign capital in the economy was reduced to 40 per cent of its pre-reform level.

As we turn from the reforms to the repercussions on the economy and the consequences for macro management and growth, we encounter immediately the simplistic quality of the understanding behind the government's policies. As Velasco took over, the economy was in quite heavy recession as a result of demand restrictions imposed by the preceding government and investment uncertainty. The assumption was that the revival would come from two main sources: foreign firms in the mining sector, where the government was applying heavy pressure to force the development of unworked mineral deposits, and local entrepreneurs freed from the influence of the 'oligarchy' and aided by an easing of credit restrictions. In the event, neither group acted in accordance with expectations.

Table 4.1
Peru: The Pattern of Enterprise Ownership in the Modern Sector
(value added as percentage of GNP[a])

	Pre-reform	Post-reform
State	11	26
Domestic private capital	30	22
Foreign capital	21	8
Co-operatives, etc.	–	6
Total Modern Sector	62	62

Source: Fitzgerald (1976), p 36.

Note:
[a] The figures have been standardized on the basis of the 1972 production structure.

Following their assumption of power, and despite the hostile foreign reaction to the IPC expropriation, the Military continued the Belaunde Government's policy of negotiating with the large foreign mining companies over the development of their unworked concessions. Despite the Military's desire to take a tough line with foreign capital, it was accepted that the technical complexity and enormous costs of mining development made it imperative to bring in the multinational companies. The contradiction between the Government's nationalist rhetoric and its desire to retain the confidence of foreign investors produced considerable uncertainty, but in late 1969 a breakthrough came when Southern Peru Copper Corporation and the Government reached an agreement for the development of the Cuajone copper mine in the south. The Cuajone contract contained a number of significant concessions to foreign capital, evidently in an attempt to establish the principle that foreign investment still had a role to play in Peru, under the new rules. Following the Cuajone agreement, the Government attempted during 1970 to pressure the other large mining companies into developing their unworked concessions, by announcing that deposits for which satisfactory development plans were not filed would revert to the State. Proposals satisfactory to the Government were not forthcoming, and at the end of 1970 all the major unworked deposits except Cuajone were taken over. Meanwhile, in April 1970 the Mining Law had established the new state company Mineroperu, initially conceived as a marketing agency; this company found itself at the beginning of 1971 placed in charge of the development of all the expropriated deposits. The point to emerge from these early moves of the Military Government in mining policy was that the original intention was not nationalisation, but partnership with foreign capital (a goal pursued with more success in oil exploration after 1971). Only after two years of negotiation and pressure had failed to result in the hoped-for new investment projects, did the Government decide to take over mining development itself. With the exception of the Cuajone contract, foreign firms had proved unwilling to commit capital to Peru under the terms offered by the Military.

Meantime, in relation to industrial investment, the Government was expecting a response to its policies from domestic entrepreneurial groups. Here was the crucial test of the Military's belief that an attack on foreign and local large-scale capital would open the way for a new stratum of dynamic local enterprises of medium scale. To the Government's evident alarm, the response was negligible. An attempt to bring banking back under local control resulted only in the Government itself being forced to take over most of the banking system.[12] Investment in agriculture remained low, since in view of the fluidity of the agrarian reform situation, no private agriculturist could feel secure. With rare exceptions, local mining investment failed to revive. Most damaging of all to government hopes, despite the apparent profitability of industry and increased tariff protection, local private investment in manufacturing remained very low. Industrial activity did pick up sharply in 1970, but this was expansion into unutilised capacity rather than the result of new investment. Apart from construction, the dominant feature of private investment during the period 1969–72 was a continuation of the long-run decline in its share of GNP which had begun in the late 1950s (see Table 4.2). Outstanding among the measures which were intended to reactivate local capitalism was the imposition of exchange control and obligatory repatriation of overseas funds, in May 1970.[13] Interestingly, as with Lleras in Colombia at the same period, the response was enough to generate a boom in the local stock exchange. The *contrast* with Lleras comes precisely in the fact that the increase in liquidity produced virtually no effect on the level of productive investment.

Faced with this abstention by private capital, the Government had to move in to take over for itself the role of the economy's main investor. From the original aim of a mixed economy with a strong private sector, the Peruvian economy moved rapidly towards state capitalism. As shown in Table 4.1 above, Fitzgerald estimates that between 1968 and 1972 roughly 34 per cent of total modern-sector output was transferred from the private sector to the Government or to co-operatives, while at the same time roughly 42 per cent of modern-sector employment was similarly transferred. This took the state/co-operative share of modern-sector output from 18 per cent before the reforms to 52 per cent by 1972. The shift in control of investment decisions was correspondingly great; as Table 4.2 shows, the state sector came to account for more than half the total investment in the economy.

Financing this public investment, however, proved extremely difficult. The two obvious sources of funds within the economy were the large liquid savings of the private sector, and the profits of companies taken over by the State. The second of these proved a disappointment, reflecting the 'static' concept of surplus which the Military had. Somehow, simply taking over a foreign firm was supposed to provide access to surplus, whereas of course such firms turned out to have been decapitalised by their foreign parent companies (e.g. IPC and Cerro). Some were of course in any case perennial loss makers, such as the

Table 4.2
Peru: Public and Private Investment as Percentage of GDP 1960–76

	1960–64	1965–68	1969–73	1974–76
Private saving[a]	16.1	14.6	9.9	8.1
less net transfer to State	–1.5	–3.9	–2.2	–1.6
gives private gross fixed investment	14.6	10.7	7.7	6.5
Public saving[b]	2.1	0.7	2.7	7.2
internal			2.0	1.5
external[b]			0.7	5.7
plus net transfer from private sector	1.5	3.9	2.2	1.6
gives public gross fixed investment	3.6	4.6	4.9	8.8

Source: Fitzgerald (1978)

Notes:
[a] Net of stockbuilding. From 1969 only, public enterprise saving has been deducted and included in public savings.
[b] Includes public external borrowing, of which a small part is publicly-guaranteed private debt.

Peruvian Corporation. In most cases following the nationalisation of major enterprises, the Government found itself faced with a heavy bill for urgently-needed investments, combined often with large compensation payments. In few cases were the enterprises profitable enough to finance these payments, let alone to subsidise other government projects. Meantime the modern-sector labour force, its expectations aroused by government propaganda surrounding the creation of 'labour communities' and ending of 'foreign exploitation', began to press for a larger slice of the cake, thereby cutting still further into available profits (given that fear of accelerating inflation placed a restraint on price increases). Particularly in the mining sector, industrial unrest became a major problem in 1972 and 1973.

This left private-sector savings as the main source of domestic finance for the Government's plans. As Table 4.2 indicates, about one quarter of private saving was typically loaned to the State. But as government investment rose as a proportion of GDP, while private savings fell, the limitations of this source of finance became evident. 'Net transfers from the private sector' financed 85 per cent of state-sector investment under Belaunde, only 46 per cent in the period 1969–73, and less than 20 per cent in 1974–6. To make up the balance, other sources of funds were required. One obvious possibility was tax reform, which in principle at least had become a serious new possibility once the country's social and political power structure had been altered by the other reforms. But to make effective changes in the yield of tax revenue inevitably meant either a sharp increase in profits tax – so discouraging the very groups on whom the reactivation policy depended – or a deep bite into the living standards of the middle classes, for example by ending the exemption from income tax of a large part of the earnings of government officials, or seriously taxing real estate. No such exercise was undertaken by the Military. Income tax had increased its share of total government revenues from 21 per cent to 28 per cent between 1965 and 1969, under the impact of the Belaunde reforms. By 1971, it had fallen back to 27 per cent.

How then was the expansion of the state sector to be maintained at a sufficiently rapid rate to ensure sustained economic growth, in the absence of a recovery of private investment? The short-run answer is immediately evident from the figures presented in Tables 4.2 and 4.3. The government's need coincided with an extraordinary increase in the availability of private bank credit to countries such as Peru. As a result, the continued rise in public investment in 1974–6 was financed entirely by public borrowing from abroad. Public foreign indebtedness increased from $945 million in 1970 to $2 170 million by the end of 1974, and $4 127 million by the end of 1976 (see Table 4.3). The ratio of debt servicing to export earnings rose accordingly, as the Government made up for its inability or unwillingness to mobilise local surplus by turning to international finance.

This rate of increase, which *ex post* appears suicidal, was made to appear reasonable on the grounds of expected petroleum resources – unfortunately, this was not to materialise.[14] It is important to note how

Table 4.3
Peru: External Public Debt 1968–76
(US$ million)

	1968	1969	1970	1971	1972	1973	1974	1975[a]	1976[a]
Gross inflow	186	221	190	184	285	574	990	1 046	1 348
Servicing	129	134	167	213	219	347	343	474	511
Net inflow	99	132	69	28	121	309	740	762	1 077
Outstanding debt	737	875	945	997	1 121	1 430	2 170	3 050	4 127
Debt service as percentage of exports	15	16	16	24	23	33	22	34	32

Source: 1968–74: Fitzgerald (1976), p. 71; 1975–76: IMF (1977).

Note:
[a] 1975–76: includes a small figure for loans repayable in local currency. The figure comparable to $3 050 million in 1975 for total debt outstanding in 1974 is $2 288 million.

far both the expectations and the borrowing were supported by external agencies, for example by a World Bank appraisal in October 1974. The borrowing permitted the continuation of a boom in imports, including a rapid rise in military equipment. This was aided by the exchange rate policy, which kept the exchange rate constant in nominal terms. (The resulting overvaluation (see Table 3.3) was of marginal importance for traditional exports, determined by the more long-run factors we describe below, but was of importance to non-traditional exports.)

The rising demand for imports plus the rise in import prices following the OPEC price rise meant that there was increasingly a foreign exchange need for borrowing. But the primary need in those years was in fact for investment funds: this is indicated by the rise in foreign exchange reserves in 1974.[15]

Predictably enough, given the hostility of the World Bank and the US government to the brand of radical nationalism displayed by Peru since 1968, there was a price to be paid for ready access to the international capital market, notwithstanding the increase in supply. In February 1974 Peru signed the 'Greene Agreement' with the US Government; the central feature of this agreement was payment by Peru of $150 million as full settlement of all outstanding disputes with US business interests (including even the IPC), in exchange for which the USA withdrew its opposition to the granting of loans to Peru. In addition to enabling the Peruvian Government to finance its operations, the agreement ended a four-year freeze on credits to Southern Peru Copper Corporation for the development of the Cuajone copper mine – the most critical of the export-expansion projects, completion of which had become dependent on the availability of US finance through the Export-Import Bank.

By early 1975, however, the escape route of 1973–74 was closed, as the international banks reversed their easy lending policies and as the extent of Peru's economic crisis became gradually more evident. The oil on which the earlier lending was based turned out to be far less than had been hoped, while the delays and long gestation time in mining meant that relief would only come at the end of the decade. We have seen that alleviation of the export supply crisis really turned on these two sectors.

Meanwhile, on the import side of the equation, local manufacturing remained very import-dependent despite the efforts at restructuring undertaken by the Military, so that the increased capacity-utilisation of the early 1970s translated rapidly into increased imports of intermediate goods. The 'basic' industries reserved to the State included a number of intermediate goods, but the process of launching new projects was slow to get going. COFIDE[16] had overall responsibility for promoting new

Table 4.4
Peru: Indices of Agricultural Production 1968–75
(1968 = 100)

	All crops	Food crops	Food crops per capita
1968	100	100	100
1969	108	110	107
1970	117	120	113
1971	119	123	112
1972	118	123	110
1973	124	129	111
1974	121	126	107
1975	126	133	109

Source: Production and Trade Yearbook (FAO, 1975).

projects, but in its early years its budget went almost entirely on feasibility studies. Further, such State enterprises as were operating had not acted in such a manner as to reduce imports, continuing to purchase overseas 'on grounds of technical requirements'.[17]

In the second place, food production recorded a dismal performance, traced in Table 4.4; after 1971 (when the transfer of coastal land out of cotton production and into food crops came to an end) food-crop production remained almost stagnant with a corresponding decline in per capita production, and need for imports. So far as foreign capital was concerned, Table 4.5 shows that the increased foreign borrowing by the Government was offset to a considerable extent by the rise of debt servicing and the net outflow of private capital.

These problems are demonstrated in Table 4.5 as they came together in the balance of payments. The acute disequilibrium resulted from the combination of stagnant export production, a cyclical decline in export prices, heavy dependence upon imports of foodstuffs and industrial intermediate goods, and an unmanageably-rapid increase in the burden of foreign debt (Table 4.3). In turn, these problems flowed from the internal contradictions of the growth model pursued: failure to promote agricultural growth, inadequate integration and rationalisation of the structure of manufacturing industry, constraints upon rapid expansion of export supply, and unwillingness of the Government to undertake tax reforms commensurate with its increased role in the economy. In addition the increase in defence spending provided a further burden, both internally and externally.

Table 4.5
Peru: Balance of Payments 1969–76
(US$ million)

	1969	1970	1971	1972	1973	1974	1975	1976
Exports	880	1 034	889	945	1 112	1 503	1 290	1 360
Imports	−659	−700	−730	−812	−1 033	−1 909	−2 390	−2 100
Visible Trade Balance	221	334	159	133	79	−406	−1 100	−740
Financial Services								
Public	−37	−31	−48	−51	−66	−104	−231[b]	
Private[a]	−147	−117	−78	−70	−115	−114		
Non-financial services and transfers	−37	−1	−67	−44	−90	−183	−206[b]	−452
Current Account Balance	0	185	−34	−32	−192	−807	−1 537	−1 192
Long-term capital								
Public	124	101	15	116	314	693	793	480
Private[a]	20	−77	−43	−5	70	202	342	196
Basic Balance	144	209	−62	79	192	88	−402	−516
Short-term capital	−56	21	−80	24	−125	244	−173[c]	−351[c]
Monetary movements, errors and omissions	−88	−230	142	−103	−67	−332	575[c]	867[c]

Source: Cuentas Nacionales del Perú 1960–1974 for balance of payments 1969–74; 1975–6 from Reynolds (1977) and from *Memoria,* Banco Central (1976).

Notes:
[a] Undistributed profits of foreign firms are here treated as outflows on current account and inflows on capital account, in accordance with present Peruvian practice. If undistributed profits are excluded, the current-account deficit is reduced to $7.2 million for 1971 and $18.8 million for 1972, with a correspondingly greater net outflow of long-term capital.
[b] Services and transfers are aggregated in the Banco Central *Memoria.* They have been disaggregated here using the relative shares shown by Reynolds.
[c] Errors and omissions are included with short-term capital in this year.

In fact, with hindsight the puzzle in interpreting all this is how the disequilibrium was allowed to become so large. There is no doubt that to the 'structural' aspects were now added 'management' aspects, as the exchange rate and food prices were kept fixed while internal prices rose and both the internal and external disequilibrium assumed huge proportions. The overall public sector deficit rose from 2 per cent of GDP in 1969 to 10 per cent in 1975. The current account deficit on the balance of payments was larger than exports by 1975 (see Table 4.5). Debt service was 16 per cent of exports in 1970 and 34 per cent by 1975.

Not surprisingly, faced with this situation and under pressure from international creditors, the only option appeared to be the even more complete abandonment of innovative policies. In August 1975 President Velasco was replaced by the more cautious General Morales Bermúdez, signifying a shift from the 'first' to the second 'phase' of the 'Revolution'. Despite assurances that the second phase represented continuance of the Revolution, in practice the significant features of the Velasco era were modified or abandoned, in a belated attempt to regain the support, politically and economically, of the private sector. The story of the conservative policies that now followed, and their continuation into the government of Belaunde, is the topic of the next chapter.

Discontinuity with how much change?

It is so easy with hindsight to point out the weaknesses and excessive simplifications in the Military's policies that it is quite possible to overlook the real change that *was* achieved. For the first time, planning began to be taken seriously, and the expansion of state activity which occurred involved much serious learning-on-the-job in relation to budgeting processes, project evaluation and the like.[18] The renegotiation with foreign firms was extremely necessary – and the raised consciousness was an important gain, even if it was not yet adequately translated into the necessary institutional control and monitoring systems. The fact that such machinery – and even consciousness – was to be severely damaged again under Belaunde should not lead us to neglect the real progress made in these years. Perhaps most significantly of all, 'consciousness-raising' extended to the grassroots, and the extraordinarily underdeveloped state of grassroots organisation received a boost the effects of which are clearly evident today. The remarkable story of what is today a district of Lima, Villa El Salvador, for example, owes its origins in part to the Military's support and is an amazing testimony of the potential that grassroots activity has in Peru. Following a land invasion by large numbers of homeless people at Pamplona on the outskirts of Lima, in May 1971, the military decided to take up the settlement as a pilot project and poured in funds and organisational resources:[19] the eventual unique level of grassroots organisation led to the awarding of the Nobel Peace Prize in 1986.

This should modify our assessment of the more negative aspects, which were several. Predictably in the light of our historical analysis, there was a failure to handle - or even to *imagine* - the complexity of what must come after radical ownership reform. Thus in area after area, the detailed management and execution were lacking to make a reality out of a promising beginning. Clear examples of this are technology policy and the agrarian reform.

What very much compounded this failure – and affected acutely the latter issue, agrarian reform - was the unwillingness to make a strong political option. As we shall see with Lleras Restrepo and with García, challenges to international orthodoxy have a direct effect, in so far as they directly change the country's relationship with the international system and its room for manoeuvre. They also have an indirect effect via their political results. The Velasco challenge made very little of this second aspect. There was definitely an incipient political gain to be made in challenging foreign control – but we have seen that failure to understand the factors affecting confidence and the sensitivity of local business groups to the growth of 'unsympathetic bureaucracy' led to little gain on that front and eventually strong disillusion. Fear of further alienating its middle-class base inhibited tax reform and was directly linked to the growth in borrowing – whereas better use of the political dividends could have consolidated that base and even permitted some improvement in the fiscal system. On the other side, the regime never had the confidence to move in a more populist direction: its reforms, we have seen, were mostly confined to the modern sector. It tended to *assume* worker support, and the insecurity even of its union support would become clear as recession grew again in the second phase. It did move to build and encourage grassroots organisation – neighbourhood groups and co-operatives – but its need for control led to constant ambiguity.[20]

The weakness of the political option really predetermined the question of redistribution. It is no surprise that redistribution was with one notable exception limited to redistribution *within* the modern sector. Figueroa has calculated that the Industry, Mining and Fishing Laws between them had the combined effect of transferring not more than 2 per cent of national income to a stratum of modern-sector workers comprising only 8 per cent of the national labour force and situated in the top quartile of the national income distribution. Workers outside the registered sector were not affected by these reforms.

The Agrarian Reform went further, spanning the boundary between the modern and traditional sectors; but even this reform took a dualistic form. Modern-sector agricultural enterprises were transferred to their modern-sector workers organised in co-operatives, while the remainder of the rural population were to have access only to the poorer lands of the Sierra estates. Even in the latter case, hacienda lands were generally transferred to the permanent workforce, leaving independent peasantry and temporary labourers altogether outside the scope of the reform. Despite the determined application of the expropriation provisions of the law, its effect was limited to the redistribution of about one-third of the country's total agricultural and pastoral land, for the benefit of between one-quarter and one-third of the rural labour force.[21] The remainder of the rural population were excluded from the benefits of the reform. Furthermore, so long as agrarian reform was restricted to redistribution of income and resources within agriculture, rather than a net transfer of resources into agriculture from other sectors, its redistributive impact was inevitably limited by the low overall productivity of the agricultural sector. In fact the Reform Law of 1969 clearly anticipated a continuing net transfer of capital out of agriculture: the agrarian bonds paid to former landowners as part-compensation for their properties were intended to be used as collateral for industrial investments, while recipients of land under the reform were required to pay the purchase price over twenty years.

Other policies continued the historical trend in their regressive character. No major effort was made to improve the availability of agricultural extension services (which reached only about 4 per cent of Sierra small farmers in 1969), while the provision of rural credit was assigned low priority, and the credit available was channelled preferentially to the large-scale 'reformed enterprises' (co-operatives and 'SAIS') and away from small peasant producers. At least one vital input – fertilizer – remained in short supply, and its allocation was hampered by bureaucratic rationing procedures.[22] To complete the picture, urban food prices were judged to be politically sensitive and were kept low, which in the absence of compensating subsidies to local producers[23] served to perpetuate the long-run unfavourable trend of the rural-urban terms of trade. In the industrial sector, the incentives to capital intensity embodied in the Industrial Promotion Law were continued.

Reviewing the 'Peruvian experiment' more than a decade after its end – and with the parallels suggested by García very much in mind – possibly the outstanding theme highlighted by this study has been the significance of the failure to understand the *modus operandi* of a mixed economy in the particular context of Peru. Yet this is only to underline once again the depth of the problems faced – not simply by the military but by *any* regime – given the nature and depth of the crisis of the model as they took over. This qualifies radically any criticism. The same point will be true as we turn to look first at the more *laissez-faire* solution which gradually replaced the Military's phase 1, and then at García's version.

Notes

1. Centro de Altos Estudios Militares: a military training school with in the 1960s a strong tradition of social science analysis. See Villaneuva (1972); Philip (1978) pp. 42–3.
2. See Philip (1975). The sources for the regime's thinking are the *First Development Plan* (1971–75), Zimmerman (1975) and the speeches of Velasco.
3. *First Development Plan* (1971), Vol. 1, p. 14.
4. *Ibid.* (1971), Vol. 1, p. 18.
5. *Ibid.* (1971), Vol. 1, p. 40.
6. *Ibid.* (1971), Vol. 1, p. 27.
7. Velasco Alvarado (1972), p. 62.
8. *First Development Plan* (1971), Vol. 1, p. 113.
9. *Ibid.* (1971), p. 28.
10. See for example the statement by Morales Bermúdez reported in *Peruvian Times*, 6 March 1970, p. 1.
11. Technically, compensation was in fact paid via funds in a blocked account, with the promise that these funds would be released when IPC paid Peru a much larger sum to compensate for past excess profits.
12. Thorp (1972).
13. *Peruvian Times*, 22nd May 1970, p. 1.
14. It seems that the original study, by a US firm, wrongly concluded that a number of separate wells indicated the existence of a huge underground basin.
15. This rise does not indicate the full extent of the excess of the internal over the external gap, since the very availability of funds in the form of foreign exchange of course influenced purchasing decisions.
16. The Corporación Financiera de Desarrollo. See Ayala and Ugarteche (1975) for an analysis of COFIDE's performance in its first three years.
17. Fitzgerald (1976a), p. 25.
18. This was made clear in numerous interviews with employees of the Ministry of Economy and the Planning Institute in May 1987.
19. The settlement was moved to a new site, infrastructure was provided (bypassing older settlements) and SINAMOS played a large role. The input of resources was such as to make the project unrepeatable on a large scale – but it does reveal the potential that exists.
20. On this see Angell and Thorp (1980), p. 876.
21. This uses the careful estimate in standardised hectares made by Caballero (1976), p. 3. Estimates of the proportion of the rural population excluded from the benefits of the reform range from two-thirds (Harding (1975), p. 220) to three-quarters (Fitzgerald (1976), p. 31).
22. See Horton (1974), Webb (1974a).
23. There were some food subsidies, but these were mainly on imports.

5 Return to Orthodoxy 1976–85

This chapter follows the fortunes of the most market-orientated period in the twenty years of economic management we are attempting to analyse in some detail. Peru from mid-1975 to mid-1985 followed increasingly orthodox policies, and a far more orthodox line than was seen at any time in these same twenty years in Colombia. Assessing this period, then, is of singular importance both in terms of our comparative themes and because as we write the most likely outcome of the 1990 elections in Peru would appear to be a victory of the right and a return to similar policies. It has recently become common currency in Peru that the problem lies in the inappropriate and excessive interventionism of the state: this view has been enshrined in a book which has achieved wide circulation both within and without the country: *El Otro Sendero* or *The Other Path*, by Hernando de Soto.[1] It is therefore of paramount importance to ask how far the problem is not only the state, but the lack of strength and competitiveness in the private sector. 'Free market' policies surely depend for their success on an ability of the system to respond, which is itself a product of history and much *prior* activity of the state.

The Military's return to orthodoxy

In June 1975 came the first serious signs that the Government was planning a shift in policies in the face of falling reserves, the huge balance-of-payments deficit and accelerating internal inflation. In that month the controlled prices of food and petroleum were raised. But this did not avert a change of presidency in August, when Morales Bermúdez, Velasco's Minister of Finance, took over from him, as it became apparent that the severity of the economic crisis necessitated a new broom: a 'second stage' in which mistakes could be blamed on the Velasco era and a new direction sought. There followed a moderate devaluation in September, but still the main solution was yet more borrowing from abroad. Budget cuts and tax increases were announced in January 1976, with further price increases: as Table 5.1 shows, however, the measures were barely enough to do more than stabilize the overall government deficit at 9 per cent of GDP. By mid-1976 urgent

Table 5.1
Peru: Public Sector Revenue and Expenditure 1974–7
(percentage GDP)

	1974	1975	1976[a]	1977[b]
Central Government				
Current expenditure	13.9	16.5	15.7	18.5
Wages and salaries	5.3	5.9	5.5	5.3
Military outlays	3.5	4.6	4.0	7.3
Other	5.1	6.0	5.3	5.9
Investment	4.5	5.1	4.8	3.8
Total Expenditure	18.4	21.6	20.4	22.2
Revenue	15.2	16.0	14.3	14.3
State Enterprises				
Current expenditure	12.7	15.4	16.8	19.8
Investment	4.7	5.3	5.0	3.6
Revenue	13.1	14.5	18.7	22.0
Total Public Sector				
Current expenditure	28.7	33.6	33.8	38.3
Investment	9.1	9.5	9.3	7.4
Revenue	31.6	32.7	35.0	36.3
Overall deficit	−6.2	−10.2	−8.6	−9.4

Source: IMF (1977), Banco Central, unpublished data.

Notes:

[a]Annual average.

[b]The total public sector figure for 1977 does not include local government and municipal budgets. The weight of these in the total is tiny, as will be seen by comparing central government and state enterprises with the totals given for earlier years.

debt repayment problems, plus net international reserves at an all-time low of −$553 million, brought Peru to negotiate directly with the major private banks. In a unique decision, the banks agreed to roll over the debt *without* the 'seal' of an IMF Standby Agreement, provided Peru co-operate[2] in a programme which was generally assessed afterwards as having been almost as stringent as the Fund's would have been.[3] The measures involved a shift toward greater fiscal and monetary restraint, devaluation, more favourable treatment of foreign investment, and a firm reversal of the anti-private sector trend of certain of Velasco's policies. There followed more increases in controlled prices, including a doubling of the price of petrol, and a further modest devaluation, and the fishing fleet was sold back to private enterprise. Table 5.1 reveals though how little was in fact done in the area of fiscal restraint. Expenditure continued to rise in real terms, the only impact on the deficit coming from the increase in public enterprise prices (chiefly the increase in petrol prices). But credit to the private sector was cut, on top of the fall in liquidity produced by the drain in reserves.

By early 1977, inflation was running more rapidly than ever, at over 40 per cent a year (see Figure 5.1 below), industrial output was falling (Table 5.7 below), real wages had fallen over 40 per cent since their peak in 1973 (Figure 5.2), and under-employment had reached over 50 per cent.[3] The balance of payments was still unfavourable and gross reserves were due to be totally exhausted by the end of July. The private banks had found their role of 'policemen' too uncomfortable.[4] This time they insisted that a standby agreement be signed with the IMF. The negotiations with the IMF produced demands by the Fund mission for targets in terms of public spending, money supply and external debt which were unacceptable to the Central Bank,[5] let alone to the country as a whole. Private sector representations as to the effect of a continued squeeze brought a new Minister of Economy from the private sector: Piazza introduced measures representing a severe dose of deflation but his attempt to deflect pressure slightly from the private industrial sector, by increasing food and petrol prices and by attacking military spending, provoked major riots in a number of provincial cities and the military were pushed into demanding his resignation. With this, and with the first general strike in twenty years, in July 1977, the stabilization policy appeared to dissolve into incoherence, price increases were rescinded, negotiations with the Fund were broken off and the Central Bank team resigned.

The government bought time – expensively – by arranging 'swap' agreements with a number of Latin American countries and by ruling that all import credits must be for 180 days instead of the previous minimum of 90 days. A mission then went to the USA to attempt to negotiate with the chief creditors without the blessing of the Fund, the incentive being the renewed commitment to elections in 1980, with a Constitutional Assembly to be elected in 1978, and a promise to reduce defence spending. The election pledge was also an attempt internally to offer circuses where bread was lacking. Not surprisingly, the reaction of the international banks and other creditors was to say that they had no confidence in existing policies and that Peru must work out a settlement with the IMF before refinancing would be forthcoming.

By October 1977 a new agreement was reached with the IMF, though it was not signed until December. The Peruvians won acceptance of the need to freeze subsidies and petrol prices; but they had to agree to a sharp deflation of public spending. The exchange rate system was reformed, with a new system of controlled depreciation introduced.

According to the agreement, the central government's current deficit was to swing from 3.4 per cent of GDP in 1977, to a surplus of 2 per cent in 1978. But the tax measures introduced were hardly enough to counterbalance, let alone outweigh, the continuing effect of the depression on tax regimes. This left expenditure to bear the brunt of the cuts; unless the Military were genuinely prepared to cut defence spending, it was obvious that the agreement must be broken. The renegotiation of the debt with international banks was postponed to February 1978.

By that date, it was abundantly clear that the agreement had not been kept. Prolonged negotiations with the IMF eventually broke down in March 1978, with the economy surviving from day to day on last-minute arrangements to roll over part of the debt. Meanwhile there was a slight improvement evident in the external balance by the end of 1977, as copper sales rose by enough to outweigh the falling world price, coffee benefited from good prices and the volume of iron ore exports rose. The depression generated a very slight fall in imports.

Nevertheless, this was still not enough to stop reserves falling: by May the country was apparently only able to avoid outright default on overdue payments by persuading Occidental Petroleum to make an advance deposit of $23 million.[6] At this point the Government achieved an agreement with the IMF and the US Treasury on tax reforms and elimination of subsidies, which it was hoped would be enough to persuade the private banks to roll over some $250 million of the debt, even though the price rises would be delayed until after the elections for a Constitutional Assembly on 6th June.[7] Meanwhile Chase Manhattan began to press more strongly for a special decree-law guaranteeing that the proceeds of the sales from the copper mine should go exclusively to the servicing and repayment of the $500 million package of loans financing Cuajone (and carrying no government guarantee), a measure strongly resisted in Peru. A cabinet shake-up produced a new Minister of Economy, who decided that the austerity measures must come at once. Accordingly price rises of 50–60 per cent in foodstuffs and transport were introduced in late May, and the elections were postponed for two weeks, in a new atmosphere of repression, with universities and schools closed and widespread arrests and deportations.[8]

It is clearly crucial to understand why the dividends from these three years of attempted adjustments were so small. We suggest that as with the earlier radical policies of the military regime, this policy too could be described as based on a number of false assumptions – reducible to two principal points. First, it presupposed that cuts in demand could be achieved basically by cuts in public and private consumption, not investment, this being the principal means of achieving compatibility between short-term and long-term goals. Second, it assumed that contraction of demand plus exchange rate adjustment would improve the balance of payments – in principle by three routes: first, the stimulus to exports both via adjustment of the price of tradables and increased supply following compressed internal demand; second, the compression of imports through the same two effects; and third, the beneficial effect on both long- and short-term foreign capital flows of removing distortions – basically, the distorted exchange rate.

Even a brief glance at the figures is sufficient to show that there must be something radically wrong with at least some of these assumptions. Table 5.2 shows how the balance-of-payments crisis initially worsened in 1976, to show a certain improvement by 1977. In both years there was a positive contribution from exports, although this was not really significant until 1977, when at last there was some recovery in the export quantum, which rose 48 per cent in 1977, almost entirely because of the major copper projects coming on stream. The volume of copper exports rose 82 per cent in 1977, while in value they formed 23 per cent of exports. Iron ore exports also recovered with the resolution of the Marcona boycott,[9] and sugar production rose. Non-traditional exports also grew rapidly though from a small base: this was the area that benefited most from the policy measures taken.

The evolution of imports is considered in detail below when we analyse the impact of policy measures; briefly, in 1976 there was a slight fall in most categories, with the ending of the extraordinary speculative boom in imports of 1974–75. But in 1977 the figure was roughly constant in dollar terms, with a further fall in capital goods being compensated by a rise in defence items. As investment fell heavily in both public and private sectors so there was a saving of $254 million on capital goods – but the 'adjustment' figure rose by more than enough to compensate – $303 million – reflecting the massive increase in defence imports in this year, while every other category rose slightly, except fuel. In 1978 the depression and fuel substitution at last significantly compressed imports.

In 1976 net long-term loans made a smaller contribution than in 1975; thus the overall result was the continuation of the massive loss in reserves which began in 1975. This was staunched towards the end of the year by the balance of payments financing which was achieved. In 1977 the main reason for the less unfavourable basic balance was the continuing improvement in current account, this coming almost entirely

Table 5.2
Peru: Balance of Payments 1975–85
(US$ millions)

	1975	1976	1977	1978	1979	1980	1981	1982	1983	1984	1985
Exports	1 330	1 341	1 726	1 972	3 676	3 916	3 249	3 293	3 015	3 147	2 978
Imports	−2 427	−2 016	−2 148	−1 668	−1 954	−3 090	−3 802	−3 721	−2 722	−2 140	−1 806
Visible Trade Balance	−1 097	−675	−422	304	1 722	826	−553	−428	293	1 007	1 171
Financial Services	−284	−375	−439	−646	−931	−909	−1 019	−1 034	−1 130	−1 165	−1 010
Non-financial Services and Transfers	−154	−22	78	178	162	−18	−156	−147	−35	−63	−36
Current Account Balance	−1 535	−1 072	−783	−164	953	−101	−1 728	−1 609	−872	−221	125
Long-term Capital	1 135	642	728	444	656	462	648	1 200	1 384	1 189	691
Public	793	446	659	405	617	371	388	995	1 431	1 392	814
Private Direct Investment	316	171	54	25	71	27	125	48	38	−89	−122
Private Loans	26	25	15	14	−32	64	135	157	−85	−114	—
Short-term Capital											—
Errors and Omissions	−177	−438	−294	−204	−30	361	576	533	−552	−721	—
Change in Reserves (increases −)	577	868	349	−76	−1 579	−722	504	−124	40	−247	−250

Source: Banco Central, *Memoria* (1985, 1987).

Table 5.3
Peru: Long-Term Public Debt and Debt Servicing 1970–85
(US$ millions)

	1970	1975	1976	1977	1978	1979	1980	1981	1982	1983	1984	1985
Gross inflow	190	1 077	846	993	848	1 084	1 208	1 620	2 043	2 554	1 525	894
Servicing due	167	474	533	635	702	825	1 323	1 756	1 600	1 791	2 492	2 036
Service paid	—	—	—	—	—	—	—	—	—	618	516	789
Outstanding debt	945	3 066	3 641	4 243	5 135	5 764	6 043	6 210	6 908	8 339	9 648	10 462
Debt service as percentage of exports	16	37	39	37	35.6	22.4	33.8	54.0	48.6	47.4[a] 20.5[b]	64.5[a] 16.4[b]	68.4[a] 26.5[b]

Sources: Banco Central, *Memoria* (1976, 1983, 1984); INE: *Compendio Estadístico* (1987).

Notes:
[a] Including debt service, which was in fact refinanced.
[b] Excluding service refinanced.

from the rise in exports, with imports constant in dollar values. But the improvement was not enough to prevent an increase in debt, with the rise in outstanding public indebtedness shown in Table 5.3, the debt-service-to-exports ratio hovering close to 40 per cent. In the newly contracted debt of 1976 and 1977 defence played an overwhelming role, accounting for more than half in 1976.[10]

However, the problem was worse than this, since short-term debt was also rising. This was primarily on account of the failure to raise petrol prices to a level to put Petroperu's financing on an adequate basis: suppliers' credits for imports of crude petroleum sent the agency's short-term debt soaring from $195 million in 1974, to $228 million in 1975, $357 million in 1976 and $421 million by the end of 1977.[11]

It will readily be seen, therefore, that the disequilibrium in the external balance was not removed by the measures taken. Why was so little adjustment achieved? One important element in the explanation is that fiscal restraint was not in fact achieved. Table 5.1 makes it very clear that whatever the intentions of the Central Bank nothing was actually done to curb public spending. Current expenditure actually rose steadily as a percentage of GDP throughout the supposed 'adjustment' period. The predominant reason was the rise in military outlays.[12] Cuts were made in real terms in the public sector wage and salary bill, but these were not enough to do more than cause a very slight fall as percentage of GDP, despite the effort involved. (In fact several elements of expenditure showed signs of levelling off in the second half of 1976: it was the 1977 failures, on top of the defence rise, which led to current expenditure reaching an all time high of 38 per cent of GDP by 1977.) By the latter year, the authorities resorted to compression of investment spending. But this was not enough to offset the effect of the depression on tax revenue. The only serious gains came from the increases in public enterprise prices, which were the main reason for the fall in the overall public sector deficit in the second half of 1976. Even these increases were not enough, though, as we have seen, to prevent the continued build-up of foreign debt.

The significance of this was not that more recession was required – it was not – but that firstly the failure to attain fiscal balance led directly to continuing increases in external debt, and secondly, that in order to succeed somewhere, failure on this front led to drastic cuts elsewhere – in private sector credit and in real wages and salaries. Thus it was the private sector which bore the brunt of credit restraint. The liquidity squeeze pushed the private sector increasingly into the informal credit market, where the higher rates formed another reason for rising unit costs with depression.

The squeeze on the private sector obviously meant that the second part of our first assumption also became invalid: private investment fell even further, as shown in Table 5.5 below – despite the fact that in a desperate attempt to woo the private investor further changes were made in 1976–77 to both the Industrial Community legislation and to Social Property – to the point where by 1977 it was generally agreed that the last traces of the original novel elements of the Revolutionary government had disappeared.

This had naturally involved also the gradual abandonment of all pretence at redistributive goals. The area of demand which it was easiest to compress was real earnings: the fall in real wages and salaries was drastic, as Figure 5.2 shows. This was reflected in what was for Peru an exceptional degree of political mobilisation and grass-roots reaction, beginning with the provincial riots of June 1977, and contributing to the lack of grasp on policy which characterised the following months.

This rather uneven compression of demand was reflected in the fall in industrial production (Table 5.7 below) and in growing unemployment. Meanwhile inflation accelerated (Figure 5.1), due to the public sector price increases, the exchange rate movement, and rising unit costs as output fell. Of the 34 per cent increase in 1976, 23 points were estimated to be 'corrective' inflation resulting from policy measures; in 1977, 27 points out of 38.[13]

The question of why so little adjustment was actually achieved in public spending derives only in part from its composition. Massive dismissals would be necessary to make a significant difference to the wage and salary figures; since it is inconceivable that the police, the military or teachers could be seriously reduced in number, this being over 70 per cent of the wage and salary bill, only quite ridiculous cuts in other Ministries would be of any avail.[14]

Nevertheless, perhaps more economies might have been achieved, especially in the public enterprises, were it not for the lack of solidarity behind the stabilization policy. It is rather clear that even in the most coherent period of policy-making (June 1976 – March 1977), the impetus came from one point, the Central Bank team, unevenly supported by the Minister of Economy. Far from identifying with and co-operating with the programme, it is only too clear that the objective of every other element of the public sector was to evade restrictions as far as possible.[15] This suggests that in addition to the obvious political preconditions for adjustment by cutting consumption and to the impossibility of stabilizing against a rising trend in defence spending, a widely-based team able

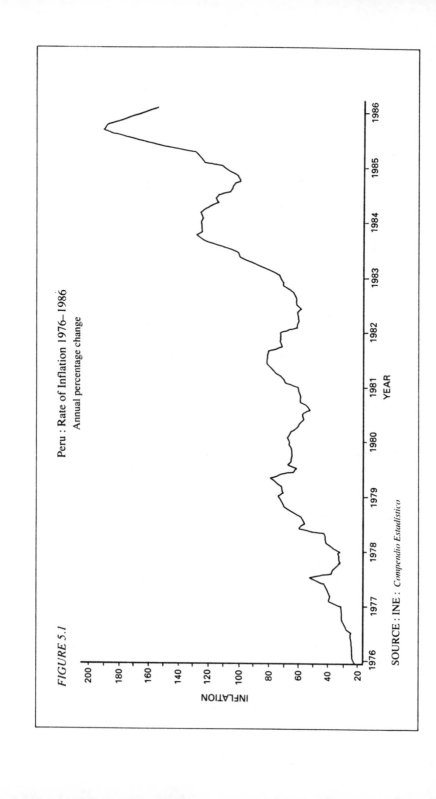

FIGURE 5.1

Peru : **Rate of Inflation 1976–1986**
Annual percentage change

SOURCE : INE : *Compendio Estadístico*

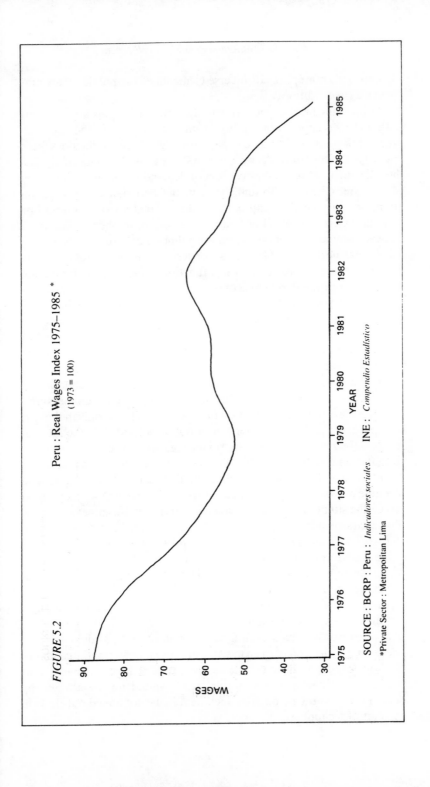

FIGURE 5.2

Peru : Real Wages Index 1975–1985 *

(1973 = 100)

WAGES

YEAR

1975 1976 1977 1978 1979 1980 1981 1982 1983 1984 1985

30 40 50 60 70 80 90

SOURCE : BCRP : Peru : *Indicadores sociales*   INE : *Compendio Estadístico*

*Private Sector : Metropolitan Lima

to control and/or speak for diverse elements of the public sector may also be a precondition.[16]

But the difficulties of the type of adjustment policy sprang not only (although perhaps principally) from the lack of the political preconditions; they also came in part from the inherent difficulties faced in this type of economy. As we saw, the strategy assumes essentially that the adjustment of relative prices and of demand will secure adjustment of the external disequilibrium, with, in the Peruvian case, particular attention to the relationship between the internal fiscal disequilibrium and the external debt. (For example, as we have shown, failure to achieve a sound financial situation for public enterprises results directly in external borrowing, often at short term.) But there are also good reasons why such measures do not function 'efficiently' in a structure such as that of the Peruvian economy.

Taking exports first, the increase might come through increased competitiveness of exports with the adjustment of the exchange rate and the restraint on internal costs following the decline in real wages, and/or increased supply following reduced internal consumption of exportables. But we have already seen that the problem with existing export lines was not lack of competitiveness but a very fundamental supply constraint which would not be affected by short-run measures. Further, the internal consumption of exportables is low: only in the case of sugar is a significant proportion of output allocated to the internal market – and by 1975 the international sugar price was falling sharply, so that even if more were offered it would do little to increase revenue. Non-traditional lines formed only around 10 per cent of the total, and in a time of world recession it was hardly to be expected that they would rescue the situation. There was some expansion in this area: as we saw above exports of manufactures rose from 5 per cent of total exports in 1975 to 7 per cent in 1976 and 9 per cent in 1977, under the impact of the exchange reform of 1976, and the increase in subsidies. The contribution on this front was important, but involved a sharp increase in subsidies to achieve it, and still the quantitative effect was not very great. The other area potentially responsive to price is small and medium mining – but the time-lag is significant.

In other words, even a painful reduction in real wages could gain just about nothing in the short run in terms of the export side of the equation.

As to foreign exchange outflows, the problem here was partly that many items showing unfavourable trends would not be affected by demand restraint. One obvious such item is the continued out-flow on account of technology.

But further, even within visible imports, the reach of the chosen instrument was very limited. When the bulk of imports are non-substitutable intermediate and capital goods, relative prices have a very small effect[17] on import demand: this is particularly true when over half of imports are for the State sector (it will only be effective here if it is combined with strict fiscal controls). And in any case, the effect of the numerous different measures of relative price adjustment is to provoke such strong cost push inflation that, unless the exchange rate is further adjusted, relative prices do not long favour import substitution.

As to demand contraction, it follows from the structure of imports which we have observed above that it is both an inefficient and extremely costly tool – yet it is the *only* means, within the policy as a whole, of moving toward equilibrium. The structure was as follows, taking the year 1974 as an example. If we take food, fuel and agricultural inputs as sacrosanct, we are left with some 7 per cent of other consumer goods, which presumably could be squeezed a little more but which will hardly solve the deficit problem. Apart from that, we have 49 per cent representing investment goods and military equipment and 27 per cent of industrial inputs excluding food. But the industrial input category is shown in Table 5.4 disaggregated by industrial sector. It shows that 60 per cent are accounted for by three sectors, which together comprise a mere 22 per cent of industrial value added. When imports are thus concentrated in a few sectors, cutting demand uniformly will clearly be a costly way to achieve economies in imports, requiring a quite disproportionate degree of recession in the industrial sector. This explains, then, the limited success we noted above with respect to imports: even leaving defence aside, a recession of the size indicated by a fall of over

Table 5.4
Peru: Imports by Selected Industrial Branches
as Percent of Total Industrial Imports 1975

Industrial Sector:	
Food products	23
Of which milk products	(6)
wheat products	(12)
Chemical products	17
Vehicles	23
Of which knocked-down kits	(21)
	63
Total imported industrial inputs	100

Source: Ministerio de Industria, unpublished data.

10 per cent in industrial production in two years, and a heavy fall in real wages has had very little effect on imports. Such economies as have been made have been achieved by cutting investment and by import substitution in fuel. Even in 1978 when imports were at last significantly reduced, 49 per cent of the reduction was from fuel, 44 per cent from defence, and only 4 per cent each from consumer goods and intermediate inputs, the two elements directly sensitive to the level of demand.

The remaining important element in the balance of payments is the capital account. The Fund's negotiations with Peru in this area have tended to emphasize the relationship between the exchange rate, confidence and short-term capital, while the underlying thinking of the Fund is clearly that a healthy undistorted economy will attract long-term capital.[18] Unfortunately it appears that in the Peruvian context capital movements, both long- and short-term, are related far more closely to more intangible variables of confidence in internal policy-making. Given this, the atmosphere of strikes and political uncertainty at least partly associated with the stabilization effort was such as to make sure that movements on the private capital account would not be favourable.

Further, even the control of the public sector deficit is exceptionally difficult, not merely because of the structure of expenditure and the lack of will to resist pressure, which we mentioned earlier, but also because the recession itself affects tax revenue sharply. This is a combination of a lower level of activity and imports depressing tax revenues, and a greater incentive to evasion as real incomes fall. Thus for example we observe that income tax was 4.9 per cent of GDP in 1974 but only 2.8 per cent in 1976. The net result of a succession of small tax changes over the last few years, plus the effect of inflation on tax brackets, has been no rise in the ratio of total tax revenue to GDP.

Yet a further reason for the lack of results arises from the fact that the initial policies were not successful (and in part because they were not sustained). The lesson of the story we have told above is that the social cost in terms of wages, employment and the fortunes of small enterprises tends to be cumulative, while short-term gains are easily reversed by subsequent events. As each programme was implemented and ran aground through failing to achieve certain targets, there were always three areas which could be affected and were: wages, employment and small business. (The extent to which the large-scale private sector was able to defend itself was reflected in the lack of major bankruptcies during those two years of recession). As we have shown, cuts in wages did little to improve the export-import balance – but the prolonged recession did mean that what good will there was available at the start to back such an effort was soon dissipated. Further, whatever the pros and cons of the crawling peg, its termination just when the initial difficulties were well over and benefits could be expected is particularly damaging, since it reduces the effect such an instrument could have another time. Again, as programme succeeds programme defence mechanisms may become better developed and certain gaps may even become wider (e.g. as short-term external borrowing continues because ambitious stabilization targets are not reached, the gap may become wider than it might have done under an alternative path with planned external borrowing at possibly lower cost).

Drawing together, then, the implications of our analysis so far, it would appear that the experience of 1976–8 lends considerable weight to the case for seeking alternative adjustment policies. Quite apart from elements of ill-luck and exogenous factors, there is a case against such policies simply based on the difficulties and unproductive nature of short-run abrupt and recessive adjustment in this type of economy. Given the very limited benefits to the balance of payments from a policy of aggregate demand compression, there was rather a case, first, for *selective* action, concentrating on the import-intensive areas, and second, for focusing on the finance problem, given its direct relation to the external debt.

It also appears clear that the further result of the difficulties of short-run adjustment was severe disruption of long-run development policies. This appears most clearly in the eventual heavy cuts in investment which were necessary, but also is evident in a less tangible fashion in the effect on policy-making effort of having to wrestle constantly with short-term problems using instruments with high social costs: long-term constructive policy planning and implementation necessarily has to suffer. Further, certain important elements of a long-term policy, such as tax reform, are virtually impossible to implement in political economy terms in a context of acute depression.

By 1978, there were signs that some of these problems were recognized both by the government and by the international financial community. At last in July 1978 there were successful negotiations for a Standby Agreement, the IMF team apparently pressing the Peruvians to plan on *more* imports and a larger public deficit than they had intended, in order to maintain the level of investment. The agreement covered a longer period than usual, and was intended to be a serious attempt at gradual adjustment, co-ordinated with an investment programme worked out with the World Bank. The short-term goals were nevertheless very ambitious. The public sector current account was in deficit to the tune of 2 per cent of GDP in 1977; the programme assumed a surplus of 5.8 per cent in 1979 and 1980, to be achieved by tax reform, increases in public enterprise prices, and cuts in current expenditure, while public investment was to maintain its share of GDP. Interest rate reforms were to bring about gradually a positive real rate of interest.

Somewhat to everyone's surprise, these targets were in general kept to, if not exceeded. Tax revenue for example by early 1979 was running at 6 per cent *above* the target figure. How was this achieved? We turn now to the boom conditions that accompanied Peru's 'return to democracy'.

'Boom' management 1979–82

Elections for the Constituent Assembly were eventually held in July 1978, and full elections followed in 1980, completing the return to democracy. These elections produced a large majority for an Acción Popular government with President Belaunde at its head, which duly took office in July 1980. The first part of our next period therefore corresponds to a 'caretaker' episode, with a civilian economic team led by Silva Ruete, which was replaced under Belaunde by a team led by Manuel Ulloa, who remained in office until December 1982.

As the title of this section indicates, conditions now changed dramatically as export proceeds began to exceed earlier projections. Led by copper prices, the export price index rose a remarkable 78 per cent between 1978 and 1980, and the terms of trade swung 43 per cent in favour of Peru.[19] This bonanza led to the apparent disappearance of 'the debt problem', and credits negotiated in 1978 were in part not drawn on or repaid before their due date. The situation was helped by the low level of imports in 1978 and 1979, as the previous policies of demand repression at last took effect, and by the still-low level of real interest rates.

The unexpectedness and size of the rise in exports are revealed by the fact that whereas in January 1979 the Central Bank's estimate of 1979 exports was $2.2 billion, by April it was no less than $3.2 billion.[20] What was no doubt contributing as well was the increase in production of coca. We shall argue in the case of Colombia that foreign exchange receipts are affected not only by the growth of the drugs trade but also by fluctuations in the price of cocaine: in Peru the income appears to be more stable as dealers remit only enough to cover local expenses. But with rising demand the substitution of coca for other crops was clearly leading to a rising income, to reach an annual inflow of some $700 or $800 million by 1982.[21]

How would Peru deal with relative affluence? And how would boom management compare with the management of the coffee bonanzas we discuss in chapters 8 and 9? We will show there that in the case of Colombia, the focus of the whole economy on coffee, and the sensitivity of policy makers to the inflationary danger arising from the widespread of potential income recipients from coffee throughout the economy, plus the concern of the Federation to 'concert' coffee policy carefully with the government, have led to elaborate mechanisms and the development of fora for discussion and concertation. We have shown how the possibility of this was opened up by the whole history of coffee management and institutional development around the coffee sector. We have seen that no such focus of policy-making evolved out of Peru's mixed export history. Certainly now as the copper price rose and fishmeal did well, there was no evidence of sensitivity to the need to manage a no-doubt short-lived boom rather carefully, so that resources could be saved for bad times and distorting effects on relative prices avoided. The Colombian problem of how far the boom should be allowed to filter through to small producers, did not of course arise: since Velasco's reforms, much of the marketing of copper was in state hands and the principal immediate effects of the boom were on government revenues and foreign exchange reserves.

Public policy statements throughout this period showed no awareness of the temporary nature of the boom, and indeed tended to play down the role of international prices altogether and claim the improving fiscal and balance-of-payments situation as a major success of the preceding orthodox measures. Much was made of the fact that the targets agreed with the IMF were being over-fulfilled. Far from avoiding the relative price shifts against tradables which is today so clearly identified as a danger of such booms, policy actively embraced the opportunity to moderate inflation by expanding imports, reducing tariffs and by continuing the previous policy of limiting exchange-rate changes to less than domestic inflation, a policy made possible by rapidly increasing international export prices. Controlled prices were not raised in line with inflation, and subsidies increased.

With the transfer from a caretaker regime to the Belaunde government, a stronger pro-market line was adopted. Private foreign investment was seen as a focal point of the development strategy, and obstacles to its entry were to be removed. Contracts were to be negotiated to get the major mining projects moving, under the lively

Minister for Energy and Mines, Pedro Pablo Kuczynski. State enterprises were to be sold when possible to the private sector. A stronger
programme of liberalisation of imports was to be pursued, starting with
the removal of quantitative controls. Financial reforms were also to
allow the market to operate more efficiently in that sphere. A
conservative monetary and fiscal policy was to be pursued. Initially,
exchange-rate management was to have deceleration of inflation as its
principal goal, since buoyant exports would permit this. In early 1981,
the attempt to restrain inflation developed into a British Labour govern-
ment-style attempt at consensus incomes policy, of which the would-be
architects were Richard Webb, president of the Central Bank, and
Alfonso Grados, Minister of Labour. The attempt broke down,
basically for want of confidence in the government's ability to fulfil its
part of the bargain. In August 1981, as inflation did not decelerate and
as export receipts weakened, a policy switch occurred: the rate of
devaluation was accelerated and the move to full 'market' policies was
strengthened by an attempt to end subsidies on critical food products.
This policy continued during 1982.

It will be seen, then, that the 'breathing space' allowed by external
trends was used basically to attempt to remove distortions and 'set the
house in order', the focus being on liberalisation of imports and to a
lesser degree on financial reforms. The space was also used to repay debt
early, in the hope presumably of improving Peru's creditworthiness, and
to push forward major export sector projects.

Of these, the last was undoubtedly of crucial importance, and a
number of major projects did make progress or get underway. In
particular, the mining projects of Cuajone and Cerro Verde progressed,
and Tintaya began. But the efforts made to attract foreign investment
were not on the whole successful: terms were liberalised and were
initially rather good, but the response was short-lived (see Table 5.2
above). Half a dozen foreign oil companies signed exploration and
development contracts, but the results they reported were disappointing.[22] Several major state projects, in particular Cobriza and the
irrigation schemes, were subsequently harshly criticised.[23]

As to the rest of the strategy, the early repayment of debt was to prove
of no avail in the face of the overwhelming influence of rising interest
rates and bankers' panic. The financial reforms aimed to simplify and
make more logical the structure of interest rates, and to raise rates to
stimulate savings; the reforms failed, however, to achieve positive real
rates of interest, for reasons we discuss below, and as a result were
powerless to slow down the increasing dollarisation of the economy in

1981 and 1982. Holdings of financial assets fell as a percentage of GDP.[24] The policy of privatisation led to the return of the media to private hands, and to a new agricultural law facilitating the sale of land. There was also some reduction in the importance of the industrial community, but overall the achievements were far less than was planned or anticipated.[25] The liberalisation of imports was the most radical of the reforms, first attacking non-tariff barriers – in December 1978 only 38 per cent of import categories were unrestricted, by December 1981 virtually all were – then reducing the average level of the tariff from 66 per cent before the reform to 39 per cent by 1980 and 32 per cent by 1981 (Banco Central, 1983). Unfortunately, there is no sign at all that it acted to stimulate in the long run the growth of a healthier and more competitive industrial sector, except in so far as certain very inefficient lines disappeared completely.[26] It is this lack of response that provides the most convincing answer to the argument that 'all that needs to be done is to remove distortions'. For industry to be able to respond, requires that there be a resilience, competitive strength and managerial and technical capacity which are the product of years of investment in education and infrastructure at many levels. There also needs to be confidence in government policy and a medium-term perspective, something that we shall return to in chapter 10 when we examine the importance of the relationship between the state and the private sector.

With regard to inflation, a Banco Central study argues that the strategy did restrain prices, since, although prices accelerated, the price of tradables rose less fast than non-tradables (Banco Central, 1983). But the resulting overvaluation was of course costly: Peru lives constantly with the dilemma that, although as we have emphasized here, the short-run dividends from devaluation are limited, it is also true that the cost of *not* devaluing are heavy and follow soon, especially for non-traditional exports.

Table 5.5 shows the evolution of the structure of demand under orthodox policies, while Table 5.6 sets out the behaviour of the public sector. In Table 5.6 a partial correction is made for the effect of inflation. A further distinction is made between 'internal' and 'external' deficit, since in a small and import-dependent economy like Peru much of state spending flows directly out of the economy on imports. It will be seen that 1979 was a year of very sluggish growth in demand in every component apart from exports, while the rise in tax income and the revenues of state companies with the export boom was sufficient to reduce the nominal fiscal deficit from 6 per cent of GDP in 1978 to a mere 1 per cent in 1979, with no cut in expenditure. Although the figures

Table 5.5
Peru: GDP by Expenditure at 1970 Prices (1974–85)
(1974 = 100)

	GDP	Consumption		Gross Fixed Investment		Exports	Imports
		Public	Private	Public	Private		
1975	102	113	102	112	129	100	115
1976	106	117	104	106	118	94	89
1977	106	117	105	77	103	109	82
1978	104	102	99	64	93	129	62
1979	108	92	99	73	107	166	65
1980	111	118	103	99	130	154	94
1981	115	116	106	123	155	150	113
1982	116	127	104	130	148	165	110
1983	102	116	93	115	92	146	82
1984	107	102	96	113	55	154	66
1985	109	106	99	87	81	160	59

Source: Banco Central, *Memoria*, 1984, 1986.

for the corrected deficits or surpluses are only suggestive, given the weakness of the data, the fact that they indicate that the deficit became a surplus of nearly 5 per cent of GDP is impressive.

In 1980 and 1981 the growth of demand was led by a boom in investment, both public and private, the latter responding to good export prospects and to a groundswell of confidence in the new government, and rising over 50 per cent above its admittedly very depressed level in 1978. Consumption was far more restrained, real wages rising a little in 1980 to fall again in 1981. There was therefore a stimulus to domestic demand from the expenditure side of the public sector in both years. In 1980, however, the more-than-doubling of fiscal income meant little change in the net effect of the public sector. In 1981 there was strong demand pressure from this source. The inflation-corrected internal surplus of 1980 of 1 per cent of GDP became − 1.5 in 1981. Monetary policy was supposedly restrictive, but even in soles money supply rose relative to GDP (see Table 5.10 below).In 1982 the rise in investment levelled off as confidence began to weaken and export prospects looked poor; the public sector expansion slowed down considerably as sources of financing looked less promising. Given the acceleration of inflation in 1982, which we discuss below, it is probable that a full inflation correction would show that the real internal deficit did not rise. There was also pressure from the IMF, as a condition for a standby signed in June 1982, 'as a precaution'. The growth in GDP was

Table 5.6
Peru: Public Sector Operations (as Percentage of GDP) 1978–84

	1978	1979	1980	1981	1982	1983	1984
Central government current revenue	15.8	18.0	20.5	17.9	17.5	14.2	16.3
Central government current expenditure	17.4	14.4	18.1	17.7	17.3	19.2	17.8
Wages and salaries	4.7	4.0	4.8	5.2	5.2	5.2	5.0
Goods and services	0.6	0.6	0.8	0.8	0.7	0.9	1.0
Military outlays	5.5	3.4	4.9	4.4	5.5	5.1	3.5
Interest	4.3	4.4	4.3	4.5	3.9	5.3	5.4
Subsidies and transfers	2.2	1.9	3.3	2.8	2.0	2.7	2.9
Capital expenditure	5.7	6.0	8.4	9.9	10.6	10.4	8.9
of which central government	3.5	4.1	5.2	5.1	4.2	3.9	4.0
Overall nominal public sector deficit (−)	−6.1	−1.1	−4.7	−8.4	−9.3	−12.1	−7.6
Total 'real' deficit or surplus[a]	−0.6	4.7	2.0	−2.4	−3.8	−5.1	−0.6
'Internal' deficit or surplus[b]	(−1.0)	(0.6)	(−1.9)	(−5.7)	−6.0	−7.6	−5.0
'Internal' deficit partially inflation-corrected[a]	(1.9)	(3.6)	(0.9)	(−2.5)	−3.2	−4.5	−3.1

Source: Banco Central (1984) and author's estimates (see notes).

Notes:
[a] This omits interest payments on the basis of methodology explained fully in Thorp and Whitehead (1987). Basically, it attempts to deduct that part of government outgoings which go to restore the value of people's real assets rather than providing income. The correction probably now *under-*estimates the deficit from the point of view of its demand-generating effects – see the discussion cited above.
[b] The calculation of the 'internal' deficit or surplus uses the innovative unpublished paper of German Alarco (1984). It makes a correction to his figures by excluding from the concept of 'internal income' the sales abroad of state enterprises, on the grounds that this does not correspond to an internal act of saving. However, figures have only been obtained for 1982–84; corrections for earlier years have been estimated only and are therefore placed in parentheses. It must be emphasised that all these 'corrections' are extremely fragile, both conceptually and in terms of the data base.

only 1.8 per cent, negative in per capita terms.The behaviour of output is shown in Table 5.7. It will be seen that agriculture continued its historically unsatisfactory if uneven performance, while the mining sector stagnated, waiting for new projects to come on stream. The most striking development was in industry, which responded in 1980 to the growth of demand with a 5 per cent growth rate, but thereafter declined in *absolute* terms as the influx of imports undermined its market position. Certain sectors did very badly, the outstanding case being textiles, which was hit by both legal and illegal imports.

Table 5.7
Peru: GDP by Productive Sectors, 1970 Prices 1975–85
(1974 = 100)

	GDP	Agric.	Fishing	Mining	Manu.	Constr.	Govt.	Other
1975	102	99	85	87	105	117	104	10
1976	106	102	103	95	109	114	107	10
1977	106	103	97	124	102	105	110	10
1978	104	99	127	143	98	88	109	10
1979	108	102	139	156	102	91	108	10
1980	111	95	132	149	108	108	110	11
1981	115	110	115	142	107	120	113	11
1982	116	113	113	154	105	123	115	11
1983	102	104	68	142	87	97	117	10
1984	107	114	130	151	89	98	117	10
1985	109	116	140	161	93	85	117	10

Source: Banco Central, *Memoria*, 1984, 1986.

Price developments are shown in Table 5.8, which gives 'relative' inflation[27] together with exchange-rate changes, and in Figure 5.1 above, which presents monthly developments, showing the percentage change each month compared with the same month in the preceding year. It will be seen that overvaluation (and increasing subsidies)[28] led to a disappointingly slight slowdown in inflation in 1980, and that prices were accelerating again by mid-year. This indicates a worrying sensitivity of prices to the rise in demand, despite the prior existence of excess capacity. Once the exchange rate and pricing policy changed in August 1981, the failure of inflation to slow down becomes no surprise. The liberalisation of imports, the weakening of export prices and the turnaround in financial markets all put pressure on the exchange rate, and the economy entered firmly into the grip of inertial inflation fed from the external sector. We analyse this process more fully in the following two sections.

Table 5.8
Peru: Exchange Rate Changes and Relative Inflation 1979–84

	Percentage change in nominal exchange rate	Relative inflation[a]	Trends in real exchange rate	Relative inflation equivalent monthly rate
Annual				
Dec. 1979–Dec. 1980	35.8	44.9 ⎫	Appreciation	3.7
Dec. 1980–Dec. 1981	47.7	69.0 ⎭		5.8
Dec. 1981–Dec. 1982	90.7	71.6	Depreciation	6.0
Quarterly				
1983				
1st quarter	23.6	27.1	Appreciation	9.0
2nd quarter	30.5	22.1 ⎫	Depreciation	7.4
3rd quarter	31.1	25.9 ⎭		8.6
4th quarter	11.4	14.4 ⎫		4.8
1984			Appreciation	
1st quarter	15.9	20.8 ⎭		6.9
2nd quarter	25.0	19.8 ⎫		6.6
3rd quarter	2.0	20.8		6.9
4th quarter	31.3	21.4 ⎬	Depreciation	7.1
1985				
1st quarter	51.4	36.6		12.2
2nd quarter	36.9	34.2 ⎭		11.4

Source: Banco Central, *Reseña Económica*, several issues, IBRD (1981).

Note:
[a] Peruvian cost of living compared with prices in main trading partners.

By the end of 1982 an acceleration in prices was part of the growing lack of confidence in the Ulloa team's approach. A further element in the growing confusion in the second half of 1982 was that as monetary policy became increasingly restrictive, so borrowing abroad increased – in particular short-term borrowing by various public sector enterprises. As this became obvious, the state of chaos in public sector financing became a scandal; as the Central Bank put it, moderately: 'part of the difficulty is that nobody knows how much the state-owned companies have borrowed'.[29] In October 1982 belated measures were introduced to control public enterprises' short-term foreign borrowing.

The emerging crisis is clearly portrayed in the balance-of-payments statistics of Table 5.2 above. The more-than-doubling of imports reflects the import liberalisation (consumer goods rose from 6 per cent of the total in 1978 to 15 per cent in 1981) and the investment boom of 1980-81.

The fall in exports in 1981 reflects the weakening of mineral prices. The two together generated a remarkable swing of the trade balance from +21 per cent of exports in 1980 to −17 per cent in 1981, a position which carried through to 1982. Still nothing was done even in 1982, in line with the pattern in country after country. In 1982, although interest rates had risen sharply and terms had shortened, the inflow of public long-term capital did increase, and the basic balance was a mere US $400 million in the red compared with $1.1 billion in 1981. The most ominous symptom was the outflow on account of debt service, 49 per cent of exports in 1982,[30] compared with 36 per cent in the preceding crisis.

From crisis to chaos, 1983–5

On the resignation of Ulloa in December 1982 the issues of confidence and relations with foreign bankers appeared paramount, and precipitated the choice of a banker from Wells Fargo, Carlos Rodríguez Pastor, to lead the new economics team. A new standby was negotiated with the IMF early in 1983, with a World Bank structural adjustment loan (a 'SAL'), on the basis of a sharp increase in the severity of orthodox policies. The IMF programme implied huge cuts in project spending, public sector wage increases were to be well below the rate of inflation, interest rates were to rise, and credit was to be effectively unobtainable either in soles or in dollars. The IMF originally pressed for a reduction in the public sector deficit to 2 per cent of GDP for 1983, but settled for 3.8 per cent (it was still thought to have been nearly 7 per cent in 1982). A 'temporary' tariff increase was accepted, to take the average tariff from 34 per cent to 41 per cent. Tax reform was planned as part of the package, which was conditional on commercial banks maintaining their exposure in Peru. The IMF and IBRD thus joined forces to try to stem the tide of falling confidence. With the agreement came a standby of US $300 million and a SAL of $200 million. Following the signing, by mid-year a substantial (if costly)[31] refinancing was achieved, shown in Table 5.3 above. The Central Bank's desire to slow down the rate of depreciation of the exchange rate and the increase in controlled prices as a deliberate anti-inflationary policy had to be abandoned for the time being as unacceptable to the Bank and the Fund.

The ensuing months were months of increasing chaos. In January and February 1983 the most severe flooding in living memory hit the North, creating disaster conditions as lives were lost and houses and crops washed away, and also destroying infrastructure and damaging installations, affecting, for example, oil production and delivery. The warm El Niño current reduced the fish catch to zero, and by mid-year drought in the South had also created disaster conditions. Weak administrative structures failed to cope with relief work, and the revenue from a special tax imposed on middle and higher income groups, in the form of 'reconstruction bonds', was generally considered not to be arriving at the points of need. The fall in the price of cocaine in 1983 (see table 9.1) may have added to the problems by further reducing the availability of dollars.

Meanwhile a number of scandals emerged over public accounting, particularly over military spending 'omitted' from the 1982 accounts, and the 1982 deficit was re-estimated as 8.6 per cent of GDP (two points more than the original estimate). Every day saw an increase in the problems of invasion of contraband, dollarisation of the economy, and capital flight.[32] Plans for tax reform and the orderly cutting of public spending were abandoned in favour of day-to-day survival. Bills were paid in the public sector increasingly by 'public investment bonds'. By mid-1983 it was claimed policy was concentrated on restrictive monetary conditions, as the only effective element left; yet with dollars now making up half of liquidity and constantly fed from illegal sources, even that claim was clearly implausible. In May at last the anti-inflationary policy pushed since the end of 1982 by the Central Bank was introduced, and the rate of mini-devaluations slowed down, to the increasing concern of the international bankers. In June Morgan Guaranty Trust refused to join a rescheduling package on the grounds that it was a 'farce'. At the end of that month the government resorted to the absurd measure of delaying public employees' wage packets for three days in order to scrape inside the IMF target on expenditure. In October the IMF rescinded the standby agreement. A new one was negotiated, as part of which the rate of mini-devaluation was accelerated, but by now the economic team had lost the government's backing and clearly lacked authority. Belaunde announced in December that he was dismissing Rodríguez Pastor, who in fact stayed on till March 1984 in an increasingly untenable and impotent position. The November municipal elections had produced the surprise result of a left-wing mayor in Lima, precipitating panic on the part of Belaunde as to the political consequences of austerity; he was also anxious to spend in order to complete at least some of his projects before the government's term of office ended in July 1985.

There followed much talk of reactivation initiatives, but in reality any possibility of producing a coherent new policy had disappeared. From late in 1983 the general sense was that any new initiative had to await a new government, despite the fact that elections were not due until April 1985 and the new government would not take office until July 1985. A so-called reactivation plan was discarded at the last moment in April 1984 to enable the signing of a new agreement with the IMF, although in Washington it was widely described as the first agreement broken even before it was signed. By August 1984 a decision was taken not to pay interest on the debt (equivalent to two months' exports). Presumably realising the inability of the present regime to put together a policy initiative, the banks did not push hard for a resolution of the problem. Existing lines of trade credit were not renewed, but what was lost was less than the savings on interest. In December 1984 the new Minister of Economy, Garido Lecca,[33] made a partial payment of $51 million as the critical 180 day limit expired.[34]

Not surprisingly, the room for manoeuvre gained by non-payment was not used to construct a coherent alternative policy – the only real rationale, surely, for risking the wrath of the bankers. The proceeds were used to pay a few public sector bills and wages which would otherwise have gone unpaid. The one sensible measure was a *cut* in taxes which, together with the slight improvement generated by the internal use of money not now needed for debt service, generated an increase in activity and so in tax yield, and hence a small increase in resources available in the later months of 1984. In general, the whole period up to the elections in April 1985 and the entry into office of the new APRA government in July was one of *absence* of policy, where new initiatives were impossible and the bankers, realising this, knew they had to wait.

Causes of the recession, 1983–5

Developments in demand are shown for 1983 in Table 5.5 above. It will be seen that every component of demand fell strongly. The impact of the public sector austerity was very deflationary, with consumption falling 9 per cent and investment 19 per cent, reflecting declining public sector wages, the cuts in investment projects and non-payment of bills.

Exports also fell, by 13 per cent, this reflecting natural disasters since the terms of trade improved somewhat in 1983. The estimated loss of $10 million in fishmeal and $42 million in sugar and cotton[35] was particularly serious for income levels. The catastrophic fall came in private investment, which fell 34 per cent in real terms as demand fell off, credit restrictions and costs increased and as the crisis of confidence deepened. Wages fell 26 per cent between November 1982 and February 1984, and salaries 16 per cent in the same period.[36] Underemployment grew, and by end 1983 was being estimated at 64 per cent.[37] The fall in labour incomes was reflected in a decline of 12 per cent in personal consumption.

Table 5.7 above shows the evolution of supply. The effect of the natural disasters is seen clearly in the figures for agriculture, fishing and mining for 1983. The fall in manufacturing reflects rather the fall-off in demand, plus the increasingly difficult position of many enterprises with the rise in financial costs, and continuing competition from contraband imports. The 19 per cent of value added in the sector, which represents processing of primary materials, was of course, affected by the natural disasters, and fell 17 per cent between the last quarter of 1982 and the first quarter of 1983; it is extremely significant, however, that the output of the rest of the industrial sector fell more heavily over the same period, by 21 per cent, and continued falling in 1984. While the special circumstances of 1983 were clearly of relevance to the disastrous outcome, it is important to note that it was the steep fall in demand which hit industry, plus the fall in investment,[38] itself related in part to loss of confidence, stemming from a sense of the government's inability to cope either with nature or with the growing problem of terrorism.[39] It is striking that this heavy fall in industrial output and in GDP secured a fall in imports of 'only' 27 per cent – an indication of the low 'efficiency' of internal recession in producing adjustment. The disaggregation shown in Table 5.9 is revealing: of the fall of 27 percentage points, the private sector fall represented 25, of which capital goods were half.[40] This was enough to lead to a positive trade balance, despite the export fall, due to the supply-side factors described above (see Table 5.2 above). The overall balance was also positive to the tune of $362 million; reserves, however, fell $40 million, indicating significant capital flight. Without the $1 billion of refinancing shown in Table 5.3 (the largest element in the inflow of new money), the situation would have been impossible.

Inflation worsened during the year, reaching an annual rate of 111 per cent, which slackened only very slightly in 1984. Surely, given the strength of the recession, we are observing not demand pressures so much as stagflationary pressures coming not from the special conditions of these two years, and certainly not from the fiscal deficit, but from cost-push circularities. It is time now to analyse more carefully this inflationary process.

The causes of inflation

The standard analysis by all government teams up to 1985, as well as by visiting missions from the IMF and the World Bank, was to see inflation

Table 5.9
Peru: Composition of Imports 1982–3
(all figures as percentage of 1982 total = 100)

	1982	1983
Total	100	73
Public	38	36
Private	62	37
Consumer goods	13	10
Public	2	3
Private	11	7
Inputs	35	27
Public	10	11
Private	25	16
Capital goods	38	24
Public	14	12
Private	24	12
'Other' and 'adjustments'	14	12
Public	12	9
Private	2	3

Source: Banco Central, *Memoria* (1983).

as caused by the fiscal deficit and by the expansion of the money supply. The 1984 Fund report stated:

> The major cause of the internal and external imbalances experienced by Peru during the past two years has been the maintenance of a public sector deficit at a level averaging 9 per cent of GDP. Public financial requirements of this magnitude led to an unsustainably high level of net foreign financing, a serious crowding out of the private sector in financial markets, and the maintenance of inflationary pressures.[41]

The report recommended major adjustments in the areas of fiscal, monetary and incomes policy.

While it is certainly true that a fiscal deficit of 9 per cent of GDP is unsustainable because of the implicit level of foreign financing, the two remaining claims are somewhat exaggerated, to say the least. Referring back to Table 5.6 above, we showed that a significant part of total public expenditure leaked directly out of the economy on imports or on debt servicing.[42] Calculating the 'internal deficit or surplus' and correcting further for the effect of inflation, we argued that on balance the demand side was deflationary in 1979 and 1980, and clearly inflationary only in 1981, when the deficit rose sharply even in real terms. The continuing deficit from 1983 on, given 'inertial' inflation and the quantity of unused resources, can hardly have played a primary causal role in inflation. The effect of devaluation alone in increasing the value in soles of liabilities denominated in dollars explains part of the increase in the deficit both in 1982 (when the rate of depreciation was particularly strong) and in 1983–4. The large public sector imports and interest payments did, of course, represent substantial pressure on the exchange rate, which in turn led to inflation and also directly inflated the deficit – but this is to enter into a very different causal analysis of inflation from that adopted by the IMF and the Peruvian authorities.

Turning to monetary policy, the analytical problem here is that, with accelerating inflation, the demand for money function would in any case shift, and no estimate of this shift exists for Peru. Thus the clear decline in real liquidity in soles in Table 5.10 cannot be taken as evidence of a drastically restrictive monetary policy, although there does exist abundant qualitative evidence of the difficulty and high cost of obtaining credit throughout our period,[43] which hardly suggests a causal role running from easy money to demand expansion to inflation.

Table 5.10
Peru: Money and Quasi-money as Percentage of
GDP 1978–85

	Money	Quasi-money		
		in soles	dollars	Total
1978	11	6	3	20
1979	10	6	5	21
1980	11	6	8	25
1981	9	9	8	26
1982	8	9	11	28
1983	8	8	13	29
1984	8	7	17	32
1985	10	8	7	25

Source: Banco Central, *Memoria* (1985).

However, what the table does show clearly is the shift into dollars, which by 1983 represented nearly half of the liquidity in the economy (and by 1985 the proportion was well over half). This suggests the following process. Although real interest rates in soles remained negative throughout the period, there were frequent increases in nominal rates and at times credit in soles became virtually unobtainable. This may actually have had a perverse effect, increasing the demand for dollars and thereby adding to exchange rate pressure and so to the inflation which continually nullified the attempts to achieve a positive real rate of interest. Table 5.10 thus suggests the declining power of monetary policy with dollarisation, and even the possibility of yet another perverse effect.

Our discussion of both monetary and fiscal aspects has brought us back to the exchange rate and to costs. This emerges as the heart of the inflationary process in Peru since 1982. Far from being demand-determined, recent inflation in Peru has derived from costs, and these costs are themselves almost all manipulated by policy. The critical elements in manufacturing costs relevant to pricing decisions are, first, the exchange rate, given the importance of imported inputs. This has been a policy instrument of prime importance. Second, various controlled prices or tariffs of public sector enterprises enter the equation. The crucial one here is petrol, but other transport and energy costs are important. The third element is wage cost, the one element which has not maintained its parity with prices, as we have seen. The fourth element is financial cost. Recent structuralist analyses have tended to place undue weight on this last element: when real interest rates are negative it seems implausible that financial costs can account for such an important part of the inflationary process. However, even with negative real rates, there may be a cost-push element operating, if two assumptions hold. First, financial costs must be a significant proportion of total costs. Second, banks must refuse to refinance the inflation-induced rise in interest costs, which they would normally do in a period of inflation. The first point is certainly true for Peru: financial costs represented 31 per cent of total costs in 1981 for the average of the industrial sector, rising to 45 per cent in 1983.[44] The lack of refinancing was also occurring by 1983, as banks faced with bad debtors struggled by any means in their power to recoup their losses.

The final factor in the mechanism of stagflation in Peru is the effect of recession itself on unit costs. As the use of installed capacity falls, so unit costs tend to rise, exerting further pressure on prices.

The remarkable aspect of the whole process is the way cost-plus pricing appears to go on raising prices even in the face of strong and growing recession. We suggest that 'expectations' account for this, since instinctively everyone knows that defense mechanisms are well enough developed for the 'privileged' market to continue to exist. The hypothesis of defense mechanisms needs fuller discussion, and it is to this theme that we turn in the following section.

It is this expectations factor which accounts for an aspect of inflation in Peru which makes it exceedingly difficult to handle in policy terms. Table 5.8 above sets out changes in the exchange rate and relative inflation. It will be seen that in the periods where an attempt was made to 'beat' inflation by rapid devaluation and interest rate changes, the policies achieved their goal in small measure only and at the price of accelerating inflation.[45] This was true between the end of 1981 and mid-1983. Unfortunately the reverse policy has, it appears, very small dividends. In 1979-81 the policy was sustained for two years during which time prices and the exchange rate were deliberately adjusted by less than the rise in prices in the preceding few months. (Pre-announcement was not used, however, which is an important point.) As we saw above (see Figure 5.1) the monthly inflation rate did slow down at first, although hardly enough to build the necessary confidence in the policy. But by mid-1980 the monthly rate was rising again: our analysis of the rise in expenditure suggests that the problem may indeed have been demand pressure. This is serious in its implications, since it suggests that a policy of reactivation risks accelerating inflation, unless careful precautions are taken. In 1983 the problem was that the policy of small and pre-announced changes in the exchange rate was sustained only for six months, and in a context of dwindling confidence. It is again disappointing, however, that the slowdown in prices in the final quarter did not seem to spread beyond controlled prices, except for non-controlled, non-traded foodstuffs, where a recovery in supply following some improvement in climatic conditions was the explanation. The relevant point in the context of late 1983 was probably the general lack of credibility of policy, the known difficulty of reversing expectations, and the continuing fall in levels of activity in industry.

Defence mechanisms

It will be our argument here that one effect of prolonged stagnation and painful adjustment policies in an economy like Peru's is that defence mechanisms get developed or more firmly entrenched. This leads, we will argue, to ever less efficiency and higher cost when orthodox adjustment measures continue to be applied.

The first two defence mechanisms we want to consider are strongly interrelated. The first is dollarisation; Table 5.10 above showed how much of liquidity was now comprised by dollars, and how this grew from

10 per cent in 1974 to over 50 per cent ten years later. In part this responds to relative prices – exchange and interest-rate policy – but far more strongly to underlying uncertainty in the face of inflation and loss of confidence in policy. But it also stems from the second defence mechanism: with the move into illegal exporting of coca and its derivatives, a steady stream of dollars becomes available. As mentioned above, a 1982 estimate put coca as the largest single export item at $800 million;[46] dollars can be either 'laundered' by smuggling in goods which can be sold cheaply, since they perform a double role, or simply used internally with increasing ease, since they are increasingly the lifeblood of the desperate economy. The cancellation in March 1983 of the 1980 law which required dollar deposits to be declared locally for tax purposes was an interesting indicator of the importance of illegal dollars to the Central Bank.[47]

Far more widespread than drugs activity, however, is the practice of shifting into 'informal' and sometimes illegal activity of many kinds. Obviously, as jobs become scarcer, a primary defence mechanism is, as it always has been, the resort to 'make work' self-employment. This is facilitated by contraband imports, which need to be peddled on every street corner. But it is also a route for firms, particularly the smaller ones: under pressure, costs can be cut by retreating out of the formal sector or by increasing the use of subcontracting. As credit becomes scarcer, firms are forced into the informal credit market. All these measures mean that total bankruptcy – the classic 'shake-out' effect – can be more or less avoided by the assiduous taking in of each other's washing.

The larger firms, while they may well use this route, also have other possibilities. First, they may benefit from increasing concentration and so greater market power as the recession grows, if weaker firms disappear; thus their ability to pass on cost increases may stay the same or even grow in a shrinking market. Probably more important than this, however, is the formation of 'economic groups'. Peruvian industrial development has always been characterised by the existence of 'empires', usually centering around a bank: the outstanding example from the 1940s to the 1960s was the Prado family empire. When it might be expected that with development and the reforms of the 1970s this characteristic would diminish in importance, in Peru recently it seems to have grown. The best known recent example is the growth of the Romero-Raffo group, centered on the Banco de Crédito and extending into insurance, property, textiles and vegetable oil.[48] (Interestingly, this group is at the heart of the modern sector of the industrial bourgeoisie, taking a leading role in ADEX, for example – the more progressive industrialists' association).[49] Each of a number of bank collapses or near-collapses has also revealed excessive in-house lending within a small group of enterprises.[50] We hypothesize that the effect of years of credit squeeze and economic difficulties is to make firms work to secure links into such groups, as a means of securing working capital and other privileged forms of access (e.g. to insurance). While this can only be hypothesised until it is further studied, we suggest it is one important means by which some firms survive when textbook economics would suggest they would long ago have been 'shaken out'.

Another route to survival for a large or medium-sized firm is division of its activities. Occasionally this is skilfully done so that unprofitable activities and debts can be concentrated in one entity which is then allowed to go bankrupt, while worthwhile assets are saved. A further mechanism which weakens the 'shake-out effect' is that of tying oneself into the public sector by means of a contract. It is fascinating in this respect to compare the 1980s with the 1930s.[51] Whereas in the 1930s public sector projects were abandoned wholesale, in the 1980s the existence of penalty clauses and other protective devices makes it just about impossible to terminate a project. Faced with the need to cut public investment, the ability of the private contractors to defend themselves (by powerful links into Congress) is such that instead of certain projects being completed and others stopped, all projects are cut by a certain amount. Since there are penalties for delay on the government side, absurd situations can begin to develop whereby the remaining funds are eaten up in interest charges and the expenses of 'ticking over'. In the next section we develop the implications of these kinds of developments for the adjustment policies Peru has typically followed.

The new mechanisms of 'adjustment' policies

The policies pursued by Peru from 1982 to mid-1985 were broadly similar, as we have seen, to those pursued in earlier adjustment crises. The primary emphasis was put on the reduction of the fiscal deficit via increased revenue and reduced expenditure, while credit restraint was to be followed with regard both to the public and private sectors. The emphasis on making the economy 'healthier', which was predominant in 1979–81, was actually lessened a little, as the invasion of imports resulting from the *apertura* had to be contained: tariffs were raised moderately. But the vision of external advisers from the World Bank and the IMF and of at least some commentators in Peru was still that swallowing the nasty medicine of recession and reducing the size of the state sector would together lead to the emergence of a leaner and more competitive economy able to compete abroad and avoid a resurgence of external disequilibrium. The recession would act as a brake on expectations, and after the necessary inflation, a conservative monetary and fiscal policy would allow prices to settle down. Earlier we showed how such measures operated extremely inefficiently on both the external and internal disequilibrium in 1975–7. The period we have now described, 1982-5, in no way modifies that analysis; in fact it strengthens it. We argued earlier that relative price shifts could be of little benefit to exports, except non-traditional products; now we see that as the mechanisms of expectations and stagflation became more entrenched, it was difficult even to achieve a relative price change, and that it could only be done by accelerating inflation. The fall in demand as usual was the only instrument that affected the balance of payments in the short term; it required a 34 per cent fall in private investment in real terms and 21 per cent fall in industrial output to achieve a 25 per cent fall in total imports in real terms (Tables 5.5 and 5.7 above). In 1984, as we have seen, survival was only possible by the precarious procedure of non-payment of interest on the debt. Meanwhile the long-term factors giving rise to the external disequilibrium – the growth in debt and its unhealthy structure, the expansion of defence commitments,[52] the long-run supply problem in exports – were not touched by these measures. Instead of an increase in competitiveness in industry, defence mechanisms were intensified.

On the internal front the more probable effect, as we have seen, was that the fiscal policy induced recession; this fed back on tax revenue which fell disastrously, from 19 per cent of GDP in 1980 to 13 per cent in 1983. We therefore have the same circularity that we usually encounter, in which policy, while in fact deflationary, is perceived as not achieving its goal, wrongly defined in terms of the budget deficit, so that further efforts at deflation must constantly be made. These partly take the form of increases in controlled prices, thus feeding the stagflationary mechanism we have described. It is interesting that public investment actually fell less severely in this than in the previous crisis. We have suggested that this was the result of one of the private sector's defence mechanisms. This led to the worst of all possible worlds, since public investment continued but was completely ineffective in terms of the need for finished projects which could contribute to the removal of bottlenecks.

We have also seen that credit policy became increasingly both ineffective and inflationary, as dollarisation removed more of the economy from internal control and as the rising cost and scarcity of formal sector credit sent enterprises to even more costly informal sources. The private sector therefore suffered increasing costs as a result of every element of the adjustment policies, and, given the growing ability of significant groups to defend themselves, inflation merrily continued. The cost was seen in worsening income distribution and increasing symptoms of distress of every kind: disease rose, infant mortality rose, and real wages fell 20 per cent in the twelve months February 1983–February 1984 (*Reseña Ecónomica*, June 1984, p. 25). We have argued elsewhere that it was only the prevalence of survival techniques in the lower strata of informal sector activity that prevented a more violent and earlier political reaction (Angell and Thorp, 1980).

For whatever reason, both economy and society tolerated a long, slow collapse into *desgobierno* between 1983 and 1985, the view being that fresh initiatives must await a fresh government – a period to be paralleled in a more exaggerated and frightening form between 1988 and 1990. Unfortunately, this long waiting period reinforced the high expectations of the alternative approach Alan García appeared to be bringing in, expectations that both in retrospect and in the light of our historical analysis here were clearly wildly unrealistic. On this basis García and the Aprista party won the elections of 1985 and came into office on July 7 that year.

Notes

1. The book here mentioned is the result of research carried out by the Instituto de Libertad y Democracia, headed by De Soto. The book's qualitative analysis is fascinating, but its statistical basis is completely unconvincing. See Rossini and Thomas (1987). More important, its conclusions are too simplistic. However, recent views expressed by the ILD suggest that they have substantially modified their initial position, and see a changed but extensive role for the state in facilitating a response from the private sector. (This is based on seminar presentations, Universidad del Pacífico, 'El Peru frente a la crisis de los 90', Lima, September 1989.)
2. Though apparently the Central Bank President insists that the programme was Peru's own idea – see Stallings (1978). Another fascinating source is Devlin (1980).
3. Ministry of Labour, cited in *Actualidad Económica*, April 1978.
4. Stallings (1978).
5. The argument between the Central Bank and the Fund was made public in several issues of *Equuns*, March and April 1977.
6. *Latin America Economic Report*, 19th May 1978.
7. *Latin America Political Report*, 19th May 1978.
8. *Financial Times*, 16th June 1978.
9. The Military's return to orthodoxy.

10. Ugarteche (1986).
11. Ministerio de Economía y Finanzas (1978).
12. In the case of military spending, purchases of equipment appear under 'current expenditure'.
13. Estimates made by Carlos Amat y Leon, Ministerio de Economía y Finanzas.
14. In mid-1978 large numbers of dismissals were in fact decreed in certain Ministeries, but the measure was rescinded after considerable protest and a number of strikes.
15. This resulted, for example, in devices such as making sure that when the budget was exhausted before December, the element left uncovered was wages and salaries. Another example is the rash of advertisements for new posts which appeared when a freeze on public appointments was known to be coming in May 1977.
16. This was one of the chief conclusions of a report written at the Government's request by Diusenberg, a Dutch economist and ex-Minister of Finance, in May 1978.
17. A study by Pirani (1977) found the price variable non-significant in explaining the behaviour of imports 1970-75.
18. See for example Spitzer (1969).
19. Data from Banco Central de la Reserva del Perú, *Memoria*, various years.
20. *Latin America Economic Report*, 13th April 1979.
21. *Andean Report*, February 1983, p. 22.
22. Latin America Bureau (1984), pp. 84-5.
23. On irrigation projects, see *Andean Report*, June 1983, p. 109.
24. Thorne (1985). He argues that the 'simplification' actually made things more complex, by introducing the difficult concept of 'capitalisable', and by treating distinct institutions in the same fashion.
25. See Scott (1986); LARR, *Andean Group Report*, 2nd September 1983: 'Velasco's Reforms are Alive and Well'.
26. Such as certain plastics. See Falconi (1983) for measures of the reverse import substitution which occurred from 1979 on.
27. Inflation in Peru compared to its principal trading partners, as calculated by the Central Bank.
28. For example, between December 1979 and December 1980, the 'real' price of rice fell 26 per cent, that of evaporated milk 22 per cent, that of gasoline 25 per cent (data from IMF, 1982, p. 45).
29. *Andean Report*, February 1983.
30. The figure was higher in 1981, but incorporated some early repayment of loans.
31. For example, rolled-over trade credits pay nearly twice the normal rate (*Andean Report*, April 1983, p. 58). But this refinancing was on more advantageous terms than the previous one Peru negotiated.
32. Using the standard method of estimating capital flight from Peru shows rather surprisingly no capital flight until 1983 – possibly because the method does not allow us to detect compensating inflows of coca dollars. But in 1983 and 1984 the method reveals a substantial outflow.
33. He replaced Benavides, who had taken over from Rodríguez Pastor in March.
34. Critical because after that period the banks must adjust their books and make additional provision against the defaulted amount.
35. Estimated in an unpublished document of the Ministerio de Economía y Finanzas.
36. *Reseña Económica*, June 1984, p. 25.
37. By the Ministry of Labour. Of the 36 per cent 'adequately employed', one-third were estimated to be in the informal sector. See LARR, *Andean Group Report*, 9th November 1984, p. 2. The figure in 1979 was 58 per cent (*Perú Económico*, July 1979).
38. Itself a component of demand, of course, but not strongly so given the large import component.

39. The Maoist-style guerrilla movement, Sendero Luminoso, had been operating in the remote and backward department of Ayacucho for some time. Only by the 1980s was it really beginning to be taken seriously. See Taylor (1983).

40. Implicit in this analysis is the assumption that shortages of imports in themselves did not *cause* the fall in production and investment. Imports were not controlled, so this would seem reasonable. However, it is possible that bureaucratic delays were used as an informal rationing system. Large and well-connected firms probably could obtain imports if they wished to invest, so the emphasis on the fall in demand may be correct.

41. IMF (1984), p. 12.

42. The analysis draws on the stimulating analysis published by Alarco (1984).

43. See, for example, *Andean Report*, September 1984, on the lack of credit in the cotton and textile sectors. The *Andean Report* of January 1983 reports on tight money policy and its effect in increasing enterprises' short-term borrowing from abroad.

44. Conasev (1982–4).

45. It is important to note, however, that in regard to interest rates this was true of the size of increase which the Peruvians attempted – usually 15 or 20 percentage points. Experience in a country like Argentina shows that with far larger increases it is eventually possible to secure positive real rates.

46. *Andean Report*, February 1983, p. 22.

47. *Andean Report*, June 1983.

48. See LAB (1984), p. 87.

49. See Ferner (1983) for an interesting discussion of the evolution of different fractions of the industrial bourgeoisie under the military government. The key moment in the groups' development was the securing of a controlling interest in the Banco de Crédito in 1979. See LAB (1984), p. 87.

50. See, for instance, LARR, *Andean Group Report*, 20th May 1983, p. 7, on the liquidation in January 1982 of the Banco de la Industria de la Construcción, to be followed by the Banco Comercial, which got into trouble when the Bertello group of companies defaulted massively on repayments to their own bank. Similar situations were revealed as several regional banks hit trouble. See *Andean Report*, February 1983 and May 1983. The June issue reports on CARSA, another example, tied into the Banco del Sur. The fact that these groups did collapse suggests that by 1983 the 'group' strategy was becoming a less successful defence mechanism.

51. This theme will be developed in a work in progress by Portocarrero, Portocarrero and Thorp.

52. See LARR, *Andean Group Report*, 5th October 1983, p. 5, on the Peruvian military's purchases. The article is entitled 'Peru Re-equips on a Grand Scale'; in 1983 military spending was 6 percent of GDP (Scott, 1986).

6 The Apra Alternative 1985–90

The García version of a radical response to Peru's problem was evolved in a context totally different to that of Velasco. We have seen how the underlying economic problems had become more severe in the interim, with new dimensions added – in particula inflation, debt and the cumulative effect of years of recession. Political and social problems had moved to a new level of severity, with the growth of the activities of Sendero Luminoso[1] and an increase in all types of violence, in part as a reaction to recession.

The room for manoeuvre that García had was narrower also in regard to *la coyuntura*, and therefore the issues and the battleground were different. The Military had been allowed virtually to ignore short-term management, thanks first to high primary product prices and then to abundant foreign loans, and then when they could no longer ignore it they gave it little attention or creativity – until there was nothing for it but to go with international pressures. The short-term crisis faced by García's government, by contrast, was so grave that it had to be the focal point for effort and for innovation. Both regimes in fact had room for manoeuvre in one sense: that given by previous recession and the resulting spare capacity in the economy. This was even greater for García than it had been in 1968, and was to be crucial to the developments of the first 18 months, as we shall see.

The Military also initially had considerable political space: García had less initially, with 46 per cent of the votes cast and an active Congress in which his party had 55 per cent of the seats. He was able rapidly to *create* more space by his initial policies, as we shall see – but this is a different matter. But in a sense he was able to do so because of a similarity with the Velasco administration: both were able to build on a strong emerging consensus in terms of policy. In Velasco's case this was the consensus on the need for ownership reform and the better 'harnessing' of the export-horse. In García's case this was the new consensus that in short-term policy management the orthodox option was bankrupt. By 1985 a remarkable consensus had developed among Peruvian academics and policy makers, that at least in the Peruvian case recession-inducing policies were inappropriate as measures to deal with inflation and exceedingly inefficient in dealing with balance-of-payments

121

disequilibrium. In Peru by July 1985 it was abundantly clear that inflation did not come from excess demand, and that the budget deficit was the symptom rather than the cause of the problem. It was clear too that the balance-of-payments disequilibrium had its roots in long-run supply problems on the export side, in weak international prices and limited possibilities of market expansion, in the difficulty of restructuring demand and industry to reduce import propensities, and in the capital flight induced by the very recession itself and the resulting lack of confidence and *desmoralización*.

We have carefully explored the arguments and evidence behind these points in the preceding chapter. The key empirical factor influencing perceptions in 1985 was the existence of substantial excess capacity in industry. This gave an illusory sense of room for manœuvre. All this paved the way for fresh thinking on the causes of inflation, parallel to that occurring in several other Latin American countries.[2] Inflation was cost-induced, in a process whereby the key prices controlled by the government were the overwhelmingly strong determinants, namely the exchange rate, the interest rate, public utility prices and some food prices, and wages – though the latter had played no active part in the process, real wages having fallen nearly 40 per cent in the years 1979–1985. Formal indexation did not exist, so the process was not identical to that identified in Brazil or Argentina – but in practice the public sector was substituting for the indexation mechanisms institutionalised elsewhere.

This analysis opened the way for the new policy approach. Given the vicious circles of recession-inflation and public sector prices-expectations-inflation, it was clear that the core of the new approach had to be to turn vice into virtue. If certain key prices had such an all-pervading effect, then at least they could be made to work for you, in the first place by a price freeze to control expectations, and in the second by using them to manipulate profitability and so generate reactivation. If recession worsened inflation, then reactivation could produce falling unit costs to assist the reversal of inflation. Meanwhile the public sector would gain from increasing revenues. The *modus operandi* of the policy was seen as the use of increased wages, lower real interest rates and a frozen exchange rate to produce first a transfer of income from financial and speculative activities towards the real sector, and then growth.

As for the external sector: since in the short term little could be done in regard to either exports or import substitution, room for manoeuvre could only be secured immediately by not paying interest on the debt. The conclusion was not, as the left would have it, that the debt should not be paid, but that it would not be, or at least only in part in the medium term. Meanwhile both in final consumption and in the industrial structure there had to be a radical shift away from imports, since no one could foresee much opportunity for increasing exports and indeed the early emphasis in the new approach was to seek a way of growing that did not depend on exports, since historically that route had brought few dividends.

The early thinking and policy statements contained a further element: history was to be reversed in yet another sense, by giving agriculture a primary role. The rural sector was actually to be the focus of reactivation, to be used to lift the urban sector. This was desirable not simply in terms of the previous perennial neglect of agriculture, but because it looked as if it would be less import-extravagant and indeed import-saving.

The 'thinness' of the team's thinking on the deepseated problems of Peru's political economy and the longer-run aspects of policy formation is already indicated by this last point, which indeed was rapidly abandoned, since no one could invent a way to implement a rural development policy in the short term – particularly when price controls on food were soon adversely affecting plantings. The team had a coherent analysis of underlying problems in terms of the way Peru had been integrated into the world economy and the need for restructuring, with some understanding of the implications of this in terms both of the industrial structure and the needs of the export sector. The detailed analysis and technical capacity to turn these perceptions into reality were not in evidence, however, and other aspects of the 'political' project – decentralisation and rural development – were even less rooted in tangible projects. Meanwhile there was little perception of the structural crisis at the political economy level which we have stressed in this book. Chapter 2 has emphasized the prolonged nature of the crisis in export supply and in investment, and the roots of both in the breakdown of the old model and the failure to develop a new class hegemony compatible with a functioning model of accumulation. By the mid-1980s the key social actors were less ready than ever, perhaps, to assume a positive role. The entrepreneurial groups had been further alienated from the state in different ways under both Velasco and Belaunde. Their negative experience with import-liberalizing policies under Belaunde had been *so* strong that they were enthusiastic in the first instance for García – but this perhaps encouraged policy makers to forget the underlying fragility of business confidence and the intense distrust of the state which were by this point deepseated characteristics. Meanwhile the social actors within the state had also been through an intensely negative experience under Belaunde (when planning, for instance, was even physically marginalised, with the Planning Institute being moved to the outskirts of Lima, in La Molina). Many of those with interesting and important experience in the government from the Velasco period had moved out to form their own NGO's or research institutes. Many of the *técnicos* remaining in the government were demoralised and unable to function for lack of resources or training. In other words, the new administration faced an incredible challenge: the need to find a fresh solution to a deep-seated problem, at a moment when the principal agents were less prepared than ever to aid in shaping that solution.

In the event, such problems were simply not at the forefront of thinking, while the treatment of public sector salaries did nothing to help the building up of the capacity of the state. Nor was the distributive contradiction considered: under the previous government investment had been unsatisfactory *notwithstanding* a shift in income distribution towards profits: profits rose as a share of GDP from 54 per cent in 1975 to 64 per cent in 1983.[3] García's populist mandate would be difficult to reconcile with a continuation of this trend. This made it even more imperative to think coherently about who was to invest and save and on what terms. The implicit assumption seems to have been that there was enough room with reactivation for all things to be possible.

The weakness of the thinking on these deeper issues was all the more serious given one of the most critical aspects of heterodox packages, namely the inherent contradiction between the short term and the long term. The short-term policy approach involves controls which threaten longer term development targets. Thus from the very beginning deliberate compensation has to be introduced to balance the resulting distortion – or the underlying contradictions will rapidly reduce the government's room for manoeuvre. Specifically, for example, the package requires that food prices must be controlled, threatening the development of local production to relieve the dependence on food imports. Interest rates typically are to be held low, threatening the scope for the long-run development of new financial structures to promote a more broadly based and equitable growth process. The exchange rate must be frozen, threatening the healthy evolution of the tradables sector. Public utility prices must be held down, threatening the pursuit of a healthy financial position and the long-term ability to grow of the state enterprises. Orthodoxy is at least simpler since short-term and long-term policy recommendations mesh! It will be clear from what we have said that to compensate for such distortions requires a sophisticated and detailed view of the specific needs of long-term policy in each area, plus the political will and institutional coherence to make such policies a high priority, when all the biases are toward attention to the short term. It hardly needs pointing out how improbable it was that these elements should be present.

When we turn to the actual measures taken to translate this model into reality, we find that, as we have indicated, the focus on the rural sector was abandoned at once – though paradoxically reality was to prove surprising. Attractive as the route of reactivation via agriculture might be, no one could begin to imagine policies that could produce this in the short term. Meanwhile the easiest measure to decree (if not to implement) – the freeze on prices – worked in the reverse direction by adversely affecting planting in the first few months. The first measures implemented the thinking behind the inflation model we have described above by freezing prices, declaring that the exchange rate would remain fixed, cutting interest rates, and in February, *reducing* the general sales tax. Wages were raised, and raised further in February. Certain additional gentle measures of reactivation were added in September 1985, and again in February, all designed to reduce firms' costs. Import controls were introduced for a few commodities. Much was made of the declaration that no more than 10 per cent of exports would be paid out in interest on the debt. The agrarian policy initially focused on credit (not always the real problem) but by February a more extended set of measures was announced which focused principally on trying to maintain adequate guaranteed prices to producers and subsidising where necessary the consumer price (deeper problems of the infrastructure were not touched). Initially, there were no controls on profit remittances and the exchange market was completely free.

These early measures resulted in an extraordinary boom in popularity for the President and for the government's policies – particularly the debt policy and the anti-inflation stance. An opinion poll in Lima in September 1985 gave the President over 90 per cent support, thus consolidating and augmenting both the sense of consensus and the political room for manoeuvre.

Policy evolution and policy results 1985-88

(i) July 1985-December 1986: reactivation and euphoria
As is well-known, the first eighteen months of the heterodox experiment were at one level months of dangerous success. Before documenting both the success and its weak points, it is important to note how policy evolved, and to some extent matured.

The key areas where the evolution was positive, if ultimately inadequate, concern the two crucial points we have been identifying throughout: the political economy of investment, and the external bottleneck.

As we shall see later, the first topic was initially left on one side with an implicit option being made for the informal sector and the smaller firm. This was the implicit logic of the price freeze, and the explicit logic of the beginning of initiatives to develop credit policies for the informal sector. There is no clear evidence that the large-scale modern sector suffered unduly, since it had many escape routes – but it *felt* discriminated against, which in terms of investment and capital flight was the relevant aspect.[4] By July 1986, the President and the economic team concluded that a clearer option was needed for an explicit and coherent accumulation model. The President called for various scenarios to be developed, including a socialist option – and a major decision was made to abandon all thought of expropriation or other socialist-style measures and to concentrate on drawing the private sector into partnership through this so-called process of *concertación*.[5] A small and highly monopolised industrial sector contributes to inflation when cost-push inflation is underway, but can be an advantage in a different scenario. It is possible for policy makers to deal individually with a handful of businessmen and achieve quantitatively interesting results.

Much talking began with leading groups in the second half of 1986 to persuade them to invest in non-traditional lines for export, with everything up for negotiation (special rates on foreign exchange transactions, credit, price adjustments, taxes, etc.). Thus in practice by special deals and by shifting many imports to the financial rate, a considerable degree of devaluation was implemented, in particular for new lines of non-traditional exports where relative profitability was felt to be important.

This policy represented a shift away from the early emphasis on the informal sector. It also involved important political developments, as the government moved increasingly away from negotiating with the trade associations, or *gremios* – CONFIEP being the principal association of entrepreneurs - towards direct talks with the so-called '12 apostles', or leaders of the 12 or 15 main groups. The result was positive in terms of the collaboration of the groups, but clearly involved resentment on the part of others.

In regard to the external sector, the early desire to break with the past by not allowing the balance of payments to dominate discussion, had to be modified for a number of reasons. First, the reality of the debt position was that much more than 10 per cent of exports was paid in 1986 – once past arrears, short-term and private sector payments are included. The Central Bank's estimate is 29 per cent of exports in 1986 and 35 per cent in 1985.[6] The payment excluding short-term and private debt was still 20 per cent in 1986, which is exactly what was in practice paid in 1984. So the extra room for manoeuvre was disappointing. Secondly, the early approach had to be recognized as a long-term goal, not a basis for short-term management. In the short term, since the industrial sector in Peru imports approximately half its inputs, imported foodstuffs are vital in urban markets, and the public sector propensity to import is high, export policy must take a high priority (thus expressing vividly the contradictions which make this style of policy so difficult).

Thus export deals became from mid-1986 on central to the *concertación* policy described above, and non-traditional exporters received very favourable treatment (mining less so). The debt policy was tightened in the second half of 1986[7] and a number of ideas developed linking debt to exporting. Basically, this took one of two forms: debt may be paid with products if the creditor is willing to buy an additional quantity of goods such that the net foreign exchange effect is positive. Or debt may be exchanged for new investment aimed at producing foreign exchange. This was an important development focusing on the active development of capacity to pay.[8]

In other areas there was no sign of policy evolution. In particular, most of the incipient contradictions of heterodox policies went unresolved through these eighteen months. As uncontrolled (and uncontrollable) prices rose, the inflation rate settled to some 4 per cent a month on average. This combined with the complete freezing of many key prices in nominal terms led to the growth of quite severe distortions – which were manageable at first but by the end of this first period were quite clearly unmanageable. But there was no evolution - here or in other heterodox experiments – in thinking on how to deal with this without re-awakening inflationary expectations. The half-heartedness of the adjustments finally introduced in December 1986 simply revealed the lack of a solution and confidence in government policies began to weaken. Meanwhile the distortions were causing problems in various areas. One of the most serious was the erosion of state revenue. As shown in Table 6.1, where it had been hoped in the heterodox logic that reactivation would bring increased revenue, in fact Central Government revenue fell as a percentage of GDP from 15 per cent to 12 per cent in 1986. The most important factor in this was the fall in revenue from the gasoline tax as the real price fell, from 100 in 1985 to 37 by 1987 (see Table 6.8 below). Other contributory factors were the extent of the participation of the informal sector in the recovery – of course not paying taxes – and the cut in sales tax rates early in 1986.[9]

Table 6.1
Peru: Public Sector Income and Expenditure 1984–9
(percent of GDP)

	1984	1985	1986	1987	1988	1989
Central Government						
Income	14.0	15.2	12.4	8.9	9.3	5.1
Expenditure	18.4	17.4	16.1	14.5	12.2	5.9
Defence	3.1	3.4	3.0	2.8	1.9	1.8
Interest	4.4	4.4[a]	2.4[a]	1.8[a]	2.2[a]	0.7[a]
Investment	3.5	2.8	3.0	2.3	1.7	0.8
Total Public Sector						
Investment	8.1	6.4	5.5	4.5	3.6	1.6
Public Sector Deficit						
as calculated by BCR	−6.6	−2.7	−5.1	−6.7	−6.7	−1.6
Deficit excluding interest[b]	−0.7	3.1	−1.8	−4.0	−3.7	−0.9

Source: Banco Central, *Memoria.*

Notes:
[a] Includes interest due but not paid. Excluding this would reduce the 1986 figure by about 3 points.
[b] Obtained by deducting all interest payments, on the argument that when real rates are negative they constitute repayment of capital, not income. (They also in large part went abroad, which raises the issue of the need to examine the internal balance of government income and expenditure. The data are not yet available to do this.) The argument is, that if we wish to evaluate possible pressure on the level of activity in the economy, this figure is more relevant than that given in the official figures.

Distortions also continued and worsened in respect of agriculture. The damaging effect of price controls on certain products continued, combined with the increasingly overvalued exchange rate which subsidised food imports. Thus one of the most negative of Peru's policies over decades – cheap imported food – was continued and reinforced. The price of bread in Lima in June 1987 was 40 per cent below its real value of 1980.[10] Meanwhile as the reactivation got underway the prices of non-controlled non-tradables rocketed, creating a historic shift in the internal terms of trade – but as an accident not an intended result of policy. The contribution of policy was to increase rural credit in unprecedented fashion. As the section below on agriculture shows in more detail, the result was clear evidence for the complexity of rural development policy: the supply response was limited by the need for other elements, such as regulation of tenure, efficient supply of inputs and better transport.

(ii) The results of policy
Reactivation was sparked in part by the improvement in wages and salaries – the rise in private sector wages by December 1986 was 35 per cent over July 1985, and 30 per cent for public sector earnings. What also stimulated demand was the income effect of certain controlled prices which fell in real terms – e.g. the gasoline prices, important for the informal transport sector as well as the middle class, and the price of kerosene and food stuffs, key prices for low income groups. In general public expenditure was not a strong source of direct demand stimulus (see Table 6.2), with new investment plans taking time to get under way and many existing projects experiencing delays because of interruptions in foreign financing and/or management problems. By the second half of 1986 private investment was a further contributor to demand expansion and public investment was picking up. Construction licences granted rose 50 per cent between March and October 1986 and sales of cement rose 40 per cent.

The initial effect of the programme on production was very flat, as manufacturers destocked, faced with uncertainty, and consumers waited to see what developed. It was with the new year that

Table 6.2
Peru: GDP Volume Index. Major Components 1984–8
(1980 = 100)

	1984	1985	1986	1987	1988
Private Consumption	104	108	120	135	127
Public Consumption	92	96	101	102	92
Gross Investment	99	84	111	127	109
– Public	152	118	118	95	109
– Private	82	73	108	137	118
Exports	92	95	83	79	71
Imports	98	91	112	124	110
GDP	102	103	114	123	112

Source: BCRP, *Memoria.*

Table 6.3
Peru: Quarterly Real Gross Domestic Product and Main Components 1985–88
(Indices 1979 = 100[a])

	1985				1986				1987				1988			
	I	II	III	IV	I	II	III	IV	I	II	III	IV	I	II	III	IV
GDP	107	105	100	100	103	112	113	120	120	122	121	121	122	118	104	85
Agriculture	107	110	106	105	105	109	116	117	118	119	113	120	126	129	133	118
Fishing	135	81	140	152	144	180	157	179	153	169	149	118	155	144	116	205
Mining	99	101	99	96	92	96	94	95	97	95	90	88	88	81	78	65
Manufacturing	102	97	93	96	98	113	115	122	121	126	131	129	130	122	103	72
Construction	96	90	82	94	98	109	117	123	124	129	134	127	138	136	113	89
Government	142	146	122	114	132	133	135	149	144	147	132	133	119	100	109	73

Source: Alerta Económica, MEF.

Note:
[a] Corrected for seasonal fluctuations.

production indices began to respond. Manufacturing production rose significantly in the first quarter of 1986 (see Table 6.3) and continued to grow. There is some evidence that the informal sector grew even faster than the formal sector in the early months – evidence for this comes, for example, from the growth in bank deposits in branches situated in the heart of the informal sector,[11] and from data showing the huge increase in formal sector sales of leather with a decline in formal sector shoe production, suggesting that leather supplies were being absorbed by informal sector firms.[12] Despite the poor performance of the export sectors (inevitable given price trends) all growth indicators became stronger month by month in the course of 1986 generating constantly revised predictions and by December an estimate of 8 per cent for the growth of GDP for 1986. The final figure proved to be 9 per cent. Agriculture and livestock grew at about 3 per cent, a somewhat better harvest in 1986 compensating for reduced plantings of some crops. Food imports rose, to US$386 million for the year 1986, and would have risen further had international grain prices not fallen significantly.

Price behaviour is shown in Table 6.4. It proved impossible to maintain the initial very low rates, but as of the end of 1986 the rate had been remarkably stable for a year at 4 per cent a month. By far the greater part of this came from nontraded agricultural goods and from services, where demand factors are important (and which were mostly not controlled). As we commented above, the monthly rate of 4 per cent was only achieved at the price of significant overvaluation of the exchange rate, and public utility prices badly out of line with costs.

Table 6.4
Lima: Index of Consumer Prices 1985–9
(monthly percentage change)

	1985	1986	1987	1988	1989
January	13.3	5.2	6.6	12.8	47.3
February	9.5	4.2	5.6	11.8	42.5
March	8.1	5.3	5.3	22.6	42.0
April	12.2	4.1	6.6	17.9	48.6
May	28.6	10.9	3.3	5.9	8.5
June	11.8	3.6	4.7	8.8	23.1
July	10.3	4.6	7.3	30.9	24.6
August	10.8	4.0	7.4	2.7	
September	3.5	3.6	6.5	114.1	
October	3.0	4.0	6.4	40.6	
November	2.7	3.6	7.1	24.4	
December	2.8	4.6	9.6	41.9	

Source: MEF, *Alerta Económica.*

What is the monetary background to these developments? With a strong deceleration in inflation, the effects on the monetary side of the economy can be quite powerful, as with the Plan Austral, for example. Summarising the effects found there, one can expect a fall in the 'inflation tax' only partially compensated by a return to normal levels of money holdings.

The Peruvian data are given in Table 6.5 which shows that M1 had in fact not fallen under the impact of inflation (in Argentina at the time of the Plan it had fallen to 3 per cent of GDP, while in Peru the figure was 26 per cent). However, this was principally because of strong dollaris-

Table 6.5
Peru: 'Real' Liquidity of Banking System, Domestic and Foreign Currency 1983–9

	Percentage Shares		Total in real terms million intis (1980 prices)	Index of real GDP 1979 = 100[a]
	Domestic	Foreign		
1983 December	58.5	41.5	1 174	92
1984 December	46.4	53.6	1 348	101
1985 March	42.9	57.1	1 264	104
June	42.9	57.1	1 085	100
September	53.9	46.1	1 056	97
December	67.8	32.2	1 161	99
1986 March	77.2	22.8	1 158	102
June	79.9	20.1	1 097	111
September	84.0	16.0	1 115	115
December	87.1	12.9	1 172	126
1987 March	88.4	11.6	1 114	121
June	89.1	9.9	1 124	122
September	93.0	7.0	1 115	123
December	88.4	11.6	1 163	124
1988 March	89.6	10.4	922	132
June	90.5	9.5	786	119
September	69.5	30.5	533	104
December	64.9	35.1	427	85
1989 March	60.5	39.5	329	92
June	62.0	38.0	331	92

Source: BCRP, *Nota Semanal* and *Reseña Económica*; MEF, *Alerta Económica*.

Note:
[a]Seasonally corrected. The figures for 1983–85 are quarterly, for 1986–89 monthly estimates.

ation: Table 6.5 shows that the strongest effect of the Peruvian measures was a quite dramatic move back to the local currency. Foreign currency deposits fell from 57 per cent of total liquidity at the start of the Plan to 16 per cent by September 1986. Meanwhile 'real liquidity' overall stayed rather stable, which in the face of such strong growth implies rather restrictive monetary policy. Credit to the private sector was constant in real terms between July 1985 and the end of 1986,[13] despite the real growth of output. The increased willingness to hold domestic currency must have eased the financing of the budget deficit.

Turning to the fiscal effects, figures are given in Table 6.1 above, comparing 1985 and 1986. As we commented above, the most disappointing aspect is the failure of revenue to rise: in fact it fell in real

Table 6.6a
Peru: The Balance of Payments 1984–9
(US$ millions)

	1984	1985	1986	1987	1988	1989–I
Current A/C	−221	125	−1 079	−1 477	−1 128	197
Exports	3 147	2 978	2 531	2 661	2 694	850
Imports	2 140	1 806	2 596	3 182	2 750	483
Public	858	703	805	1 070	960	186
Private	1 282	1 103	1 791	2 112	1 790	297
Trade Balance	1 007	1 172	−65	−521	−56	367
Services and Transfers	−1 228	−1 047	−1 014	−956	−1 072	−170
Long-Term Capital	1 189	691	603	767	814	141
Net Basic Balance	968	816	−449	−710	−341	338
Changes in Net						
Foreign Reserves	247	280	−517	−785	−389	286

Table 6.6b
Peru: Imports, Per Cent Change 1986–9

	1986/85	1987/86	1988/87	1989/88 I Quarter
Total	44	23	−14	−33
Public	15	33	−10	−26
Private	62	18	−15	−37
Consumer Goods	193	8	−33	−36
Inputs	51	18	8	−32
Capital Goods	36	28	−30	−33
Defence	−27	56	−39	−41
Principal Food Imports	89	9	−1	−36

Source: Banco Central, *Memoria.*

terms despite the recovery in activity. The result has been some increase in the deficit despite very moderate increases in expenditure.

The external sector only benefited somewhat by the increasing restrictions on debt repayment. The balance of payments figures are given in Table 6.6a. A quite significant overall worsening can be seen in 1986, reflecting increased private sector imports not compensated elsewhere. Capital flight appeared to rise towards the end of 1986 and there was a loss of reserves. Cocaine income was probably the largest single source of foreign exchange, at some $700 million, and was undoubtedly crucial to the foreign exchange equation.[14] The results of 1986 would have been worse, had not the public sector grown so slowly – note that public sector imports rose a modest 14 per cent compared with a massive 56 per cent for the private sector (in current dollars). The generation of new or expanded exports must inevitably be a slow process and the reactivation of demand diminished *supplies* of some of Peru's non-traditional exports. It is hard to regain markets once lost, so this may have been a high cost. Non-traditional exports in 1986 were $649 million, compared with $719 million in 1985. New lending obviously could not step in to ease the situation; indeed the 'Declaration of Ineligibility' by the IMF even further dried up access. Not all foreign investment stopped and indeed reactivation brought some interest.

Turning to distribution, we have seen that it appears that policy-induced improvements in earnings aided the reactivation and that this reactivation was at least less skewed against small and informal sector firms than usual. A serious evaluation of who gained and who lost in this process is impossible given the quality of the data, and the importance of illegal activity and informality.[15] The evidence from wage data for considerable improvement in the first two years (Table 6.7) is consistent with a small but significant piece of evidence: a survey of low-income families in four of Lima's slums, carried out in July 1985 and repeated in October 1986, found that real family income increased 25 per cent between those dates. The principal reason was the higher earnings of those already in wage employment.[16] What is harder to judge is whether there was any significant loss in relative income shares by other groups, or whether 9 per cent real growth allowed all to gain. To explore this more fully, we looked at various indicators of the consumption of the upper-middle class: luxury housing, demand for private schools, sales of new cars and travel abroad. While each of these markets is complex and affected by relative price shifts also, the surge in consumption during 1986 (and up to the middle of 1987) is strong and widespread enough to suggest that the well-to-do were certainly prospering.[17]

Table 6.7
Peru: Real Earnings 1987–9
(Indices: November 1987 = 100)

	Private Sector	Central Government	Legal min. income
1987			
January	131.0	122.0	115.0
February	130.0	116.0	109.0
March	129.0	110.0	104.0
April	139.0	136.0	136.0
May	135.0	128.0	129.0
June	133.0	122.0	123.0
July	145.0	152.0	156.0
August	141.0	142.0	145.0
September	139.0	135.0	136.0
October	138.0	202.0	128.0
November	145.0	189.0	154.0
December	139.0	168.0	140.0
1988			
January	132.0	155.0	124.0
February	126.0	140.0	111.0
March	130.0	163.0	145.0
April	120.0	139.0	123.0
May	118.0	128.0	113.0
June	116.0	118.0	104.0
July	115.0	139.0	136.0
August	103.0	114.0	112.0
September	88.0	81.0	139.0
October	71.0	57.0	99.0
November	82.0	67.0	119.0
December	69.0	52.0	84.0
1989			
January	69.0	52.0	81.0
February	64.0	41.0	70.0
March	59.0	38.0	63.0
April	53.0	31.8	55.5
May	51.9	39.3	55.1

Source: INE, *Informe Estadístico.*

(iii) An interregnum and a lost opportunity: January–September 1987
We have identified a number of crucial policy issues needing enormous care as of the beginning of 1987. The two crucial issues of accumulation and foreign exchange were now delicately poised following the decision to develop a policy of *concertación* with big business centred on export

projects – but the detailed policy implementation necessary for the generation of confidence was still to come. It was made the more crucial by the narrowing of the room for manoeuvre, as excess capacity declined and foreign exchange reserves fell. The latter led to the decision at the end of 1986 to introduce extensive import controls – possibly of all policies the one most needing careful concerting with the private sector in an atmosphere of confidence. In January 1987 there was still considerable private sector goodwill and expectation in regard to *concertación* – but the policies lacked the decrees necessary to give them flesh. The third issue we have identified is relative prices: the need for a policy was sharply evident by the end of 1986 but so too was the lack of a clear strategy.

However, what followed was not careful consolidation based on good communication and consensus-building – but a period of near-vacuum in economic policy-making while political considerations dominated.[18] By May the private sector was thoroughly confused by inconsistencies and failures to follow through. For example, an apparently interesting initiative, and the apparent core of the *concertación* policy, the *Fondo de Inversión e Empleo*,[19] was announced in April 1987, but the concrete regulations did not follow, while lack of policy co-ordination resulted in the almost simultaneous announcement of *bonos compulsivos*, compulsory bond purchases for all sectors with (initially) a poor rate of return. Subsequently the compulsory element was removed and the rate of return much improved – but the damage was done.

This was one among many such instances which led to reduced credibility and confidence, which showed up in the parallel market rate. Between January and June 1987, this moved from some 20 intis to 40 intis to the dollar. As it moved, it in turn generated adverse expectations. Manufacturers, watching the black market rate, began to adjust prices. Inflation moved to a new plateau of 6–7 per cent a month. Shortages were beginning to play some role in price increases, and there was beginning to be a case for slowing the expansion – but the figures on continuing capacity margins suggest that some of the acceleration was based on subjective and psychological factors.

As political pressures on García developed, so this situation worsened. A policy document of May 1987, prepared by García's advisers and aimed at a reassertion of a coherent heterodox policy line,[20] was eventually not implemented, because it did not answer the political need as the President saw it. Eventually, a single policy became the exclusive focus – for political reasons – and 'fine-tuning' was neglected while the state takeover of the banking system dominated policy attention. This was announced in the President's Independence Day speech on July 28th, and resulted in a by-now well-known story: the measure was so ill-prepared that its implementation produced chaos and disruption and it failed politically. Economically, its main significance was twofold: first, it made effectively impossible the serious and delicate management of the economy that was imperative months before: instead, inflation and the black market rate both took off and foreign exchange reserves fell, while the *concertación* policy was totally undermined.[21]

The cost of this interregnum can hardly be overestimated. What had been a rectifiable situation at the beginning of the year, with monthly inflation at 4 per cent, gross reserves at over $2 billion and expectations generally still favourable, had become by the end of the year far more volatile, with monthly inflation at 10 per cent, gross reserves at $1.4 billion, and credibility disastrously low. Meanwhile an incredible and expensive sensitivity to the street market rate had developed, whereby it both had become the single indicator of credibility for the private sector, and at the same time the prey of speculative forces. Its legalisation led to an amazing visible extension of the street market.

(iii) 'Muddling-through': September 1987–August 1988

As the dust settled from the bank takeover, a fresh initiative was of course desperately needed. In fact, the following year saw a lacklustre period of policy-making leading to considerable demoralisation. The theory was that relative price adjustments were needed but that there was no need to curb demand, and meanwhile *concertación* had to be revived. The practice was depressingly familiar: a succession of packages which used devaluation and partial relative price adjustments to cut real incomes via their inflationary repercussions. The monthly data on earnings are given in Table 6.7. It will be seen that earnings peaked around the third quarter of 1987, and then fell an astonishing 20 per cent in the space of six months.

The recession was further aggravated by lack of liquidity: the fall in the amount of credit available in real terms through the formal banking sector was 32 per cent in six months, while increasingly people moved into the informal system and began again to use dollars. The huge exchange losses created by the multiple exchange rate system were leading to substantial generation of intis by the Central Bank. But given the fall in 'real liquidity' and the decline in all components of demand it is difficult to interpret this as other than accommodating the price increases coming from relative price adjustment and the movement of the *ocoña* or street[22] rate. Comparing the first six months of 1988 with the same period in 1987, investment fell slightly and consumption per capita fell 2 per cent.

The reduction in demand led to some slackening in the demand for imports, though the reserves kept on falling – to $1 169 million (gross) by June 1988. Yet the worst of all worlds obtained, since the relative price readjustments were not sufficient to remove distortions, with the exception of the export exchange rate. The central prices are given in Table 6.8, while the monthly variation in the cost of living is shown in Table 6.4 above. It will be seen that the measures were successful in achieving significant 'real' devaluation by mid-1988, but that all other key controlled prices fell in real terms. By mid-1988 the import rate was less than half and petrol only 20 per cent of the 1985 level. The price of imported wheat was at its lowest level for 20 years. The interest rate was absurdly low in real terms, while in practice most firms had to operate in the informal credit market. By July 1988 interfirm lending was occurring at a rate of 400 per cent for a three month loan.[23]

The monthly inflation rate given in Table 6.4 reflects each attempted adjustment in relative prices. In fact the subsequent *reduction* in inflation, particularly after the March package, is quite impressive and indicates the depression in demand and the tight liquidity situation.

The real wage fall of 20 per cent in six months was creating acute hardship and unrest – man hours lost in strikes in May 1987 were 85 per cent over the level of May 1986.[24] Production was widely affected by slack demand, and by shortages of parts as well as increasing labour unrest. The provisional estimates for the first half of 1988 show manufacturing output stagnating and gross domestic product 0.5 per cent below the level of the first half of 1987. By mid-year it was probably true that all the elements of intervention in the economy were having perverse results: where money was being made, it was typically from the lack of logic in the system. Smuggling and evasion of taxes were every day more commonplace, and a strong popular sentiment was in evidence in favour of *moralización*, or an improvement in standards of behaviour.

The atmosphere in which policy was being made was one of lack of co-ordination and confidence. Each policy initiative, in December, March and July, was in some way mishandled, with last minute adjustments producing incoherence or with individual measures being implemented in isolation and so failing again in coherence. Thus, in December 1987, a careful plan was being developed in collaboration with a World Bank Mission, when on 14th December a devaluation was announced without other measures and without co-ordination with agencies setting

Table 6.8
Peru: Relative Prices with Respect to the Average Cost-of-Living Index 1986–9
(July 1985 = 100)

	1986	1987	1988	1989 I Quarter
Food and Drink	100	89	87	83
Gasoline	66	46	58	53
Electricity (industrial use)	67	73	44	46
Import Exchange Rate	58	63	71	45
Export Rate	58	68	53	45
Export Rate, non-traditional priority	86	73	57	56
Informal (street) exchange rate	74	159	161	50
Terms of trade agricultural/industry	118	129	55	53
Real interest rate (loans) per cent	−13.5	−17.7	−40.4	−47.5

Source: MEF, *Alerta Económica*, Instituto Nacional de Estadística, *Informe Estadístico*.

prices. In March, the original package implied stiff relative price adjustments and careful compensation for price increases in the essential consumption basket: the details were floated in a contrived leak and the subsequent package made much weaker. In July the disarticulation was extremely obvious, with the Central Bank raising the interest rate without consultation, and again devaluation being carried out without co-ordination: in the words of one disillusioned public official 'policy was made by the person who could get to *El Peruano* to put out a decree first.'[25] Obviously, none of this remedied in any way the underlying political economy problems of confidence and credibility, and the move into dollars, speculation on the exchange rate, and prices informally indexing themselves to the parallel market rate, all continued.

This acceleration of inflation triggered a decision to implement in August a packet of measures which was far more drastic, combined with a major decision to unify the exchange rate. The package was orthodox in using *huge* relative price adjustments to create even more recession – but unorthodox in announcing a price freeze to follow the adjustments.

Turning to the distributive aspect, again we have the problem of data. Our 'informal indicators' of wealth and poverty, however, show an impressively consistent picture of falling incomes on *every* front, from somewhere in the second half of 1987.[26]

(iv) 'Orthodoxy' without external support: September 1988–September 1989

By September 1988 the falling level of reserves led to a decision to implement a more serious corrective policy. Two *paquetazos* followed, in September and November, implementing large readjustments in relative prices. The results can be seen in the tables of the previous section. Table 6.4 shows how inflation accelerated, to 114 per cent in the month of September alone. Real wages fell as shown in Table 6.7, some 60 per cent between November 1987 and May 1989. GDP fell by one-third between the first quarter of 1988 and the second quarter of 1989 (Table 6.3 above). Manufacturing production fell 33 per cent between the first quarter of 1988 and the same months in 1989 (INE, *Informe Estadistico*). The number of strikes rose, the hours lost rising from a monthly average of 756 000 in 1987 to 9 743 000 in November of 1988 (*Alerta Económica*, June–July 1989, p. 45). Nutritional levels fell and the incidence of illnesses such as tuberculosis rose.[27]

The fall in incomes was driven in part by falling government expenditure (see Table 6.1); central government current expenditure fell from 12 per cent of GDP in 1987 to a mere 4 per cent by the first half of 1989. But with inflation plus recession and the continuing decline in the coherence of government policy, revenue declined still more sharply. Much of the deficit was financed by nonpayment of bills, which amounted to 2 per cent of GDP in 1988.[28] Credit to the private sector was made extremely scarce, and seriously affected output both in agriculture and in industry.

With the recession, imports fell: comparing the first six months of 1988 and 1989 the fall was 38 per cent (*Alerta Económica*, June–July 1989, p. 123). As a result and as the copper price improved in early 1989, so the foreign exchange reserves began to recuperate. This allowed a moderation of policy in 1989: the rate of devaluation of the inti was slowed down and there were even *sales* of dollars from official sources to moderate the movement of the parallel market. Adjustments of the various public sector prices were also moderated (though as Table 6.7 shows wages continued to fall). The result was the slow-down in inflation shown in Table 6.4, from a monthly rate in the mid-40's at the turn of the year to some 25 per cent a month by mid-1989.

The monetisation of the increase in reserves allowed inflation to continue at this rate. The slow-down was achieved basically at the cost of a renewed accumulation of distortions.[29]

Though the decline in wages continued, there was some levelling off of the recessionary process: monthly output figures levelled off from February 1989, (*Alerta Económica, op cit.*, p. 30) and the number of strikes fell. No major fresh initiatives were taken, however, and the general sense was that none could be expected during the remainder of the government. Elections were due in March 1990 and a victory for the right was predicted on all sides.

Conclusion: The lessons to be learnt

The first three years of the APRA administration represented an important experiment in innovatory economic management. Their evaluation needs to be done with care, since the policies clearly failed. Does this failure imply that a heterodox policy route should be dismissed altogether for the future?

We identified at the start of this chapter a number of important areas needing attention and care for heterodox shock policies to work in the Peruvian context. First, the closely-related areas of accumulation and foreign-exchange generation needed careful attention, and at the level of political economy as we have explained. Second, the contradictions between short- and long-term needs had to be somehow accommodated. And third, closely related with the second, some mechanism of accord had to be found to move from price freeze to freer markets without a renewed price inflation. In fact we have seen the policy failing increasingly with time to handle any of these three areas. Surely the correct conclusion is, not that the goals were impossible, but that with more awareness, more consensus-building, more coherence and credibility, more progress could have been made? Again we remind the reader that when alternative and more orthodox policies have been tried, these have typically produced stagnation and accelerating inflation, except where an externally-induced export boom has happened to rescue the economy.

To explore thoroughly what would make possible such desirable goals as consensus, coherence and credibility requires a fuller and more sensitive political analysis than can be undertaken here: it surely must concern learning how to build proper links between society and government, so that energies that are clearly there can be channelled and coherence develop from a valid basis. This points to a crucial role for political parties as well as to a need for institutional reform to introduce greater transparency and accountability. The quality of the state and the public administration are therefore crucial, though their transformation will only come effectively 'from below'. The centrality of state capacity is underlined by the following chapter: Alan García probably would not choose him as his model, but Lleras' understanding of the importance of institutions has undoubtedly been very important in the story to which we now turn.

Notes

1. See Chapter 5, endnote 39.
2. Indeed, there was clear cross-fertilization: a key influence in the construction of the García plan was an Argentine economist, Daniel Carbonetto, resident in Lima since the 1970s. The visit of Alfonsin to Lima immediately before García's accession was also apparently important in convincing the President of the need for swift action.
3. *INE, Compendio Estadistico*, 1987, p. 138.
4. The share of profits in GDP, which was 64 per cent in 1985, was 63 per cent in both 1986 and 1987 (*INE, Compendio Estadístico*, 1987, p. 138).
5. The Spanish terms 'concertación' and 'concertar' have no direct equivalent in English. But the same word is used in 'concert our plans', i.e. harmonize.
6. Central Bank data dated 26th March 1987, published in *The Peru Report*, Vol. 1, No. 4, April 1987.
7. The private sector was brought into the 10 per cent limitation. A decision to pay only a very small amount to the IMF brought about a declaration of Peru's inelegibility to draw from the Fund – a problem because of its spin-off effects on other sources of cash.
8. A typical example is the deal with Metropolitan Investments Corporation where the MIC assumed old debt (US$35mn) related to the Chira-Piura irrigation scheme, is itself exporting products, and actively creating or financing projects to produce export revenue (*The Peru Report*, April 1987).
9. Apparently a further factor was the ability of firms to set 1986 profits against earlier losses.
10. *INE, Compendio Estadístico*, 1987.
11. J. Schuldt, 'Desinflación selectiva y Reactivación Generalizada en el Perú 1985-86', paper presented at a seminar on 'Anti-inflationary Policies in Argentina, Bolivia, Brazil and Peru', Bogotá, 7th–8th January 1987, p. 42.
12. Between August 1985 and June 1986, the index for leather production rose 23 per cent while that for formal sector shoe production fell 18 per cent.
13. *Alerta Económica*, June 1988.
14. Instituto Peruano de Administración de Empresas (1988), p. 26. The figure is based on rough estimates of the area cultivated.
15. Richard Webb's study for the INP shows a strong improvement in 1986 – but his own assessment is that this is simply a best guess. (Webb, 1987).
16. BCRP, *Reseña Económica*, October 1986. The survey covered 450 families in Villa El Salvador, Villa Maria, San Juan de Miraflores and Carabayllo.
17. This is a very preliminary report on work in progress. Briefly:
    (i) Real estate: the market in upper-middle-class housing boomed from mid-1985 to the middle of 1987 (this is evidenced by prices and confirmed in interviews with real estate agents).
    (ii) Private schooling: our key indictor is the demand for places at schools such as San Silvestre and Markham. This fell a little in 1986 but in response to the first fee increase in years (in terms of dollars).
    (iii) Private cars: total sales rose 17 per cent comparing the second half of 1986 with the first half of 1985 (data for APIA members only).
    (iv) Tourism: the huge increase in Peruvians travelling abroad reflects the favourable exchange rate but also suggests prosperity.
18. This paragraph is based on interviews with the private and public sector carried out in May 1987. The political pressures on García culminated in the police strike and the national strike in early May. The economic team seems to have lacked leadership through this period.
19. An arrangement whereby anyone buying a bond at the standard rate of interest might exchange it for a share in an approved project, upon which the government would contribute an additional 5 per cent to the rate of return – a subsidy raising

the effective return to about 27 per cent in dollar terms. 'Approved projects' must be outside Lima and in accordance with the priorities of industrial policy.

20.   Published as a supplement to the *Peru Report*, July 1988.

21.   It should be borne in mind that most credit was previously under the management of the public sector in any case, so that the measure's *direct* economic importance was less than might be expected.

22.   So-called after the street where the parallel market first developed. The street market was legalised in 1987.

23.   Macroconsult, *REM*.

24.   *Alerta Económica*, June 1988.

25.   This section is based on interviews conducted in August 1988 with various public sector officials and ex-officials.

26.   In regard to the rich and better off, the market in luxury housing turned down after mid-1987; while the number of emigrants rose, this was considered a marginal factor (interview with real estate agent, August 1988). Sales of new cars dropped dramatically, though price was probably the key determinant here. The number of applicants to private schools dropped, in one case, to less than half the level of 1988.

27.   Based on interviews in September 1989 with the directors of 'popular kitchens', who reported many families unable to continue paying the sum required to purchase a portion (about 15 cents), while the nutritional value of the portions also declined. The calorie content was found to have fallen 13 per cent between November 1988 and June 1989, according to a survey by FOVIDA.

28.   Figure provided by the Banco Central de la Reserva.

29.   For interesting recent analyses of the process from a variety of points of view, see the special issue of *Economía*, June 1989, Jimenez (1989), Cáceres (1989).

7 Colombia 1967–70: Change with some Continuity?

In the Peruvian case we have seen that one can identify a discontinuity in the country's economic history in the late 1960s, and that in terms of the theme of this monograph that moment coincides with a new stage in the ISI model – though the 'crisis' we have described goes far deeper than the standard limitations or problems of ISI, involving the whole economic and political structure of the country. We have seen that the search for a new impetus to ISI was in Peru's case a fairly minor part of a much more radical search for a new economic and political model, embodied in three radically different regimes and still today unsuccessful. In Colombia's case also it is customary to identify a discontinuity in economic trends and policy-making in the late 1960s, with the administration of Carlos Lleras Restrepo, his challenge to the International Monetary Fund in late 1966, the innovation of the crawling peg and many more institutional innovations. This did indeed also take Colombia through to a 'new stage' of the ISI model. The discontinuity is seen differently by different authors. For Ranis and Fei (1990) it marks the beginning of Colombia's entry into a mature 'liberalisation' phase; for the IMF too, with hindsight, that has been their view, once recovered from the discord of 1966. For others, including this author, the significance is somewhat different, as we shall see.

Obviously, however, the differences with the Peruvian case are many. Our whole argument has been that the pattern of history created in the one case a country weakly prepared in political economy terms to deal with the faltering dynamism of the traditional model, while in the other in many diverse ways the characteristics of the predominant export sector helped create a political economy favourably endowed for responsive and coherent policy management, as well as a healthier base for industrial growth. In Colombia with hindsight we find neither of our key indicators of crisis: the index of export volume was rising at a reasonable rate (7 per cent in real terms between 1965–70), and the share of private investment in GDP showed no sign of falling through the 1960s. None of the reasons which led in the Peruvian case to the strong focus on ownership reform were present in Colombia. The different economic structure and the permanent bias against foreign capital led by the 1960s to the very low participation of foreign ownership which we commented on in Chapter 3. Land reform had rightly been an important policy issue in the 1960s – but given the predominance of small farmers in the key export sector, could not stand out as the key issue in the generation and control of economic surplus, as it did in Peru. The generation of surplus was rather seen as critically tied to the management of coffee, both internally and externally: in the 1960s, this appeared to turn on taxation and exchange rate policy – on efficiency and policy management issues, rather than ownership. ISI was widely criticized in Colombia in the 1960s, for its employment effects or the lack of them and for its inefficiency, but the issue again was seen as management, not ownership.

The issue that perhaps brings the two countries closest is that of 'autonomy'. Colombia had always followed a rather self-consciously independent line, which was being contaminated, it might be said, by her showcase status under the Alliance for Progress. Being the only country ready with a 10-year plan to present to the Alliance, Colombia had been taken up at the beginning of the 1960s as a pilot case, with heavy involvement also of the World Bank (the World Bank Consultative Group was the first of its kind).[1] As the IMF began to press in 1966 for a substantial devaluation, the issue of policy autonomy was very definitely on the agenda – as it was in Velasco's Peru.

This chapter first tells the story of the Lleras challenge and the policy innovations that followed, then examines the economic record of the Administration, before attempting in the final part some evaluation of the kind of discontinuity involved, if any.

The measures and the political context

In contrast to Velasco, the immediate preoccupation of the new administration which took office in August 1966 had to be the balance of payments. With coffee prices falling and reserves low, reaction had to be rapid. Various foreign loans were in the pipeline, but a precondition in each case was an agreement with the IMF.

The background to the fight that now ensued is given by previous experiences with devaluation. The strength of the prejudice against devaluation as of 1966 is at first sight curious in a country dominated by one major export sector, and thus apparently by export interests. The total conviction that devaluation would simply lead to inflation and so undermine itself is fascinating in the light of the 1980s pre-occupation with inertial inflation. Like many views of inflation, by this point it had become virtually self-validating. The subjective memory of the 1951 devaluation was that it was eroded within two years; one of the strongest opponents of devaluation in the Lleras episode, his Minister of Development, had suffered the consequences as the then Minister of Finance.[2] The experience under Valencia in 1962 and again in 1965 was similar.

Curiously, the data do not sustain this view of 1951: there was in fact a real devaluation sustained for a long period, but at the cost of some acceleration in inflation. The same is true of 1957, which did not seem to feature in people's memories. By the 1960s, the perception was indeed self-validating: the devaluation of December 1962 was 34 per cent in the import rate: by mid 1964 the cost of living had risen 55 per cent above the predevaluation rate. The devaluation of July 1965 had led by March 1966 to 13 per cent inflation.[3] As Diaz Alejandro shows, the subsequent inflation was in each case more than that narrowly accounted for by import prices – representing expectations variables. By 1966 the opponents of devaluation were vociferous[4] and quick to point out the political consequences: Rojas Pinilla was losing no opportunity to point out the record of the National Front on devaluation and inflation.

What of coffee interests? The coffee sector was – and is – critically preoccupied with the internal coffee price as against internal input costs:[5] the sector's experience has been that the benefits of devaluation may well be siphoned off in tax (implicit or explicit) while rising costs rapidly complete the process. The sector has typically been more concerned to monitor the panoply of measures that affect coffee profits and their distribution, than to fight for politically unpopular overt devaluation, linked as it is ineradicably to the fear of inflation – a fear that some claim goes back to the horrors of the Thousand Days' War.

Given the degree of severity of the balance-of-payments problem – the current account deficit in 1966 was over 50 per cent of export revenue – the first measure the regime took was somewhat surprising: a quite drastic *liberalisation* of imports. What it represented, however, was precisely a disguised attempt to devalue without too much inflation. The differential rate for coffee was abolished (completing a process begun in 1965) and coffee exports moved to the rate of 13.50 pesos to the dollar.[6] To 'balance' that market, many of the goods previously imported at that rate were now passed to the 'free' rate and freed from restrictions. This was a bargain offered to the major importers in return for an assurance that prices would not be raised.[7] The result however was a flood of imports and by the end of October intolerable pressure (from the IMF and others) to devalue by a very substantial figure.

The break with the Fund which now ensued is of special interest to us for its parallel in the García administration in Peru. Looking toward the comparative analysis which we attempt later, we need to examine, first the political role of the challenge to the Fund, second the technical use made of it, and third its repercussions in the international economic relations of the country. We turn to these questions in the final section below. First we describe the economic measures of the Lleras Restrepo administration, and its economic achievements.

The decision to break off negotiations with the Fund was announced to the nation by the President in a now-famous television speech of 29th November 1966.[8] The speech is notable for its calm and dignity. The word 'break' does not figure: there are 'unfortunate differences' with the Fund. The differences are over technical aspects of management and over Colombia's right to determine its own economic policy. The tone is never demagogic. The strongest criticism of the Fund is a nicely-chosen phrase: the Fund's advocacy of automatic devaluation in response to paper criteria is 'antitechnical'. He is confident that Colombia's own solution will work – pragmatic exchange rate management, responding to circumstances, careful control of the capital account and of imports combined with budgetary equilibrium, a credit policy to help production, careful incomes and coffee policy.

The immediate emergency legislation provided for control of imports, in line with an assigned budget, and exchange rate management responding to circumstances, and made it from then on illegal for private citizens to hold foreign exchange. Within a given space of time amounts were to be declared and arrangements made to return money to the country. The next three months were completely given over to the creation of 'Decree 444', the famous *estatuto cambiario* which still governs every aspect of Colombia's foreign exchange and trade transactions.[9] This in itself was only part of an even wider programme of institutional reform.

Based in the decree, the core institutions to promote non-traditional exports (PROEXPO) and to administer the control of imports (INCOMEX) were now developed. Both institutions were made accountable to CONPES – the Council of Economic Policy – now strengthened, as we describe below. The allocation of the foreign exchange budget to INCOMEX was to be decided by the Junta Monetaria.[10]

The weakest aspect of the control of imports related to the public sector, since in practice many loopholes were to be found:[11] it is interesting however that at least in principle there was awareness of the need to monitor state agency purchasing. Lleras in a 1967 speech showed awareness of the 'key role' of public sector purchases.[12]

Control of all foreign exchange, including capital transactions, was institutionalised, based in the Banco de la República and overseen by the Junta Monetaria. All exporters had to declare in advance their foreign exchange earnings and remit them to the Bank, with one significant exception: the petroleum sector. All the extensive regulation of foreign investment which was now developed in the decree made a complete exception of petroleum: an exception based in its large capital needs.[13] (This measure, which gave virtual autonomy to the state oil company, Ecopetrol and provided for a special dollar rate for oil transactions, is now proving of considerable importance: curiously, it attracted little attention at the time.)

The control of foreign capital in general provided the substantial basis for what was to become Decision 24 of the Andean Pact: mechanisms and criteria were developed continually over the period 1967–70, heavily influenced by the work of Constantino Vaitos in Colombia in these years. Much of the pathbreaking work in detecting and monitoring overpricing dates from this time.[14]

The slow evolution of the monitoring and control of the coffee sector also continued: the transformation of the exchange differential into an ad valorem tax on coffee was now confirmed, and the Junta Monetaria was given control over the important decision as to the level of the *reintegro*, the official quantity per sack of coffee that has to be paid to the government to get a licence to export. This key variable had been decided by the Coffee Federation since 1940: its transfer to the Junta Monetaria was a significant change.

In other areas the legislative base was already there, and what was needed was effective development. This now happened in regard to planning and industrial development. Alberto Lleras had created the Department of Planning in 1958; Lleras Restrepo now gave it backing and teeth. The Jefe was given strong backing in gathering bright young Colombians to staff the department;[15] special rates of pay were arranged.[16] The Department was given control over the investment budget and over foreign sources of finance, and responsibility for the evaluation of foreign investment projects. It was given participation in all the key 'Juntas'. The Instituto Financiero Industrial – IFI – had been created by Lleras himself in 1940, and now for the first time came to life.[17] It played a central role in Lleras' concept of indicative planning. Sectoral committees were developed to 'concert' with the private sector. Their role was not necessarily to plan in detail, but to give confidence and orientation to the private sector. The committees for paper, chemicals and steel were launched successfully at this time.

Lleras also activated the Council for Economic Policy (CONPES) – created again by Alberto Lleras – and made it the fundamental organ of economic policy-making. The President presided in person at the weekly meetings, and again used it for institutional changes. Its first two decisions under him created ISA and CORELCA, the basic institutions to plan and coordinate the electricity sector.[18] But perhaps the most basic reform was intangible: the constant pressure to manage, to be accountable, to 'run a tight ship', in the words of one economic advisor:[19] all a new experience for the Colombian public sector.[20]

In terms of day-to-day economic management, the emphasis was on fiscal and monetary 'prudence'. Tax revenues were raised considerably, from 8 per cent of GDP in 1966 to 13.4 per cent by 1970. Direct taxes in particular rose from 3.7 per cent of GDP in 1966 to 5.3 per cent in 1967. In 1968 an important tax reform amplified taxation at source and extended it to the corporate sector.[21] There were other minor changes, and a major review of the whole fiscal system was commissioned.[22] But the main immediate thrust of policy was to reduce evasion – helped of course by the extension of taxation at source. This was achieved largely by the personal commitment of the President, who proposed on television in June 1967 that tax declarations should be made public, and announced again on TV in October that he personally had examined hundreds of tax declarations, several of which (obviously fraudulent) he proceeded to describe in detail – without names, but suggesting the introduction of Congressional hearings with names.[23] Such was the credibility of the President that receipts rose.

Table 7.1
Colombia: GDP by Expenditure, 1970 prices, 1965–70
(1965 = 100)

| | GDP | Consumption | | Investment | | Exports | Imports |
		Private	Public	Public Construction	Total		
1966	105.4	109.2	104.5	143.5	108.0	98.3	132.8
1967	109.8	110.7	109.9	189.7	115.2	106.9	104.2
1968	116.5	117.4	113.7	216.5	132.4	115.8	130.7
1969	123.9	126.7	122.6	225.8	135.7	121.2	138.8
1970	132.3	136.4	140.0	242.3	153.6	122.3	162.5

Source: Banco de la República, *Cuentas Nacionales.*

Public spending was able to rise quite strongly: the then Minister of Finance claims that there was no austerity,[24] and this is clear in Table 7.1, which shows public sector current spending and public construction both rising more rapidly than GDP 1966–70. How much deficit spending there was is hard to say. The accounts for the Central Government which the authorities would have had available to them show a small surplus, and this was the boast of the authorities. However, subsequent reworking suggests a deficit for the whole of the public sector.[25] The net effect is perhaps best shown by the public sector borrowing requirement, which shows net Central Bank lending to the public sector varying between 0.2 and 0.6 per cent of GDP in the years in question.[26]

In respect of credit, too, the myth and the reality diverged somewhat. The rhetoric was all that of strict credit control – and indeed there was much care taken to moderate credit expansion. The minutes of the Junta Monetaria reflect the constant battle. In this it was important, first, that the coffee *reintegro* was no longer decided by the Federation, and second, that the international coffee price soon stabilized and even recovered slightly. The key mechanism whereby excess credit expansion had typically come about was through the Federation's demands for credit to finance the difference between its outgoings in purchasing the harvest and its receipts on the international market. Although some credit continued to be granted to the Federation, the producer price was reduced in December, January and February,[27] and was the principal source of the recession experienced in the first months of 1967.[28] The recovery in exports soon alleviated the situation, however.

Other credit needs were often responded to: non-coffee agriculture and productive investment in agriculture received generous treatment,[29] and supply responded accordingly. Table 7.2 shows the liquidity

Table 7.2
Colombia: Money and Quasi-money
as Per Cent of GDP 1965–70

1965	20.1
1966	18.6
1967	19.3
1968	20.0
1969	19.9
1970	19.7

Source: Banco de la República, *Cuentas Nacionales* and IMF, *International Financial Statistics.*

Table 7.3
Colombia: Means of Payment and Prices, Percentage Change 1962–70
(May–May)

	Means of payment		Prices	
1962–3	19.4		25.2	
1963–4	27.8	18.7	17.6	16.8
1964–5	11.5		5.5	
1965–6	16.1		19.0	
1966–7	18.2		7.3	
1967–8	20.3	18.7	8.7	7.5
1968–9	14.1		6.4	
1969–70	22.0		7.4	

Source: Espinosa (1970) p. viii.

coefficient 1966–70, and Table 7.3 reproduces the Minister of Finance's own demonstration of his non-orthodox management.

Wage policy was aimed at achieving constancy in the real wage: the fact that it did this with a declared increase of only 7 per cent in the first year reflects development on the inflation front, to appraise which we must turn to the economic record. But it also raises the issue of politics and the political strength and legitimacy of Lleras. His reforms subsequently commanded such respect that it is hard to reconstruct the context, which is one where he alienated in turn most organised sectors of the population.

Lleras was determined from the outset to restore strength to the Executive. Inevitably, this meant challenging traditional political interests and the privileged position both of Congress and the regional *gamonales*, or powerful local figures. But there were few groups he did not alienate at some point, and while he achieved his central reforms he was actually unable to benefit from them in the remaining time as much as one might have expected. In the final year of his Presidency, 1969, with the new structures in place and finding by then considerable acceptability among business and technocratic groups, the surge of popular unrest seriously limited his ability to use his new instruments.

His strategy was from the beginning one of 'direct democracy', involving much travel and a wholly novel and effective use of television in a direct appeal to the people. This alienated from the start the traditional political interests. He proceeded to appoint regional governors without consulting the regional leaders, and still worse, embodied his new structures in regional committees organised from the centre and bypassing the *gamonales*. Even where the latter were formally incorporated, they had no resources, either political or technical, to make their participation real. The creation of 'decentralized agencies' was also used to bypass existing interests and structures.[30]

Congress fought tooth and nail against the constitutional reforms, which initially would have robbed them of all their spending power. In fact Lleras had to compromise and give them substantial funds under their own control: this compromise has since been seen as a very high price to have paid. From this point, it is claimed, date such abuses as first class and often unnecessary travel abroad for congressmen which are so heavily criticised today.

There was opposition also within the business classes, focused by the incident in 1968 when Lleras intervened personally in the sale of a US corporation to Colombian interests at a scandalously high price. The President of Bavaria, Alberto Samper, ended up in gaol and was denounced personally on television by Lleras. The next such scandal led to a scathing denunciation by Lleras, claiming that these events 'put in question both the capacity of our industrialists and their degree of identity with national interests'.[31] He failed in his project for a National Savings Fund which would have involved the takeover by the state of private pensions funds.[32] It is interesting though that, notwithstanding these battles, by December 1968 the ANDI was publicly recognising the beneficial effect of the majority of the Lleras reforms.[33]

But while business opposition lessened, the opposition from the working class and from peasants grew, despite land reform and the creation of ANUC, a federation of peasant unions. From the beginning, his methods of confronting student unrest and his repression of traditional methods of protest (marches, strikes that were technically illegal) was appreciated by much of the middle class but resisted by the unions. 1967 saw also an increase in the extent of armed struggle on the left. In January 1969 increases in urban transport prices concentrated many elements of incipient protest in widespread popular manifestations, forcing the moderation of the increases. From that point on the degree of opposition effectively limited what Lleras could achieve in the final year of the Presidency.

These considerations, then, shed light on the management of wages and other variables crucial to the economic record which we must now consider.

The economic record 1966–70

The developments in demand are shown in Table 7.1. The decline in the real internal coffee price is reflected in the fall in per capita private

Table 7.4
Colombia: GDP by Origin, Principal Components, 1970 Prices 1966–70
(1965 = 100)

	GDP	Agriculture	Mining	Manufacturing	Construction	Commerce	Banking	Government
1966	105	103	96	107	119	107	105	104
1967	110	107	97	110	142	109	109	107
1968	116	116	94	117	157	116	117	110
1969	124	120	111	126	172	124	128	116
1970	132	126	108	136	178	134	150	127

Source: Banco de la República, *Cuentas Nacionales.*

consumption in 1967. Even in 1967, the indices of investment and public sector spending continued to grow; in the next three years they grew strongly, backed by the recovery in exports. Thus consumption picked up in real terms in 1968 and demand grew strongly on every front 1968–70. Real wages for unskilled workers stayed roughly constant and the share of labour in GDP fell slightly.

The production response was strong, as shown in Table 7.4. GDP grew in real terms some 8 per cent a year, industry at 9–10 per cent, agriculture at 5 per cent. Unemployment, having risen in 1967, returned to its customary level thereafter.[34]

It is remarkable that growth was even possible in 1967 when imports were cut drastically, by 26 per cent in dollar terms, the bulk of the cut being in intermediate goods. The explanation lies in the high level of inventories resulting from the boom in imports in 1966 following liberalisation. By 1968 imports could recover, almost to their all-time peak of 1966, as exports recovered and capital inflows rose, including the resumption of aid. The remarkable response to the regime's demand for capital repatriation eased the balance of payments and created a stock exchange boom.[35] The index of import liberalisation created by García, which fell from 14 to 7 in 1967 under the impact of the severe restrictions, crept back up to 9 by 1970.[36]

Both the import licensing system and the new sectoral committees were used to encourage the new stage of ISI: intermediate and capital goods production accounted for 41 per cent of the total increase in manufacturing production 1966–70, compared with its share of 33 per cent in 1966.

Perhaps the most interesting figures are those on inflation and the consequences for the real exchange rate, shown in Table 7.5. It will be seen that inflation actually slowed during the period,[37] and that the exchange rate was devalued in real terms – a trend that persisted through to 1975. In terms of comparable efforts at economic management elsewhere in Latin America, this is a very remarkable achievement – and certainly not achieved via recession, but in fact with strong growth. What was the secret?

As we noted above, the conventional analysis in Colombia, among those responsible for economic policy, has focused on monetary and fiscal policy. But we have seen that neither instrument was used in the conventional manner to bring inflation *down*. Both were used – prudently – to facilitate and encourage the expansion of production. Fiscal policy in particular was expansionary, using foreign borrowing to provide the appearance of balance. Admittedly considerable restraint

Table 7.5
Colombia: Inflation and the Real Exchange Rate 1965–75
(1965 = 100)

	Internal inflation[a]	Relative inflation[b]	Real exchange rate[c]
1965	100	100	100
1966	120	117	91
1967	130	124	90
1968	137	129	84
1969	151	138	84
1970	162	141	80
1971	176	149	78
1972	201	165	79
1973	232	165	73
1974	294	167	67
1975	347	175	59

Source: IFS, Banco de la República.

Notes:
[a] Wholesale price index.
[b] UK, US and German export prices weighted by 1960 trade shares, divided by index of Colombian inflation.
[b] Dollars per peso, divided by index of relative inflation.

was enforced to prevent demand running unreasonably ahead of production – but the actual deceleration was not due to orthodoxy *per se*.
Rather, we would emphasize the variables of confidence and expectations. Very strong signals were given – focusing on Presidential public
statements - that inflation was coming down, that businessmen could
trust this and act accordingly,[38] and that a 7 per cent wage increase for
1967 could be taken as adequate to maintain wages in real terms. Such
was the credibility of the regime – and especially the President – that this
had effect,[39] backed as it was by strong authoritarian measures in regard
to illegal strikes and popular protest of all kinds. What also helped
modify businessmen's behaviour was the high level of stocks following
the import boom, the inflow of imports funded by borrowing, and the
adequate harvests of these years. It should also be remembered that the
constancy of real wages given the rapid rate of growth, must have
reduced pressure on prices as well as permitting the share of capital to
rise.

How much of a challenge?

We turn now to evaluate the significance of the original break with the
IMF, in the light of this review of events 1966–70. In political terms, its

significance was clearly considerable. For one author, Maullin, the entire episode should be understood *purely* in terms of Lleras' need for internal political support. His reform plans faced every prospect of endless frustration by Congress: as he complained in December 1966, '... not one single executive bill has been passed by Congress, while in four months of government I have had to sign numerous regional aid laws ... which if totalled up would represent the national budget for 10 to 20 years'.[40] The challenge to the Fund did not give him carte blanche – on 13th December 1966 Congress refused him the extraordinary powers he was seeking.[41] But it clearly did give him exceptional authority and credibility – in the machista phrase of the time, he was seen as 'having trousers on'.[42]

But to *explain* the entire event in such terms is to take too superficial a view. To insist on confronting Colombia's problems not, yet again, with a shift in relative prices but rather with far reaching institutional reforms and pragmatic interventionism was something deep at the heart of Lleras' approach. The way he insisted was cleverly used to win support for what he was set on doing anyway – but the motivation went far beyond the need to create support.

This is one element in a balanced evaluation of the 'challenge'; the second is to realise that the measures in no way came out of the blue. We have emphasized the tradition of pragmatic interventionism, going back to the 1929 crisis. The idea of a flexible exchange rate was not novel either: experience had been building up over a number of years. In the President's analysis of July 1967, he pointed out that the country had in principle had a flexible rate since 1957 but that it had been mishandled – in particular through inappropriate demand management and through lack of controls on capital. This was the reason for his fear expressed in 1960, that a flexible rate would lead to gradual devaluation which would grow '... as the poet Jorge Rojas says, more or less insensibly like the roses' (Diaz-Alejandro (1974) p. 187). Precisely why such a major piece of legislation as Decree 444 was able to be constructed in 3 months, is because many strands were already there, 'needing to be put together like a quilt'.[43] Indeed, even the IMF had in 1965 contemplated a flexible system of small steps as a solution for Colombia – though only as a means of approaching equilibrium.[44]

Now that we have seen the solid and serious content of the reforms, it is hardly surprising to learn that the effect on Colombia's external relations was actually positive. Lleras and Espinosa stressed from the first the desire to continue talking, and informal dialogue continued all the time. By early 1967, quiet messages were coming through to the

Fund and Bank from other agencies and the private banks that 'this thing looks good'. By February the Fund had been persuaded to accept the Colombian answer: by then the official transactions rate was nearing the free market rate so it was relatively easy for the Fund to find the situation acceptable. 'It represents perhaps a unique instance of a man reaping all the political benefits of such a move and none of the costs.'[45]

How much of a challenge to orthodoxy are we left with then? The tendency has been among some writers to assimilate Colombia from 1967 rather firmly into the 'liberalisation' epoch in Latin America, emphasizing the liberalisation of imports after the first months, the fiscal and monetary conservatism and suggesting a greater role for 'market forces' than pre-1967[46] – at least as exemplified in the 'realistic' exchange rate. Our own summing up is a little different: we have argued that fiscal and monetary 'conservatism' is hardly a fair description, though policy was very 'prudent'. The policy in fact *used* growth to create virtuous circles, in a manner similar to García's intentions in Peru in the 1980s.[47] The liberalisation of imports reached nowhere near the level of 1966. And the whole emphasis of policy was on pragmatic interventionism and on creating and improving mechanisms and institutions to make this more efficient – challenging, where necessary, not only traditional elite interests but also popular and democratic elements. Lleras himself was clear that the state would often be a better instrument than the market: '*quisiera, de una vez por todas, ayudar a borrar esa idea de que el Estado aqui siempre es mal administrador y que, en cambio, los empresarios privados son sabios*'.[48] His most important reform, he considers today, is the one he failed in: the introduction of long-term planning machinery.[49] We cannot emphasize too strongly the difference between the 'getting the prices right' approach implicit in the international agencies' recommendation, and the Colombian concentration on far-reaching institutional reform to improve interventionist policies as well as to strengthen the market sector.[50]

We also need to be clear that these reforms, admirable as they were, were achieved at considerable cost in terms of suppression of popular interests and pressures. Although Lleras' challenge to the *gamonales* was to cost him his candidacy to the Presidency in 1974, the challenge was radical only in a limited sense. The traditional two-party system and the National Front were made more solid and more credible, not less, by the Lleras reforms.

Notes

1. More formal groups were already in existence – e.g. for India and Pakistan. The Colombian arrangement was new in being informal and consultative.
2. Interview, Antonio Alvarez Restrepo, Bogota, July 1987.
3. See Dunkerley (1968), Diaz-Alejandro (1976) for detailed accounts.
4. See the numerous writings of Palacios Rudas at this time, for instance, collected in *Las Columnas de Cofrade.*
5. Jorge Cárdenas, interview, Bogotá, July 1987. Cardenas is President of the FNCC.
6. The exchange rate for coffee was about 20 per cent below the official rate. Fedesarrollo (1987), p. 503.
7. Minutes, Junta Monetaria, 9th August 1966.
8. Lleras, Restrepo (1970), Tomo IV, Anexo Segundo, Vol. I.
9. The intensity of work – and the direct personal involvement of the President – is recalled by all who took part. Ministers not directly concerned simply had no access to the President for these three months.
10. These institutions and all other aspects of the regulation of foreign trade are fully described in Diaz-Alejandro (1976).
11. See Chapter 10 below.
12. Lleras, Restrepo (1981), p. 147.
13. Lleras, Restrepo, interview, Bogotá, August 1987. He argues that the record of foreign investment in oil in Colombia has fully justified that exception.
14. Chudnovsky (1974), Vaitsos (1970).
15. Interview, Edgar Gutierrez Castro, Bogotá, 7th July 1987. Head of Planning for the first part of the Lleras Administration.
16. The new decentralised agencies were not subject to the same pay rules as central government, so salaries could be increased when people moved. (Interview, Enrique Peñalosa, Minister of Agriculture in the Lleras Administration, 8th July 1987).
17. Interview, Hugo Millan, present Director of Projects IFI, 17th July 1987, Bogotá.
18. Interview, Edgar Gutierrez, Head of Planning in the Lleras Administration.
19. Interview, Rodrigo Botero, advisor to the President on economic matters 1966–70, Bogotá, 9th July 1987.
20. The reforms were not achieved without cost, as we describe below. Many of them strengthened the control of the Executive – but a price had to be paid to achieve this.
21. Taxation at source had been introduced in 1957, but the opposition was such it was not applied. A further unsuccessful attempt was made in 1963. It was only now it became effective (Fedesarrollo 1987, Ch. 2, p. 19).
22. The Musgrave Report (1971) is a major source document on the Colombian fiscal system.
23. Lleras, Restrepo 1970, speeches of June and October (p. 208).
24. Interview, Abdon Espinosa, Bogotá, 10th August 1987.
25. The BIRD–Wiesner report calculates a deficit of 3.6 per cent of GDP for 1967 for the consolidated public sector. (For later years, when other sources also estimate the deficit, the BIRD–Wiesner figure is by far the highest – see García (1987), p. 174.
26. Fedesarrollo (1987), ch. 2; *Finanzas Publicas* 1950–1984, graph 14 and p. 56.
27. The coffee price was reduced in December 1966 from 762.5 pesos per *carga* to 737.5 in January to 715. Its level in 1967 as a whole was the lowest in real terms in many years (Espinosa 1970, p. X).
28. Minutes, Junta Monetaria, 24th May 1967.
29. This is insisted on by Abdon Espinosa, Minister of Finance 1966–70 (interview, Bogotá 1987).
30. On this see Collins (1987).
31. Quoted in Pecaut (1989), p. 59 (my translation).
32. He succeeded only in creating a fund for public employees.
33. Pecaut (1984), p. 61.

34.   Reyes Posada (1986).
35.   Document A14 of the assessors of the Junta Monetaria records that 'a considerable sum' had already been repatriated as of 28th March 1967.
36.   García (1986), Table 1.11. The index attempts to measure the effect of changes in tariffs, changes in direct controls and changes in classification.
37.   The increase in the cost-of-living index for manual workers was 17 per cent in 1966, 8 per cent in 1967 and 7 per cent in each of 1968–70.
38.   See Lleras, Restrepo (1970) Tomo IV, *Anexo Segundo*, Vol. I, p. 150.
39.   Many stories are told to demonstrate this credibility. The one which approaches legendary status is the occasion in 1970 when it appeared Rojas Pinilla might have won the election: in a situation of high tension, Lleras appeared on TV and pointed to his watch: it was then 7 p.m. and he wanted everyone in their homes by 8 p.m.. To enforce such an order was impossible – but the streets were empty by 8. The watch was later auctioned.
40.   Speech to FNCC, December 1966, cited by Maullin (1967), p. 10.
41.   Banco de la Republica (1987), p. 26.
42.   Maullin (1967), p. 43.
43.   Rodrigo Botero, interview, Bogotá, July 1987.
44.   A. López Mejía (1987), p. 44, cites an IMF document dated 1965. López' analysis traces in great detail the historical roots of Decree 444.
45.   Botero, interview.
46.   See Ranis and Fei (1990).
47.   See the speech of 29th November 1966 for the need to expand supply, not reduce demand (Lleras, Restrepo, Anexo Segundo, Tomo IV, (1970), p. 74).
48.   Speech, television, 21st November 1967.
49.   Interview, Bogotá, 6th August 1987. The failure was due to Congressional resistance.
50.   The point is well made by Lleras himself in a television speech of 30th December 1966, where he insists on how much far-reaching change is needed, and denounces the falsity of the assumption that balance of payments problems can be solved by devaluations (Lleras, Restrepo, (1981) p. 97).

8 Colombia in the 1970s: The Coffee Boom and 'Liberalisation'

In terms of our theme of short-term macro management, the focus of interest of the decade of the 1970s is the enormous boom in coffee which developed from 1975 on, resulting from frost in Brazil. What would happen to the tradition of prudence and the new structures of management and control put in place by Lleras? Would an export boom nevertheless infect the economy with classic 'Dutch disease'? This is the topic of part two of this chapter. In part one we consider briefly the Pastrana years, which were years that presented no obvious challenge in terms of macro management. Coffee prices were quite favourable: what dominated policy was not any immediate adjustment issue but the need for a political initiative, in a context of reasonable room for manoeuvre. The trends in policy and their consequences were important in shaping the contrasting policies of the López regime, which took office in late 1974.

Developments in demand and policy initiatives in the Pastrana years

Pastrana's presidency began in difficult circumstances, and he desperately needed political support, since it was not even clear that he had won the election.[1] His response was to seek 'populist' policies, albeit in muted Colombian style, with a considerable openness to foreign financing. The role of the World Bank and the IDB both grew, from an inflow of $472 million in 1980 prices 1967–70, to $778 million 1971–74.[2] It should be noted that an increased role for foreign financing was perfectly possible, since the restrictions introduced by Lleras with Decree 444 were all *discretionary*: they also did not apply to credits under one year. With foreign financing, there was expansion of programmes such as that for food distribution, through IDEMA.

Gradually, the government's programme shifted to focus on the remarkable 'Currie Plan'. Lauchlin Currie has been almost the only foreigner to achieve status in Colombia as a policy adviser – and he in due course took Colombian nationality. The core of Currie's thinking was that migration to urban centres was the necessary solution to rural development, and that urban construction was the key to urban

161

employment and growth. The Plan therefore centred on a major financial innovation for that date: indexed bonds known as UPACs,[3] for the finance of the construction sector.

Table 8.1
Colombia: GDP by Expenditure 1970–4
(Indices 1970 = 100)

| | GDP | Consumption | | Investment | | | |
		Private	Public	Total	Public Construction	Exports	Imports
1970	100	100	100	100	100	100	100
1971	106	106	118	104	107	145	120
1972	114	116	114	102	112	172	104
1973	122	128	123	111	117	204	108
1974	130	135	120	133	118	223	119

Source: DANE (1988), *Cuentas Nacionales.*

This policy began to have powerful economic consequences in the second half of Pastrana's Presidency.[4] Of the rise in investment of 18 per cent in real terms 1972–74, 13.5 points came from the rise in construction.[5] Table 8.1 shows the structure of demand. The role of public spending does not appear to have been the major factor (contrary to the later image propagated). Tax revenue fell as a percentage of GDP, as the efficiency demanded by Lleras slackened off again, but expenditure fell somewhat too, and the overall deficit was roughly constant (see Figure 8.1).[6] In addition to construction, the buoyancy of demand came from private consumption, aided in part by reduced tax collections but more by growing employment although real wages fell, and from exports. Exports were not particularly dynamic, falling as a proportion of GDP. But within the export total, manufactures did respond to the growth in world demand in 1973–74 and their rise in price. Colombia's exports of manufactures almost doubled as a percent of exports between 1970 and 1975, rising from 10.7 per cent to 21 per cent. This was comparable to the experience of Argentina and Brazil in the same years. The average for the LAFTA countries as a group rose from 10.6 per cent to 15.2 per cent.[7] The comparability of Colombia's performance with others of the more industrialised LAFTA members tends to confirm the finding of Echavarría[8] that international demand was more important than the exchange rate in causing the expansion.[9]

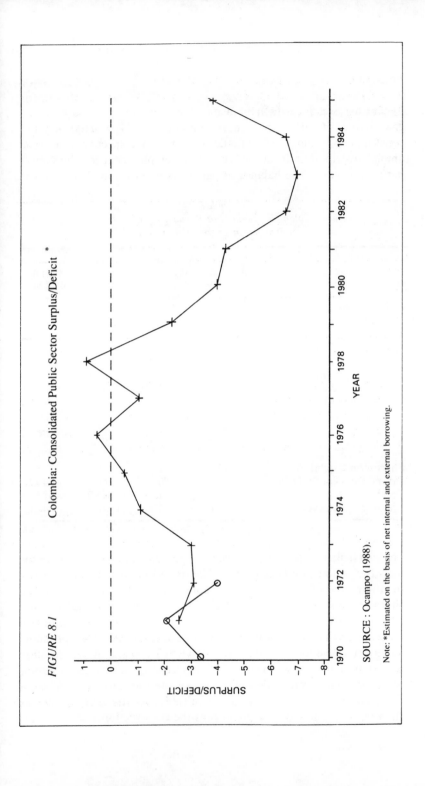

FIGURE 8.1

Colombia: Consolidated Public Sector Surplus/Deficit *

SOURCE : Ocampo (1988).

Note: *Estimated on the basis of net internal and external borrowing.

The results

The rather steady growth in demand produced a very satisfactory growth rate of GDP of 7 per cent per annum 1970–74, with industry and construction leading with 11 and 10 per cent respectively, average annual growth (data from DANE). Urban employment rose by some 4 per cent a year.[10] The balance of payments is shown in Table 8.2: the

Table 8.2
Colombia: Balance of Payments 1965–84
(Five year averages, US$ values)

	5 Year Average 1965–69	5 Year Average 1970–74	5 Year Average 1975–79	5 Year Average 1980–84
Goods Exports	592.8	1 055	2 716	3 549
Goods Imports	− 559.2	− 1 008.6	− 2 125.8	− 4 572.4
Trade Balance	33.6	46.4	590.2	− 1 023.4
Financial Services	− 105.4	− 191.8	− 281	− 730
Non-financial Services	− 89.6	− 160.2	− 63.4	− 550.3
Transfer Payments	22.0	14.8	63.8	207.8
Current Account Balance	− 138.6	− 290.8	309.6	− 1 875.8
Foreign Direct Investment	37.8	31	52	334.8
Long-term Capital Flows				
Net Private	36.6	3.8	5.2	303.6
Net Public	70.4	216.8	205.8	845.8
Basic Balance	6.2	− 39.2	572.6	− 391.6
Short-term Capital Flow	− 12.2	− 42.6	− 75.8	− 5
Errors, Omissions, SDRs	11.4	50.4	149.4	− 43.2
Total	5.4	− 31.4	646.2	− 439.8
Changes in Reserves	− 5.6	31.4	− 646.6	441.6

Source: Banco de la República, *Revista, Informe Anual.*

growing deficit on the service account was more or less balanced by the increased inflow of official capital. The rise in exports balanced the rise in imports responding to the rise in consumption, the latter reflecting a sharp rise in import prices as well as rising demand and liberalisation.[11] This latter was principally seen as an anti-inflation measure: unfortunately given the sharp rise in international prices in 1973–74 it probably had a perverse effect. The data are shown in Table 8.3; the acceleration of inflation from 7 per cent to 25 per cent in this period was unprecedented in recent Colombian history and was a principal focus of criticism when the next administration took over. Its analysis stressed the role of public sector demand plus the construction boom and the financial expansion. Businessmen tended to blame higher interest rates. In fact interest rates in general fell in real terms and public expenditure was not a prime factor, as we have seen. The construction boom was creating pressure in the final two years – but so, most importantly, was the huge rise in dollar import prices. Food prices also rose in 1972 and 1973 in response to poor harvests – food production fell 3 per cent in per capita terms in 1973.[12] The food price component of the cost of living rose 29 per cent in 1973 (see Table 8.3).

Table 8.3
Colombia: Prices 1970–4

	a Unit import values	b Food	c General	d Real interest rates (loans)
	annual percentage change			
1971	+2%	+12.6	+11.8	3.4
1972	+6%	+15.4	+13.8	2.7
1973	+18%	+28.8	+22.0	1.2
1974	+28%	+29.2	+25.2	−2.4

Source: (a) IMF, *IFS*. Figures for Colombia.
(b) (c) Blue collar, DANE *Boletin Mensual de Estadistico*.
(d) Carrizosa (1985).

As the next administration took over, there were a number of real points of threat. Not only had inflation accelerated, but also the rise in the oil price came just as Colombia moved from self sufficiency to become again an oil importer. However, there was a further political need for a redefinition of policy, as the following section will explain.

Economic management under López 1974–78

The election campaign of López took place in the context of the ending of the National Front. In effect, it was the first time in twenty years that the previous government did not substantially control the next. The liberal campaign therefore needed to and was free to define itself in opposition to the Pastrana record. From the account we have given it will be obvious that the natural focus was the unacceptable level of inflation, the supposed misuse of foreign credits for the fiscal deficit, and the need for greater autonomy and self sufficiency. What gave an edge to the last point was that AID was about to reduce substantially its commitment in Colombia, and it was seen as politic to anticipate this move. But the policy was more profound than that: it consciously sought greater autonomy through increased savings and exports, and saw Colombia as moving through to a new stature on the international stage.[13] Tax and financial reforms were thus central to the policy, as well as a radical tightening of the procedures for borrowing abroad.

The assembled team was a strong one, and comprised people identified on the whole with the more conservative line in Colombian economic management. But it will be seen immediately from the preceding brief description that in fact the policies were anything but simplistically orthodox. What has sometimes been described as the Colombian version of a Chicago-boy experiment, bore very little relation to the standard model.

At the heart of the policy were the reforms in respect of foreign borrowing. The key was the reform of Decree 155, setting out the system of contracting public foreign credit. This law, part of the Lleras reforms, had always made it deliberately difficult to borrow abroad. But its implementation had been lax in the Pastrana years and as we pointed out above the decree did not apply to credit of less than one year. Now, this loophole was closed, but more importantly the key administrators in *Credito Público* were encouraged and supported in being very tough. Bureaucratic procedures were deliberately used as weapons to control the Ministries and public enterprises – who of course resisted strenuously – notably Ecopetrol and IDEMA – as did the Armed Forces.[14] There was collusion among these various actors and the banks, both national and foreign, who all stood to lose profit opportunities. The department fought the foreign banks directly also, on fees, on where negotiations should take place, on who should produce the first draft of a loan contract.[15] They also fought on similar issues with the international agencies – over the contracting system and the preference for foreigners, for instance.

The concrete results were a significant fall in the contracting of foreign debt – the total debt to GDP ratio fell from 0.28 in 1975 to 0.18 in 1978[16] – and a reinforcing of a tradition of toughness and the legitimacy of this type of stand.

The second notable policy of the new Administration was a major tax reform, which raised revenue as a percent of GDP from 19.2 per cent in 1973 to 21.5 per cent in 1975.[17] The main emphasis was on reducing exemptions and allowances against income other than from work, and on improving collection. This reform, popular with no President for obvious reasons, was accepted by López partly because it incorporated changes affecting and facilitating foreign investment in petroleum – a bottleneck which with good reason was a preoccupation as oil imports began to rise.

The third major element of policy was the financial 'liberalisation' policy. This, although labelled and sold as such, was in fact an extremely Colombian version, being coupled with the Colombianisation of the banks and *increased* control of the financial sector. In practice it was a policy to raise interest rates not to free them.[18]

The Colombianisation of the banks is worth a little space, for it illustrates vividly some typical characteristics of Colombian policy-making. The idea was to achieve majority Colombian shareholding. The motivation was fear that as the foreign banks grew they would unduly limit monetary policy and would give preference to the foreign investor. It is not clear whether a full 'fade out' of foreign ownership was the original intention, but the form the policy took in practice meant a limit of 49 per cent foreign ownership.[19] What is revealing is the debate on the nature of the Colombian shareholding: the Liberals wanted this to be widespread, the Conservatives saw with reason that this would simply permit the foreign owner to continue to dominate. The result is no surprise: the Colombian side was concentrated in a few elite hands, and excellent relations developed with the foreign partners.[20] This is consistent with the shift in attitude on foreign investment which was now coming about in the energy field, in response to the oil price rise, both in relation to oil and coal.[21]

The liberalisation of imports, however, was intended to be a much more classically orthodox process. Ironically, it was not, simply because it failed. It had two goals: increased efficiency and reduction of inflation. The private sector was ready to fight it tooth and nail and the administration was prepared to be tough with the ANDI, the principal industrial association: in fact it never came to this, as the desire of the CONPES was that the new tariff structure should be harmonized with the pending Andean Pact reforms. Not surprisingly, the bureaucratic delays and the weak administrative mechanisms of the Pact ensured that the reforms proposed were never implemented.[22] The 'index of liberalisation' of imports constructed by García shows no change 1974–1978 (García, 1986, Table 1.11).

The remarkable part of the above measures was that apart from the import liberalization, they were all in place *before* the principal challenge to the team's management capacity occurred: the rise in the coffee price to an historic high in 1977, rising by 164 per cent in two years and leading to an almost 100 per cent improvement in the country's terms of trade.

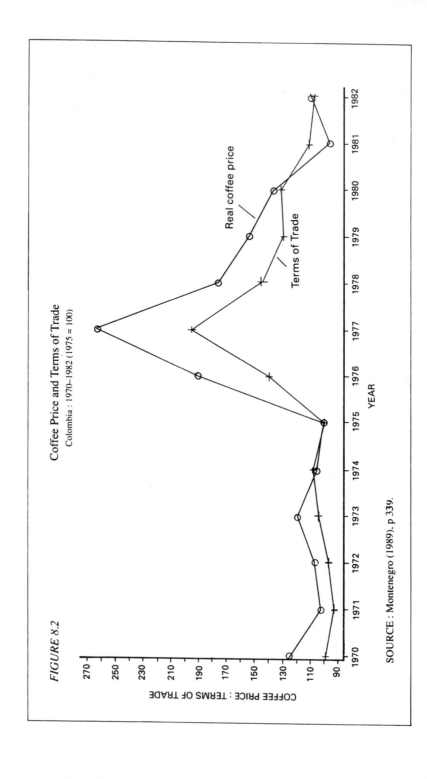

FIGURE 8.2

Coffee Price and Terms of Trade
Colombia : 1970–1982 (1975 = 100)

Real coffee price

Terms of Trade

COFFEE PRICE : TERMS OF TRADE

270
250
230
210
190
170
150
130
110
90

1970 1971 1972 1973 1974 1975 1976 1977 1978 1979 1980 1981 1982

YEAR

SOURCE : Montenegro (1989), p. 339.

The price fell in real terms after 1977 but in 1980 was still above the level of the early 1970s (see Figure 8.2). The reason was frost in Brazil.

As if this was not enough, a second element of 'boom' began to make itself felt for the first time: dollars earned from drugs. Neither drugs production nor illegal dollars were new to Colombia: smuggling of cattle, coffee and emeralds had been a constant over many decades,[23] and the cultivation of marijuana went back to the 1940s. The initial stimulus to growth seems to have come with the arrival of Cuban drug traffickers following the Cuban revolution.[24] But real growth only came in the 1970s with booming international demand for marijuana, which led to an enormous expansion of production, especially in the Sierra Nevada of Santa Marta. By the peak of the coffee boom, estimates of total income from drugs range from $500 million (Junguito and Caballero, 1982) for 1977 – one-third of coffee exports – to 126 per cent of coffee exports in 1978 (Ruiz and López, 1981). Both of course refer to total income, not value returned to Colombia, which would have been much lower – though at this date the sales were almost entirely marijuana, widely produced by small producers.

The development literature abounds in case studies of the problems, known as 'Dutch disease', which tend to result from such bonanzas. Before we explore how the Colombian team coped with such problems, we should note the by-now standard expectations of such a situation, and ask if the products in question in themselves make any difference.

The standard predictions of the nature of Dutch disease are that the boom will lead to appreciation of the exchange rate – hard to modify by policy – and thereby to disparate effects on tradables and non-tradables. In particular, non-booming exports, and industry insofar as it is tradable, typically decline in relative and even absolute terms and the economy becomes less diversified. Less attention is typically given to the 'political economy' level, whereby an export bonanza makes possible and encourages foreign borrowing with usually distorting effects on the pattern of public sector spending. A key point in the whole analysis concerns to whom the bonanza accrues in the first instance: the relative roles of the different social actors and their likely behaviour. In this case the key actors will be foreign investors, domestic producers and the national government.

It will be seen immediately that the two products we are dealing with – coffee and drugs – have some important particular characteristics which affect the political economy of management. In neither case does the government have the direct access to the surplus that it has, say, in the state-controlled Venezuelan oil industry. In coffee, the role of the

Federación of course becomes crucial – and it is interesting that the FNCC feels that it experiences *more* conflict with the Government in times of boom than in times of poor prices.[25] Both coffee and marijuana – but especially coffee – involve small producers and therefore have a potentially wide demand impact. The distribution of the bonanza in the case of coffee is carefully controlled through a number of policy instruments, each negotiated with the Federación. To have *any* control on drugs involves difficult questions of admitting the dependence of the economy on illegal income. There are obviously non-economic issues related to illegality which have emerged more recently as central problems for Colombia:[26] at least however, the supply of foreign loans is unlikely to increase with a drug money bonanza! One interesting dimension is the effect on industry: in countries such as Colombia the definition of industry as either tradable or non-tradable is always a problem, since the reality is that it is largely *partially* tradable. But the growth of drugs tends to be associated with growth of smuggling, so that effectively the degree to which industry is tradable (and therefore vulnerable to Dutch disease) increases. What do we learn about Colombian short-term management capacity, faced by this amazing bonanza? Would the 'prudence' and desire to preserve autonomy which by now we are beginning to associate as peculiarly Colombian characteristics withstand the onslaught represented by a 164 per cent rise in the price of the main export?

Figure 3.3 shows that the classic and predicted effect did occur: the exchange rate appreciated in real terms by some 30 per cent between 1975 and 1978. This was not however the result simply of market forces – nor was the appreciation as much as the forces of the market would have generated.[27] Policy thinking was rather clearcut: the principal preoccupations remained the two original goals of reducing inflation and increasing autonomy. It was also clearly perceived that the boom was temporary. The thinking was that for the long run as small a relative price shift as possible was desirable, since the boom was temporary.[28] Yet to allow all the boom to be felt as a flood of foreign exchange would be beyond the authorities' capacity for sterilisation and would result in inflationary pressures. So some appreciation was needed, to help limit such pressures, while the still-inevitable influx of dollars would have to be carefully neutralised by stringent monetary, fiscal and stabilisation policies. Meanwhile all the machinery so fortunately already in place would need to be used to see that an additional influx on capital account did not upset this management as well as undermining other goals.

The problem was that in terms of demand management some hostages to fortune were already given or were soon to be given. First, there was a political commitment that much of the boom would accrue to the producers, which limited the manipulation of the internal coffee price, which in fact rose very substantially (Thomas (1985) p. 108). Secondly, and perhaps because of the previous tax reform, an increased tax on coffee appears to have been unthinkable.[29]

Apart from a modest increase in the rate applied to the part of the coffee tax paid in kind, demand mangement policy measures were basically limited to two areas: sterilisation operated both on the primary increase in reserves and on its secondary effects. For the first, prior import deposits and open market operations were used. For the second, reserve requirements were used, being raised to 100 per cent at the margin in 1977–80. Such measures led inevitably to financial innovations to circumvent them.[30]

More powerful were the measures to induce savings. The fiscal deficit was moved into surplus by cutting expenditure (Figure 8.1 above) and the private sector was both compelled and induced to save. Exporters were made to accept Exchange Certificates, of 30 days' maturity, for example, and 'Exchangeable Bonds' were introduced, partly taken up by agreement by the Federación and partly by financial intermediaries.[31] Private and public sector savings are shown in Figure 8.3. Wage policy helped to increase savings, since wages fell somewhat up to 1977, although in the election year of 1978 they rose (see Table 8.4).

The results: how severe a dose?

The key undesirable results on industry and on non-booming exports were certainly not avoided. Legal exports other than coffee of course fell

Table 8.4
Colombia: Real Urban Wages 1974–80 (annual percentage change)

	Manual workers manufacturing	Construction[a]
1975	−1.8	1.7
1976	2.3	−4.6
1977	−5.6	−6.1
1978	11.6	15.6
1979	6.5	17.0
1980	0.7	5.6

Source: DANE.

Note;
[a] Weighted average of master bricklayer, bricklayers' and labourers' income.

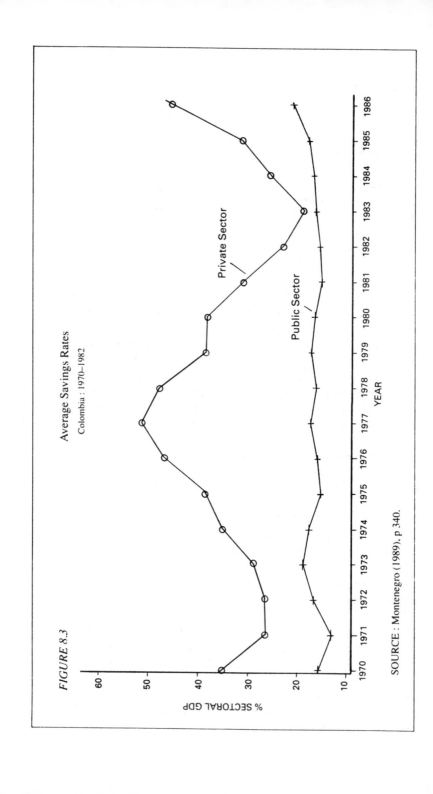

FIGURE 8.3

Average Savings Rates
Colombia : 1970–1982

Private Sector

Public Sector

% SECTORAL GDP

YEAR

SOURCE : Montenegro (1989), p 340.

as a share of dollar receipts – from 51 per cent in 1975 to 40 per cent by 1979–81 – in volume terms they rose only very slowly. Industry as a share of GDP fell from 20 per cent in 1974 to 17 per cent by 1978.[32] The analysis of industry is very much complicated by the fact that there are non-tariff barriers, transport costs, etc. which have an uneven incidence in the sector, while appreciation of the exchange rate *helps* insofar as a firm imports inputs and capital goods. The most helpful analysis is one by Kamas, which by ranking industry as more or less tradable, is able to show that the more tradable end of the spectrum suffers most.[33] What the role of increased smuggling is in this, is not clear.

Inflation also rose, to 35 per cent in 1977, despite the authorities' care. Supply side factors, however, played an important role in this, independently of the rise in demand. A severe drought sent food prices jumping by an unprecedented amount in 1976 and 1977 (see Table 8.5). This is a recurring theme in Colombian inflation: we saw in 1972/3 the importance of food prices in the acceleration of inflation. What is *also* important is that it seems that at the next round some supply response is typically forthcoming: that is, the commercialised products (rice, soya, potatoes)[34] play enough of a role in consumption that the price rise can be damped quite rapidly. (It presumably helps that while maize, beans, and yuca, for instance, are not commercialised and may respond less readily, there is substitution in consumption between such products and, say, rice and potatoes, which are commercially produced.)[35] This leads to the phenomenon which Montenegro identifies: the food price rise in 1977 is reversed without a noticeable effect on the rest of the economy.[36] (The process contrasts strongly with Peru's, where an increase in food prices produces very little supply response, and strong effects on real wages, and an increase in imports with consequent balance-of-payments problems.)

The combination of the temporary nature of the food price rise, the beneficial effect on prices of the appreciating exchange rate, and the fall in real wages up to and including 1977, results in inflation moderating to only 17 per cent in 1978.

Obviously, the boom ideally could have been better managed even in these early years (we turn to the next administration in the final section of this chapter). The increase in savings was not reflected in increased investment: investment as a percent of GDP fell from an average of 19.5 per cent in 1970–74 to an average of 17.9 per cent 1975–79.[37] The damage done to export products like cotton and sugar is obvious and could have been avoided. To have industrial production actually fall in absolute terms, as it did in 1977, while GDP was rising at 4 per cent, is

Table 8.5
Colombia: Retail Prices and Cost of Living, Manual Workers 1974–80
(*percentage increase*)

	Food prices	Cost of living
1974	30.8	26.9
1975	19.7	17.9
1976	27.9	25.9
1977	35.1	29.3
1978	12.0	17.9
1979	32.1	29.8
1980	25.4	26.5

Source: DANE, *Colombia Estadística* 1985, *Revista del Banco de la República.*

a rather seriously adverse result. The boom produced an unhealthily rapid expansion of the finance sector, with increased speculation and many new intermediaries lacking experience.[38] Nevertheless, there were healthy results too – in particular the avoidance of an inflationary spiral and the firm controls on borrowing. Unfortunately these elements of policy were weakening even in the last year of the López administration.

The Turbay Administration: even Colombia is vulnerable

The Turbay Administration took office with the coffee price beginning to wane. Although cash was abundant (perhaps drugs were contributing more than was realised) there was a perception that a new stimulus was needed. There was also considerable awareness that one major cost of 'prudence' had been public investment foregone: there were clear signs of deterioration in infrastructure.[39] The World Bank was anxious to increase lending to Colombia – and *encouraged* her to look for private sector finance too.[40] The boom in the international supply of credit was still strong – so, against all tradition, the government fell at last into the typical Dutch disease syndrome and borrowed heavily abroad – at the Latin American rate.[41] The theory was that big projects would have 'trickle-down' effects.

The data are shown in Table 8.6. The increase in the two ratios 1980–82 is rather remarkable, though it should be noted that debt service was high partly because, unlike most other Latin American countries, Colombia continued to amortize the debt as well as pay interest.

The new credits were very large, and came principally to the public sector and from commercial banks, whose balance with the public sector

Table 8.6
Colombia: Indicators of External Indebtedness 1970–82

	Net debt _____ Exports of goods	Interest plus amortization as percentage of exports of goods
1970	2.2	28
1975	1.8	22
1980	0.3	10
1981	0.8	25
1982	1.5	33

Source: Ocampo and Lora (1988), p. 87.

rose at 50 per cent a year 1978–82. The average interest rate on new loans rose from 5.9 per cent in 1976 to 12.2 per cent by 1980. The electricity sector received the lion's share, at 40 per cent. Mining and transport received 11 and 8 per cent respectively, and defence only 6 per cent, well below the typical Latin American figure.

The private sector was, however, now allowed to participate, with the López rulings being modified to permit this. Private debt rose three times 1978–1982, with borrowing being heavily concentrated: 43 per cent went to no more than five firms.[42] Typically, the terms required repayment in seven or eight years, with no grace period (Garay, 1984), despite the long gestation period of the typical project financed.

We thus encounter all the typical characteristics of the debt story in Latin America in this period: rising cost, short repayment period and heavy overindebtedness of a few firms and institutions. Only the late start meant that nevertheless in 1982 Colombia's debt structure was more manageable than elsewhere. The debt export ratio in 1982 was still only 1.84 while the average ratio for Latin America was 3.16 (ECLA, 1984, p. 54).

With this inflow of resources, the budget moved from surplus to deficit (see Figure 8.1 above). For once, the usual Colombian preoccupation with monetary caution was not to the forefront. The thinking on inflation was that import liberalisation would be a powerful instrument to restrain it. Turbay now implemented several policies which López had promised – but at quite the worst time, since imports rose strongly just as exports were moving into recession.

The liberalisation of imports was not only attempted with more rigour, but extended to new groups of industries. Ocampo (1989) estimates that while in 1976–9 the increment in imports was responsible for an annual contraction of industrial production of 1.2 per cent, this doubled in 1979–82 to 2.4 per cent (pp. 132–3). Newer lines suffered particularly, the contraction being 9 per cent a year, with *metal mecánica* being the most severely affected (*Econometría*, 1985).

The Turbay government also took further and implemented more radically the financial 'liberalisation' of López – again at an unfortunate time, since international rates rose abruptly in the early 1980s. Toro (1987) shows how international rates influenced internal rates quite strongly at those times when the economy was financially more open. Whereas the ratio of the internal to the external cost of borrowing, was on average 1.64 in 1978, in 1981 it was 1.07 (Toro, 1987, pp. 157–8).

Thus when the US prime rate rose from 6.8 per cent in 1977 to 15.3 per cent in 1980 and 18.9 per cent in 1982, Colombia suffered on the service amount of the balance of payments. But the effect was *also* felt in the internal financial system. Domestic interest rates are shown in Table 8.7. This effect meshed with the desire to maintain a tight monetary policy, while allowing fiscal expansion. The consequences are easy to imagine. The negative aspects already identified under López continued. Industry suffered now that liberalisation was added to exchange rate appreciation, and after a recovery in 1980 fell back again to a mere 17 per cent of GDP by 1982. But what was added was the 'Latin Americanisation' of Colombia as debt service rose, to 33 per cent of exports in 1982 from its remarkably low level of 18 per cent in 1977,[43] foreign finance was used to fund the public sector deficit, and imports rose.

More important however than the specific measures, there was a loss of control and efficiency in public sector management. Corruption grew, particularly around the financial sector. With the boom, there had been an increase in the phenomenon of 'financial groups' as well as a growing

Table 8.7
Colombia: The Cost of Credit in Nominal Terms and the GDP Deflator
1970–84

	Commercial Banks	Financial Corporations	GDP Deflator
1970	23.8	26.6	17.1
1979	26.4	28.7	24.0
1980	35.6	37.6	27.6
1981	34.7	35.9	22.8
1982	32.6	35.3	24.8
1983	31.0	35.8	20.4
1984	29.5	32.7	21.5

Source: Carrizosa (1985).

loss of control of the financial sector;[44] the familiar consequence of groups is that particular firms are allowed to overborrow. As market conditions turned around, so there was increased pressure to borrow to help firms through the bad time: indices of bad loans were rising by 1982 while bank profits were falling. This was one among a number of elements of increased fragility, a topic to which we will return in the next chapter where we analyse policy management faced with growing crisis instead of boom.

Notes

1. As the polls closed it appeared that Rojas Pinilla was in the lead. The following day Pastrana's victory was announced, amid some scepticism.
2. Ocampo (1988), Table 7.
3. UPACs, or *Unidades de Poder Adquisitivo Constante*, were issued by the newly-created Corporaciones de Ahorro y Vivienda. They were indexed to a 3-month moving average of the combined blue and white-collar cost-of-living index, on a daily basis (the system has since been modified several times). See Sandilands (1976).
4. The political consequences were also marked: Pastrana achieved the unusual feat of *increasing* his party's support at the mid-term elections.
5. DANE (1985).
6. The data are so conflicting on this issue that it is hard to draw a conclusion. The estimates vary widely. The estimate of the public sector deficit varies from 2 per cent to 6 per cent of GDP during these years. But the most recent and authoritative estimate (Ocampo and Montenegro, 1987) is shown in Figure 8.1 – based on data on internal and external borrowing.
7. Uruguay's share rose more, by 14.6 points. Peru *more* than doubled its share – the only country to do so – but this reflected its low level in 1970 – 1.4 per cent, rising to 3.8 per cent. (Data from ECLA, *Statistical Yearbook for Latin America and the Caribbean*.)
8. Echavarría (1987), p. 73.
9. The rate of real devaluation (shown in Figure 3.3 above) slowed down compared with 1967–70.
10. Reyes Posada (1986).
11. Martínez (1986).
12. Calculated from FAO *Yearbook*.
13. For example, membership in OECD was proposed.
14. This account is based on interviews with two of the Directors of Public Credit through this period: Rudolph Hommes and Christian Mosquera.
15. Before this date, for instance, Colombian negotiators had had to go to the USA. They now refused, and foreign banks had to set up local offices of representation. First drafts of contracts had previously come from the banks; now Crédito Público produced the first draft and even developed a standard form.
16. Data from ECLA, *Statistical Yearbook* (1979). Debt service as a percentage of exports fell from 16 per cent in 1974 to 10 per cent in 1978.
17. BIRD-Wiesner (1982). See Perry (1977) for an account of the reforms, which affected 75 per cent of Central Government tax revenues.
18. Although some rates were free, all lending rates remained fixed.
19. The alternative interpretation was that there was to be *no* further DFI in banking so that with the growth of the banks the original 49 per cent would 'fade out'.

(Interview, March 1988, Christian Mosquera, Director of Public Credit during part of López administration.)

20.   See Plata (1979) for a full account of the whole experience.
21.   The controversial negotiation over El Carrejón, the huge coal deposit in La Guajira, was concluded only in the next Administration but began under López. On this see Kline (1987).
22.   Interview, Bogotá, September 1987, Tomas Mosquera, Director of Planeación during part of the López administration.
23.   Junguito and Caballero (1982).
24.   Gómez (1988).
25.   Interview, Jorge Cárdenas, Manager of FNCC, Bogotá, April 1988.
26.   As is well-known, Colombia today is suffering serious problems from the undermining of the Judiciary via the power of the drug interests.
27.   This is an intuitive judgement but seems reasonable, given the size of the rise in coffee and drug sales.
28.   Sarmiento (1982).
29.   An increase in the ad valorem tax on coffee was proposed by the economic team, but rejected by the President.
30.   This account draws on Montenegro (1983) and Montenegro (1989). The latter work contains a brilliant formalization of the effects of the coffee bonanza.
31.   Montenegro (1989), p. 333.
32.   Data from Thomas (1985), pp. 220–1.
33.   Kamas (1986).
34.   50 per cent commercialised.
35.   Junguito (1980) finds statistical evidence of a supply response *even* for traditional products.
36.   Montenegro (1989), p. 336. He attributes this to timely supply-side policies, which is doubtful, since increased credit was the main tool and is typically ineffective in the traditional sector. This area is an important one for more micro-level work, to understand the mechanics of Colombian inflation.
37.   This is the principal criticism made by Ocampo (1987a). The data are from DANE.
38.   Montenegro (1983).
39.   Just before Turbay took office, for instance, there was much publicity over the congested state of the port of Buenaventura – so bad that much-needed wheat imports could not get through.
40.   Roberto Junguito, Minister of Finance in the Betancur administration, interview Bogotá, April 1988.
41.   Echavarria (1987), p. 8, Ocampo and Lora (1988).
42.   Avianca, Inversiones Samper, Coltejer, Acerias Paz del Rio and Fabricato. See Ocampo and Lora (1988), p. 93.
43.   Ocampo and Lora (1988) p. 87.
44.   Jaramillo, J. C. (1982); Montenegro (1983).

9 Colombia in the Rough Seas of the 1980s

Colombia's 'debt crisis'

Between 1982 and 1985 – that is for most of the administration of Belisario Betancur – Colombia had to deal with both an external and an internal imbalance, which, while mild compared to that of most other Latin American countries, still challenged the management capability of the economic team. It led to the downfall of one team, with the resignation of Edgar Gutierrez in mid-1984 as Minister of Economy, and the entry into office of Roberto Junguito.

Table 9.1
Colombia: Export Prices 1977–88

	Coffee ($ per lb)	Cocaine ($ 000 per kilo, wholesale)
1977	2.35	
1980	1.54	
1981	1.28	20.0
1982	1.40	20.0
1983	1.32	7.2
1984	1.44	10.0
1985	1.46	8.0
1986	2.33	–
1987	1.15	–
1988	1.45	–

Source: Junguito (1986), p. 97, Gómez (1988), p. 99, *Revista del Banco de la República.*

The elements of crisis show some interesting similarities and contrasts with the rest of Latin America. The coffee price was quite unsatisfactory, as shown in Table 9.1, but had already fallen by 1980 and was not a major cause of further crisis as the 1980s progressed. A new export product was on the horizon – coal – but in 1982 was not yet ready to contribute significantly.[1] Imports had risen very strongly under the liberalisation programme, and continued to rise in 1982, accounting for most of the worsening trade balance shown in Table 9.2. As with the rest of Latin America, what also affected the balance of payments in the

Table 9.2
Colombia: Balance of Payments 1981–88
(US$ millions)

	1981	1982	1983	1984	1985	1986	1987	1988
Exports	3 158	3 114	2 970	4 273	3 550	5 331	5 254	5 339
Imports	-4 730	-5 358	-4 464	-4 027	-3 673	-3 490	-3 794	-4 515
Trade Balance	-1 572	-2 244	-1 494	246	-23	1 841	1 461	824
Interest Payment	-306	-649	-739	-1 055	-1 151	-1 315	-1 347	-1 355
Current A/C Balance	-1 961	-3 054	-3 003	-1 401	-1 809	302	128	-353
Capital A/C Balance	1 901	2 204	1 158	1 016	1 916	968	-150	697
Overall Balance (Excluding Reserves, exceptional financing and liabilities constricting foreign exchange authorities)	-60	-850	-1 845	-385	155	1 270	415	—
Total change in Reserves (increase minus)	-218	722	1 753	1 166	-285	-1 354	22	-344

Source: IMF, *International Financial Statistics*, 1988, Junguito (1986), Table 1, p. 107, *Coyuntura Económica*, June 1989.

1980s was the move into deficit of the service account, as we argued in the previous chapter. Colombia, having at last entered the overborrowing game in 1979–82, was vulnerable to the rise in international rates which followed.

This vulnerability may have extended to the internal financial system. It is interesting to note that Colombia avoided a severe external debt problem, only to suffer instead an internal banking crisis. Domestic interest rates were given in Table 8.3. The rise came on top of the collapse of the Venezuelan market and the two factors together were added to the effect of the revalued exchange rate, the import liberalisation and the growth of smuggling, all of which we described in the previous chapter. The problems in the textile sector were particularly severe. These problems fed through in turn to the banks, and compounded the problems arising from a rash of bad practices and corruption, which now began to be exposed. The first collapse came at the end of the Turbay administration, with the failure of the Banco Nacional. The financial panic that followed exposed for the first time the new fragility in the financial system.

Table 9.3
Colombia: An Estimate of Drug Traffic as Percentage of GDP

	Total $ billion	% GDP
1981	1.5	4.1
1982	2.5	6.4
1983	1.5	3.9
1984	1.0	2.6
1985	.9	2.6

Source: Gómez (1988).

Note:
[a] This is *not* returned value, but an attempt to estimate the income received by Colombians. It assumes arbitrarily that 50 per cent of the Colombian sales are made at the wholesale level in the US, 50 per cent at the Colombian border.

Returning to the external crisis, a further and specifically Colombian element in the developing problem is by its very nature difficult to appraise: the fall in the price of cocaine shown in Table 9.1. It was certainly not recognised as part of the problem at the time, and the understandable unwillingness to recognize officially the size of the problem plus its illegality both make a quantitative analysis extremely difficult. But by the 1980s, cocaine had become very significant for Colombia. By this point, the marijuana sales that had been part of the 'Dutch Disease' of the 1970s had been almost totally replaced in the US market by Californian production; however, in the meantime another and vastly more lucrative business had grown up. In 1975, coca paste produced in Peru and Bolivia had begun to be processed in Colombia:[2] by the 1980s the shift in international fashion had produced a booming market, a dramatic rise in price and a whole new export for Colombia. The huge income had a lower and less stable proportion of returned value than marijuana had had, which in the 1980s made macro management much more difficult. The contrast with Peru is clear: the income was not only far less stable than Peru's drug income, but also less equally distributed – and increasingly less so as cocaine replaced marijuana.[3]

Table 9.4
Colombia: The Service Account and the Black Dollar Premium 1980–85

	Income from services	Expenditure	Net service account	Premium on black dollars
	$ million			
1980	1 864	1 307	557	− 5.75
1981	1 734	1 675	59	− 4.20
1982	1 317	1 934	− 617	− 0.37
1983	852	1 931	− 1 079	12.29
1984	614	1 770	− 1 156	15.85
1985	974	1 732	− 758	6.68

Source: Gómez (1988).

Estimating the value of drug sales is of course difficult: estimates tend to fall anywhere within a range of 2 to 8 per cent of GDP in the 1980s. One estimate as early as 1978 makes drug income 126 per cent of coffee exports – surely too high.[4] (This refers to total income, not to returned value.)

What is clearer, however, and more important to the economic management issue, is the degree of instability at the margin which cocaine has brought.[5] Table 9.3 shows one estimate of total income from drugs 1980–85. Table 9.4 shows net income from services and the premium on the 'black' dollar in Colombia. Income from services is normally taken as the main means of remitting drug-related dollars to Colombia, so that the fall in income as the cocaine price falls appears significant. In fact the service account does *not* straightforwardly record variations at the margin, since an interesting arbitrage occurs, related to the movement of the black market exchange rate.[6] Once the 'left-hand window'[7] was introduced in 1979, it became relatively safe to sell drug-related dollars as if they were income from services. But if the premium on black market dollars rises, (in part probably *because* of a fall in drug income) there will be a shift at the margin to the black market. Observing the huge variations in the premium on the black market dollar given in Table 9.4, it can be guessed that the fall in cocaine income with the fall in price, the increased supply from other sources and the increased policing activities in 1983–85 led to a fall in drug-related income and a shortage of black market dollars which shifted the premium and led to a *further* fall in service income as receipts were switched to the black market.

We can therefore draw no simple conclusion from the fall in service income. But a *fall* in estimated gross revenue from drugs from $2.5 billion in 1982 to a 'mere' $885 million in 1985, *must*, however far out in absolute terms, have had a profound effect on the severity of the adjustment crisis which developed after 1982.

A more readily acknowledged part of the growing crisis was the increasing fiscal imbalance. A consolidated public sector deficit of 3 per cent in 1980 and 6.3 per cent in 1981 had caused little comment when external funding was easily available. With the Mexican declaration of a moratorium on debt servicing in September 1982, suddenly even Colombia was to feel the 'contagion effect' and find external credit less available: meanwhile the fiscal deficit was even larger, as shown in Figure 8.1 above. Central government revenue rose as a per cent of GDP more than expenditure,[8] but the massive increase in infrastructure spending of the public enterprises under Turbay was still feeding through into the consolidated deficit.

The initial strategy of the Betancur administration

In their first few months in office, the new economic team concentrated attention on the financial panic: on the need to improve credit to the private sector and to cut the fiscal deficit, which was seen as crowding out the private sector.[9] In October 1982 an 'economic emergency' was decreed to allow a strengthening of controls on financial institutions and to permit the government to 'bail out' banks. Subsequently, a large number of banks and other intermediaries were taken over. Special rediscount lines were created, with interesting and novel provisions to try to induce firms to increase their level of capitalisation. Refinancing provisions for private foreign debts were also introduced. In the early period all this had little concrete effect: confidence was low and it would take much time and stronger action to restore credibility to the financial sector. Meanwhile the Venezuelan devaluation of February 1983 was the catalyst to force more attention to the external problem. The analysis of the economic team was still, however, that while it was crucially important to tackle the problems in the banking, industrial and fiscal areas, there was no direct connection between the fiscal imbalance and the external problem. The latter came from external events and from the import liberalisation and could be dealt with directly while maintaining the level of activity. There was thus a deliberate option for a 'heterodox' solution, the kingpin of which was to be an institutional reinforcement of INCOMEX, the foreign trade agency, and a strong policy of import control applied to both the public and private sectors.

The import policy succeeded both in reversing the increase in imports and in facilitating a long overdue recovery in industrial production. Industrial production rose slightly in 1983, for the first time in three years and by 8 per cent in 1984 (helped also by the disincentive to smuggling as the black market premium rose in response to the fall in supply of cocaine dollars). Businessmen, initially apprehensive of the strengthened INCOMEX, were subsequently unanimous in their praise for the way the policy was handled.[10] The fall in imports shown in Table 9.2 would have been even more impressive if more headway could have been made in controlling the *public* sector – a topic we return to in the following chapter.

At the same time that import controls were reintroduced and tightened, exchange controls were tightened, and export subsidies increased. On the internal front, a substantial tax reform was passed, increasing income, sales and local taxes. Although this was subsequently to improve revenue significantly, it did nothing to improve the position until well into 1984, so that the overall fiscal deficit increased in 1983 and 1984.

These developments meant that Colombia entered 1984 with strong and growing crisis signals. The fiscal deficit was still growing, and most important of all, international reserves were falling. The cut in imports was more than outweighed by the continued unfavourable trend on the service account, the black market premium was high, confidence was low and there is evidence of capital flight further worsening the situation. Gutierrez' confidence that he could raise foreign credit was turning out to be falsely based. As the situation worsened it became evidently impossible to raise credit, since external agencies' clear perception was that adjustment was a necessary pre-condition.

With reserves down to three months of imports and falling at a monthly rate of nearly $150 million, Roberto Junguito was asked to take over as Minister of Economy. He accepted on condition that he could have a free hand to make it clear how bad the situation was and implement a severe adjustment programme. Colombia for once entered a rather 'orthodox' phase of policy management. As usual, however, as we shall see, there were Colombian nuances to orthodoxy.

July 1984–September 1985

The analysis of this period is made unusually fascinating and rewarding by the existence of an exceptional document. There can be few official documents as insightful and revealing, both in technical and human terms, as the *Memoria del Ministro de Hacienda* for July 1984 to September 1985. The following account draws heavily on this publication and on discussions with its author.

The Minister's justifiable pride in the adjustment experience comes through clearly: 'the sequence of measures adopted were exceptionally effective and worthy of study from the point of view of economic theory' (p. 11). The most remarkable achievement was a 30 per cent real devaluation in the course of 1985, without the acceleration in internal prices which is the customary price in recent Latin American experience: as the *Memoria* states, 'this experience had no precedents in Latin America' (p. 30). The second achievement was a continuation of growth through the adjustment period. The third was an agreement with the international banks without the formal participation of the IMF.

The political context in which the team took office was one in which the one impossible answer to the economic crisis was the usual form of IMF Standby. The President was strongly opposed to such an agreement, and in terms of the legacy of the Lleras success of 1967 *vis-à-vis* the Fund, it would have been politically extremely damaging. The team was also determined to avoid a sharp devaluation, the typical IMF recommendation, and above all determined to stamp out *expectations* of such a devaluation, which conversations with the Fund would have aroused. The team knew that if they were to achieve their principal goal, an acceleration of the crawling peg without acceleration of internal prices, then complete secrecy was essential: an agreement with the Fund would have required spelling out in detail the exchange rate policy, which would have undermined it from the start.[11] They also knew they had to act at once, and Standbys take months to negotiate.[12]

The central goals of the team were, therefore, the real devaluation as described above, and a loan agreement with the private international banks without formal IMF participation. Fiscal austerity was seen as necessary but more for its role in relation to the above two goals than because the level of activity was unduly high. All were agreed on the medium-term importance of 'setting the house in order' in regard to the fiscal deficit.

The first initiative by the team was to convince the country and in particular Congress of the severity of the crisis *and* of the team's determination that the crawling peg could be maintained. Fears of devaluation and the associated capital flight had to be killed. The *Memoria* describes explicitly how the focus on the fiscal deficit was used 'to distract attention' from the exchange rate front, 'as the government's priority area of action'. So effective was the rhetoric, that Congress actually implemented *all* the fiscal measures suggested by the team! This was not anticipated, so that the degree of fiscal austerity went beyond the team's plans, as the *Memoria* admits (p. 18).[13] Tariff and gasoline price increases and reductions in fiscal exemptions were accepted, new bond issues approved, and a strict wage policy passed, implying a sharp fall in earnings in real terms for both the public and private sectors.[14] Controls on the spending of public enterprises were introduced and/or tightened.

These measures meant that expenditure as a percent of GDP fell marginally in 1985. Meanwhile the new tax changes, added to the fiscal reform of the previous team, led to a rise in revenue of 49 per cent in 1985,[15] while prices rose 21 per cent. All this led to a fall in the Central Government deficit from 5 per cent of GDP in 1984 to 2.8 per cent in 1985. The consolidated deficit fell from 7.6 per cent to 4.9 per cent in the same period.[16]

With the country 'distracted' by the black picture painted and the severe fiscal package, the way was now prepared for the discreet manipulation of the rate of crawl. First, though, the coffee situation had to be organised. Here was a delicate problem: as the devaluation was accomplished, there would be gains to the coffee sector, which would need to be carefully regulated so as not to generate excess demand. But as it could not be indicated in any quarter that there was to be devaluation, how could this be negotiated with the Federación? As the

Memoria describes (p. 35), a way through was found in the form of a commitment to maintain the real internal producer price and an agreement in general that any excess resources in the Fondo Nacional del Café would go to three main uses: the *capitalización* of the Banco Cafetero, the reduction of the Fondo's *internal* debt and the creation of National Savings Bonds.

With this, the way was cleared for the adjustment of the crawl. 'Discretion' was helped by the fact that the rate published daily was annualised, so people failed to perceive immediately what was happening to the monthly rate. The success was so great that a distinguished economist sent the Minister several notes during 1985 urging him to devalue![17] The result we have already mentioned: a 30 per cent real devaluation in the course of 1985. As Table 9.5 shows, this was achieved with scarcely any variation in the rate of inflation.

Table 9.5
Colombia: Real Exchange Rate and Consumer Prices 1980–88

	Real Exchange Rate Index 1985 = 100	Cost of living % change in year
December 1980	79.12	26.0
December 1981	76.50	26.3
December 1982	70.98	24.0
December 1983	72.86	16.6
December 1984	77.84	18.3
December 1985	100.00	22.5
December 1986	108.21	21.6
December 1987	107.91	24.6
December 1988	105.25	28.3

Source: Junguito, p. 990, *Boletín de Estadística, Colombia Estadística.*

The right environment was also now considered to exist to negotiate external funding – for medium- rather than short-term purposes. The lengthy negotiations are described in considerable detail in the *Memoria*. There are many interesting elements, not least the positive role of the World Bank in trying to encourage the IMF to be more flexible (pp. 63–64). Finally, it appeared that the banks required something more formal, and the argument resolved into whether there should be an actual signing of a 'comfort Standby' – the IMF's suggestion – i.e. a Standby to become effective in case of need - or a 'monitoring' plus a statement of intention to proceed to a Standby should it become necessary (p. 76). It took the personal intervention of Betancur to achieve the latter, which then allowed the signing of a 'Jumbo' credit from a consortium of international banks, for US $1 billion – finally concluded only in December 1985.

Meanwhile, a further important line of policy concerned the financial sector. The measures implemented by the previous team to rescue many banks and firms were strengthened and more resources were made available. This has been the most controversial part of the Junguito policies, since many felt that the rescue operations were far too generous when they involved 'rescues' from some fairly shady operations.

By the time the credit came through, it was of no relevance to the balance of payments since as we describe below the coffee price began to rise in October 1985, taking the economy through once more to a quite different phase of economic management. More important was the continued careful use of import controls. Even under increasing pressure from the World Bank, careful management meant that it was possible to reduce the number of prohibited products significantly without damage either to domestic production or to the external account.[18] The growth of domestic oil production also helped the import bill.

The results

We have indicated already the principal results. The GDP data are given in Table 9.6.

It will be seen that the fiscal and wage policies did slow down growth but only fractionally: GDP rose 3 per cent in 1985 compared with 3.3 per cent in 1984, while industrial production rose 3 per cent compared with 8 per cent. Investment fell 5 per cent, the heaviest fall coming in the private sector. The recovery in agricultural production in the second half of 1985 helped – and helped prices even more. Food prices rose sharply in the early months but fell again as sharply, a phenomenon we have noted repeatedly. Considering the degree of recession in demand implicit in the wage and fiscal policies, however, the slow down was surprisingly mild, possibly reflecting the renewed confidence generated by the policy management we have described.[19] It was also helped by credit policy: the reduction in lending to the government permitted increased lending to the private sector.[20]

The supply side expansion, even though modest, helped to reinforce the strong signals coming from policy and the wage restraint, and prices rose a mere 22 per cent compared with 18 per cent in 1984.

The balance of payments turned around, as shown in Table 9.2 above. This owed little to exports until the coffee price rose: exports other than

Table 9.6
Colombia: GDP by Expenditure 1980–88
(constant 1975 prices)
1982 = 100

	1980	1981	1982	1983	1984	1985	1986	1987[b]	1988[b]
GDP	96.8	99.1	100.0	101.6	105.0	108.2	113.8	119.8	124.3
Consumption	95.3	98.2	100.0	100.3	103.3	105.6	108.6	113.1	118.0
private	95.8	98.5	100.0	100.5	103.3	105.3	108.4	112.5	116.8
public	92.1	95.6	100.0	99.4	103.5	108.2	110.1	116.8	126.1
Investment	91.4	97.1	100.0	101.2	102.4	97.1	104.9	111.9	122.4
private	99.2	105.7	100.0	106.2	95.3	86.5	98.0	104.0	108.2
public[a]	82.4	87.3	100.0	95.3	110.8	109.4	113.0	117.1	137.3
Exports	115.2	101.6	100.0	99.1	109.3	125.0	143.4	155.3	153.6
Imports	88.3	92.6	100.0	90.9	87.3	81.6	83.9	87.1	93.7

Source: DANE, *Cuentas Nacionales.*

Notes:
[a] For 1980–86 no such breakdown is given by DANE at constant prices. These figures have been calculated from current price data, using the DANE investment deflator and making heroic assumptions about which institutional components of investment are principally public.
[b] Fedesarrollo, *Coyuntura Económica*, September 1989.

coffee, oil and coal rose only 6 per cent in 1985 despite the large devaluation. More impressive was the fall of 25 per cent in imports despite rising production. The result was that reserves began to rise by the first quarter of 1985.

Evaluation: adjustment Colombian-style

The economic team's own evaluation of their programme emphasizes sequencing, expectations and surprise. Junguito stresses the importance of *first* affecting expectations by means of the fiscal adjustment, *then* proceeding to take people unawares with the crawling peg adjustment. These elements are clearly crucial, and were well-managed though with fiscal overkill and a cost in investment.[21] We would add other points, however, remarkable for their similarity with the Lleras experience we have described earlier. First, growth *continued*, so that many vicious circles were avoided. This was partly the result of policy, particularly credit policy, which in a selective fashion strongly promoted continued expansion in the private sector (as in 1968–69).[22] It was also partly the result of a particularly Colombian characteristic: the rapid supply response in food stuffs to a rise in prices. This was certainly encouraged by credit but seems to owe more to underlying production character- istics. Continuing expansion was also helped insofar as the increased resources of the Coffee Fund did feed through – e.g. by repayment of internal debt.

Second, the continuing expansion was aided by the extent to which sudden cuts in public sector projects were avoided. Public investment in fact rose; the cut in the fiscal deficit came partly from the prior tax reform.

Third, we would underline the importance of a very unorthodox element: import controls. To achieve a 25 per cent cut in imports with industrial production rising 3 per cent is an unusual success. The 'orthodox' aspect, the response of exports to devaluation, was actually rather weak.

Fourth, of course, it is important to note the extent to which the working class paid the price: the fall of real wages of some 4–5 per cent is moderate compared with, say, Southern Cone experiences but represented a serious cut in living standards for those affected. Fortunately, and finally, the whole experience did not have to last long. The rise in coffee prices in the last few months of the Administration ushered in another period where the challenge was rather how to manage and distribute prosperity. This is the story of the remaining section of this chapter.

Epilogue: the next bonanza

The coffee price rise was given in Table 9.1 above: it generated a rise in dollar export income from coffee of 69 per cent in 1986 compared with 1984, while total dollar export income rose 47 per cent.

The management of this next boom was exemplary in terms of short-run macro balances. The key groups co-ordinating policy, from the Federación and from the economic team, were convinced that in the previous boom, the treatment of producers had been generous to the point of danger: this time, high savings were the top priority, and for the Federación, the retention of control over the use of such savings was fundamental.

The real internal coffee price is shown in Table 9.7. It can be seen that it rose very modestly compared to the increase in international prices. The enormous proceeds were handled under an agreement between the Federación and the Government, in a manner which resulted in much the greater part being saved. Part was lent on to various enterprises to

Table 9.7
Colombia: Internal Coffee Price[a] 1977–88
(1978 prices)

1977	8 940
1978	7 300
1979	6 214
1980	5 814
1981	4 975
1982	4 714
1983	4 509
1984	4 775
1985	5 565
1986	7 783
1987	6 697
1988	6 532

Source: Thomas (1985) and *Revista* del Banco de
la República.

Note:
[a] Pesos per bag of 125 kg.

repay their foreign debt, the repayments to be made when the Jumbo
loan was available, and then put back into the Fondo Nacional del
Café.[23] Bonds were issued to producers, which could be used as security
for productive credit, to settle existing debts or to buy fertilizer from the
Federación.[24] The surplus accumulated by the Coffee Fund through this
agreement came to 2 per cent of GDP, a phenomenon 'without historical
precedent'.[25] The consequences of the coffee boom were the higher
income of producers, the strengthening of the coffee fund and a
favourable impact on the balance of payments and the earnings of the
state.[26]

The high savings induced in 1986 were an appropriate response to
what was correctly perceived as a temporary shock: by early 1987 coffee
prices had fallen again – though oil and coal were by now rising sharply
in volume and exports in 1987 were 7 per cent higher than in 1986. The
rather steady evolution of all variables through the boom and its end is
shown in Tables 9.5 and 9.6. Particularly impressive is the continuing
slight depreciation of the real exchange rate and the steady rate of
growth of output. The growth of output slowed in 1988 to a 'mere' 3.3
per cent, provoking talk of *un año de quiebre* and *recesión*.[27] But the
growth was still positive in per capita terms. Inflation has continued at
its customary 22–25 per cent.

This has given rise to an accepted view in Colombia, that 'our
problems are not economic but political'. While the economy grows

steadily, the crisis in public order seems to have grown steadily worse. This story is for others to tell: briefly, the attempt at a Peace Plan under the Betancur Administration merely seems to have given the guerrilla forces an opportunity to re-arm and refocus their activities, while the drug trade and its associated violence have become steadily more menacing. The well-publicized assassinations, including a Minister of Justice, and countless threats and attempted murders, have undermined the judicial process. The result by the end of the 1980s is a sense of loss of direction and deep uncertainty. Most recently, the assassination of the popular and charismatic Presidential candidate, Luis Carlos Galán, in August 1989, has brought a new determination to confront drug interests.

Is it even true, however, that the problems are not economic? We turn in the next chapter to issues of poverty and distribution, to encounter some striking results. Even at the level of economic management, there are questions to be asked. The first concerns trade prospects and management. Table 9.8 shows the shift in composition of exports in the course of the 1980s (leaving aside for the moment the issue of drugs). It will be seen that by 1987 oil and coal together came to 30.5 per cent of total exports, almost equalling coffee at 31 per cent.

The fascinating issues this raises at the political economy level will be obvious by now: the coffee sector has evolved over fifty years extraordinarily sophisticated mechanisms for control of fluctuations, based on a subtle interweaving of private and public power and interests. No such mechanisms exist for oil and coal. In both cases, the income accruing directly to the state is very large, and not mediated by any local group. In both cases, foreign companies feature largely, in direct contrast to coffee. In the case of oil, the absence of control machinery is particularly marked, since companies are exempt from the provisions of Decree 444 in regard to foreign exchange earnings. This was argued by Lleras to be vital in order to generate the necessary inflow of foreign investment to the sector – which simply demonstrates in the most vivid way possible the difference with coffee. In other words, Colombia is facing for the first time a situation which Peru has suffered for a century. None of the various instruments so carefully developed to manage coffee-led growth can simply be assumed to transfer to the management of a more standard natural-resource-led model.[28] These doubts are made the more serious by the breakdown of the International Coffee Agreement in 1989: for the first time ever, both meetings, in March and September, failed to secure an accord.

The second area for questioning concerns the debt. Colombia has adamantly resisted the general tendency to reschedule and is paying in

Table 9.8
Colombia: Composition of Exports 1981–8
(Percentage shares in US$ millions)

	1981	1982	1983	1984	1985	1986	1987	1988
Coffee	46.2	45.9	47.9	44.6	50.0	57.7	31.0	30.1
Petroleum and Petroleum products	6.5	13.8	12.3	10.7	11.2	8.8	25.5	18.3
Coal	0.4	0.5	0.1	3.3	3.5	4.3	5.0	5.8
Minor Exports	41.8	32.7	30.3	30.4	26.2	29.3	29.6	34.7

Source: *Revista* del Banco del la República, September 1987. Fedesarollo *Conyuntura Económica*, March 1989, IMF, IFS, 1988 *Supplement* on Trade Statistics.

full and on time. Debt service has increased from 13 per cent of total export to 38 per cent in 1985 and 26.4 per cent in 1987. But the issue is surely more serious when considered in terms of the burden on the budget of state enterprises. It is reasonable to assume that for a given state enterprise, the opportunity costs of interest payments are maintenance and investment expenses. The interview data reported on in the following chapter produced many examples of a lack of cash for routine maintenance. This may be the most serious long-run dimension of the debt situation.

The reasons for the refusal to consider debt rescheduling parallel in a curious way the issues raised by the new exports of oil and coal. Colombia has been pursuing a policy of decentralisation not backed by adequate funds. Hence local governments, regional development agencies etc. feel acutely that they have responsibility without financial capacity. Much of the debt is in the hands of these actors. Hence, a sudden reduction in debt obligations would inject spending power at the decentralised level improving the budget position of local governments and state agencies in a way beyond the control of the central government, which is unacceptable to the traditions of tight management developed at the centre.[29] It is clear that quite a deep conflict of interest prevents the resolution of this issue.

Notes

1. Oil would only become an additional favourable prospect in 1984, with the Caño Limón strike.
2. Puyana (1988).
3. This effect was muted a little as small-scale production of coca also began in Colombia in the 1980s.
4. Ruiz (1979); Ruiz and López (1981). At the opposite end is the estimate of Junguito and Caballero for 1977: $500 million.
5. There are also strong local effects, on land and labour markets in certain regions. See Gómez (1988).
6. This idea is explored in Gómez (1988).
7. The *ventanilla sinestra* refers to a no-questions-asked arrangement for purchasing dollars.
8. See data in OANE, *Boletín de Estadística*.
9. Ocampo and Lora (1987).
10. Based on numerous interviews in Bogotá in 1987.
11. 'We could tell no one – not even the president' is Junguito's description of the process. (Interview, September 1988).
12. BCRP, *Memoria*, p. 59.
13. 'Se legisló en materia fiscal más allá de lo esperado por el mismo Gobierno' – p. 18.
14. For details, see *Memoria*, pp. 17–19.
15. BCRP, *Memoria*, p. 108.
16. BCRP, *Memoria*, p. 20.
17. Interview with Roberto Junguito, Bogotá , September 1988.
18. E.g. removing from the prohibited or restricted list products not imported anyway.
19. Ocampo and Lora (1987) suggest that falling markups aided the recovery, by generating redistribution. But their data for profits show a rise in 1985, (p. 83) and their markup data only goes to 1984, so the argument is not clearly confirmed.
20. BCRP, *Memoria*, p. 87.
21. Junguito claims this was true but inevitable (interview, Bogotá , September 1987).
22. Commercial bank credit to agriculture rose 14 per cent in real terms in 1985, to industry 37 per cent, according to the *Revista* del Banco de la República, April 1987. This is based on an imperfect classification, so is not conclusive.
23. Notas Editoriales, *Revista* del Banco de la República, March 1986.
24. Notas Editoriales, *Revista* del Banco de al República, April 1986.
25. Notas Editoriales, *Revista* del Banco de la República, December 1986.
26. Notas Editoriales, *ibid.*
27. Fedesarollo, *Coyuntura Económica*, June 1989, p. 34.
28. This argument is made formally and with considerable elegance by Eduardo Lora (1989), using a CGE model to simulate shocks with different products.
29. I owe this perception to Eduardo Lora, in a seminar paper on 'Economic Prospects for Colombia', Oxford, June 1989.

10 In Conclusion: Macro Management, Distribution and Welfare

Implicit in much of the analysis of the preceding chapters has been the idea that somehow the Colombian economy functions 'better' than the Peruvian economy, at the level of macro management both of crises and booms. This leaves completely aside issues of distribution and development, though it may well have implications for such issues. This chapter aims first to explore more deeply the 'macro management' issue, and secondly to balance what would otherwise be too favourable a picture of Colombia, by looking at the evidence on deeper aspects of planning, structural change, distribution and welfare. The analysis is suggestive, not conclusive. I am deliberately raising issues which go far beyond economics and where the research does not yet exist to provide conclusive answers.

The notion of Colombia as 'functioning better' has emerged in the previous chapters as based in two interrelated comparative features of the two countries. The first is that policy in the case of Colombia has *relatively* speaking responded pragmatically, sensibly and prudently to changing circumstances, with behind this a sense of accumulated experience and ability to learn from the past. The second is the relationship between the state and the private sector, which in Colombia's case has been characterised by greater mutual confidence and respect, a situation which facilitates policy and in turn is sustained by greater coherence and 'success' in policy. I turn now to try to amplify these two notions, before offering some explanations.

'Better' policy

If we summarise the substantive points made in earlier chapters about policy-making in the two countries, we find the following: *1)* The identical policy – ISI – was handled in the two cases in quite divergent ways. In Peru, once the policy was adopted (very late), all the 'standard' problems were very much in evidence (discrimination against agriculture, overvaluation of the exchange rate, extreme cases of negative protection, exaggerated capital intensity, inefficiency, excess capacity, little employment generation). Foreign investment in industry and banking accentuated some of these problems and there was no attempt either at control of foreign investment or at sensible planning of the domestic sector. By contrast, although Colombia was by no means free of all these problems, up to 1975 agriculture was *promoted*, the effective exchange rate *favoured* exporting, and there was an unusually coherent beginning of planning and regulation of foreign investment. *2)* The identical crises – in 1929, in 1966–7, in the 1980s – produced in the Colombian case a more pragmatic response with greater priority given to growth and to continuity as an asset in itself – and ultimately greater success in recovering and maintaining growth and 'forcing' the balance of payments to accommodate. On most occasions the more stereotyped Peruvian response produced an adjustment crisis which with time became more pernicious in its stagflation characteristics and more damaging to long-run prospects. With time the repercussions became such, of course, that the paths of the two economies diverged so much that contrast becomes virtually meaningless. *3)* The management of booms also showed divergence. Although Colombia's management of the coffee bonanza of the 1970s can be severely criticized, interestingly Colombian policy makers themselves learnt from the experience and this was in evidence in the 1980s bonanza. We have been able to find no evidence of a similar learning process for Peru, where the most recent bonanza – copper prices in 1979–80 – produced the standard mistaken analysis and response.

This historical record is the substance behind the hypothesis I would now like to put forward – that the greater coherence and credibility of Colombian macro-economic management is perhaps the outstanding difference between the two economies, and that this coherence and credibility is based not on a purer adherence to the market but on pragmatic interventionist policies based on the second comparative characteristic I wish to emphasize: the relationship with the private sector. The next section fills out this point.

The state-private sector relation

In Peru, interviews with the private sector thrust to the foreground the element of distrust of the state. There is a sense of an almost unbridgeable gap, of a lack of communication. 'No one in the government understands the world of business.'[1] The gap is seen as extending back 'at least to Beltrán'. It was widened with the military, as we have seen in Chapter 4.[2] Interestingly, it was in no way closed with Belaunde: the liberal policies of 1981–82 were so savage in their impact on business that six years later businessmen were still talking of them with horror. The technocrats who ran that policy were seen as *impermeable* – dogmatic and ideological.[3] There was simply no access for businessmen.[4]

With the advent of the García administration, the whole problem was thrown into sharp relief. As we have shown, by the end of the first year, the decision had been clearly taken to strengthen the links with the private sector and to build *concertación*. There was even enormous goodwill to draw on, since the experience with the previous government had been so bad that businessmen longed to believe in the new alternative. There was also a huge effort to consult, beginning in August 1986. But at the same time it proved intensely difficult to reverse the trend of history: as one businessman commented: 'there's a tremendous gap between the concept and its execution. People hear this marvellous stuff about "concertación" and the FIE, but when they go to COFIDE, to the price control committee, to the BCR for imports, they get a negative response.'[5] The weak institutional framework affected both sides: the government began by negotiating with the *gremios*, but as of January 1987 began to bypass the *gremios* to deal directly with 'the apostles' – presumably because of the ineffectiveness of the *gremios*. It was of course a step which had negative repercussions on the whole process, for the resentment it created.

Thus the weak historical development on both sides of the equation was itself naturally a problem as an historic attempt was made to introduce a discontinuity and a new relationship. The fragility of this relationship was exposed and accentuated by the disastrously handled decision of July 1987 to nationalise the banks.

Turning to Colombia, the contrast of attitude can hardly be overemphasized. The private sector feels it has – and typically has had – excellent access to the public sector. The *gremios* – particularly ANDI – are enormously influential. There is 'equal and amazing access under *any* Presidency – even to the President himself.'[6] ANDI is invited by the government to hold fora on issues such as tax reforms; their role in moulding opinion is consciously used and respected. Of course the degree of influence of different sectors varies with different regimes: the manufacturing sector was not centre-stage during Turbay or López, for example. Yet it is striking that all insist that access remained good. There is widespread confidence that the web of friendships and contacts is such that interests will be sensibly looked after. Thus with regard to an import control policy, for example, there is trust that the system will be 'reasonably' operated. This does not mean that some abstract and neutral system will arbitrate, but that reasonable common sense and practicality will prevail. The positive view of import controls held by the Colombian private sector contrasts strikingly with the apprehension felt in Peru as García reintroduced and tightened such controls in January 1987.

The degree to which access is independent of particular administrations rests of course partly on the much-analysed poli-classist nature of the Colombian political system: its members all speak to and know each other. The openness of the Colombian system also allows experts to join administrations not of their party with remarkable freedom.

Of course many both inside and outside the public sector are extremely critical both of policy-making and of the state apparatus – and with good reason, as we have seen and shall see further below. And the views and attitudes expressed here are those only of the minority, who are part of the system. Nevertheless, *comparatively* speaking, the confidence in and the acceptance of the state is at a different level from that in Peru. This clearly affects many areas of policy-making and many key economic variables. It would be quite untrue to claim that there is no export of capital from Colombia[7] – but the 'capital-*flight*' reaction so typical of Peru, Mexico and Argentina is not found. The continuance of investment in circumstances which elsewhere would lead to recession is surely fundamentally related to this confidence. In turn, it reinforces the level of policy competence, since entering government is prestigious and further develops the crucial networks. In Colombia one's career is *advanced* by moving between the state and the private sector.[8] And as the system succeeds, so it is reinforced.

The self-reinforcing elements in the system explain part of the difference encountered in our two cases. In Peru the cumulative processes work in the opposite direction: as the degree of crisis worsens, so it becomes increasingly unlikely that time spent in the public sector increases one's prestige. But cumulative processes have to originate somewhere. The serious explanation of the origins of such striking differences requires a socio-political analysis beyond the scope of this study: some suggestions can however be found in the historical analysis of Chapters 1 and 2. I would propose as hypotheses for further research that *part* of the contrast as we have identified it here can be explained first in terms of the endowment and character of the export economy in the two cases, and second in terms of the varying strength of regional interests.

As Chapter 1 made clear, coffee in the context of Colombia has been a very special crop. Summarising the conclusions of that chapter, the large number of small producers plus the management needs of marketing high quality coffee required institutional development of a very special sort, linking local, regional and national levels. Out of this grew a network of participation and an attitude of acceptance of the importance of participation in terms of self interest that must surely have 'spilt over' into other areas. The answer in coffee was a unique organisation – the Coffee Federation: the success of and centrality of its relation to the state built into Colombian consciousness the positive dimension of the state's role. By contrast, in Peru, no export crop played this role. Typically, infrastructure and marketing functions were supplied by foreign capital. The Colombian relationship of reciprocity and symbiosis is echoed in Peru's case by the relationship between the domestic private sector and foreign capital. Elite groups during the successful export-led decades could certainly typically dominate the state – but did not need to in the Colombian sense. We have shown how for decades export-led growth in Peru required little of the state beyond the passive maintenance of order. We have shown the relevance of the resulting lack of experience in techniques of intervention or state management, to the failures of the ISI model and the weakness of attempts at unorthodoxy. What we also might conclude is that its very passivity failed to generate the slow growth of links of mutual self interest that one day would be vitally necessary to sustain a mixed-economy model – links which did develop in Colombia.

Let us stress again: such links are not market integrating in the normal sense of the word; we are not talking about more-or-less-perfect market economies. Rather, they often are extra-market, or represent in themselves market distortions. But their existence is vital to the functioning of a mixed economy in the *context* of extreme imperfections.

This vitality has been supported by the strength of regional interests in the Colombian case, compared with the extreme degree of centralisation experienced in Peru. This we have shown did not originate with coffee but was enormously enhanced by the characteristics of coffee. Geography has been perhaps the single strongest causal factor. The consequences for policy-making and the state are first, the continued life of the regions, which feeds through into grassroots activity and participation at all levels. But perhaps more important has been the continued strength of regional elites, requiring as they do sophisticated bargaining mechanisms and trade-offs to conciliate their interests at a national level.[9]

We have suggested, however, at several points that it would be easy to overemphasize the significance of such a 'well-functioning' system.

Colombia remains an underdeveloped economy with acute problems of distribution, violence, illegality and so forth: this was shown in Chapters 1 and 3. Let us look now at a different area of 'management': that of public investment, and see how the comparative picture looks.

The political economy of public investment

If we are looking for ways of appraising the 'quality' of economic policy, then public sector investment decisions would seem an obvious topic to take as a case study, given the crucial role of public investment in a mixed economy in complementing and compensating for private investment and its potential role in goals of welfare and structural change. We explore here the institutional setting of investment planning and pay particular attention to the role of international agencies.[10]

In the case of Peru, public investment is in principle monitored and co-ordinated by the Planning Institute, within the framework of the short-term and medium-term plans. A process of 'dynamic interaction' is supposed to occur with the Ministry of Finance in the process of generating the budget, which is the key instrument in so far as it provides funds. The responsibility for ranking investment projects also lies with the Planning Institute, working in collaboration with the agency that supervises the State enterprises – CONADE – and the sectoral planning offices of the different ministries.

The reality is inevitably different – to the point where one can legitimately query whether anyone plans public investment. We can identify four areas of problems – two concerning institutional aspects on the Peruvian side, two concerning 'structural' aspects of public investment *per se*.

The first arises, as we would expect, out of the weakness of government mechanisms in general in Peru. Planning and intervention in general, as we have seen, were comparatively underdeveloped in Peru by the 1960s. The military government of General Velasco gave planning an abrupt boost, and the Planning Institute came to the fore for the first time, only to be marginalised again in the Belaunde government – to the point of being geographically displaced. In March 1982 the Institute was actually moved physically from the centre of Lima out to La Molina – an excellent way of effecting and symbolising its renewed marginal status. The Belaunde years were a period of demoralisation, when many talented people left the Instituto Nacional de Planificación and the germs of a learning process of planning and assessment were stifled. (Sectoral planning offices in the different ministries were similarly weakened through this time.)

With the advent of García and heterodox policies, the decline was reversed – but when salaries cannot be raised substantially because of economic crisis, reversing such a decline is difficult. The whole process of continual short-term crisis also creates a climate hostile to serious investment in planning: since the short term is inevitably the key issue in debate, to have weight an institution *must* involve itself in the short term. The INP has not escaped this irresistible pressure at the price of the development of techniques of serious planning and re-planning of public investment.

The second institutional aspect concerns the delicate relationship with other institutions involved in planning public investment. Since budgetary control lies elsewhere, and the detailed management of particular projects also resides elsewhere, good inter-institutional relations are required to make any sense at all of the planning process. Needless to say, the reality is different, with institutional rivalries and lack of collaboration the typical state of affairs. But it is not true either that the Treasury wins the day: in fact the vulnerability and lack of authority of the planning process make it relatively easy for political pressures to overrule technical considerations at the final count.

But even were all these institutional aspects healthier than in fact they are, there would still be serious deficiencies in the outcome. These arise first from our third problem area: the simple fact of 'inertia'. Public investment projects are often large and take a long time: this tends to mean that in a given year easily 70 per cent or 80 per cent of the investment budget may be already committed to existing projects[11] – the figure in a time of recession can well be higher. The cost of cancelling a project, in terms of penalty clauses and sunk costs, is usually such as to make it appear not to be an option. So 'planning' in the sense of giving shape to investment expenditure can only happen at the margin. This problem is also responsible for pressures which further undermine serious planning: since it is far more profitable both politically and in terms of 'commissions' to start new projects than to finish old, there is an almost irresistible pressure both to overspend and to cut back irrationally on existing projects.[12] Thus *maintenance* budgets come under extreme pressure.[13]

The fourth and final problem relates to the source of funding. Almost all funding of public sector investment involves international agencies – overwhelmingly for our case studies the World Bank and the Inter-American Development Bank. Evaluating the Peruvian planning process – and as we shall see shortly the Colombian also – produces yet more evidence of how effectively the autonomy of 'national planning processes', such as it is, is undermined in these circumstances. These agencies, by the way they back certain projects and not others, encourage some groups and not others, insist on contract specifications and so forth, have a major effect on which projects actually come to fruition, as well as on the form of the project. The latter involves the interrelated aspects of size, technology and source of supplies. The basic bias on the part of the World Bank and IADB is in favour of large projects:[14] the technical aspects and the role of foreign suppliers probably follow from this, rather than representing a conscious response to private sector pressures.

Only very recently has Peru begun to take account of this problem and to attempt to deal with it. In 1987 a project to develop a 'Bolsa de Subcontratación' was launched to facilitate local purchases in public contracts – an idea originating with the Sociedad Nacional de Industrias[15] – and *all* projects with the World Bank were suspended pending their re-evaluation and possible renegotiation.[16]

Given our earlier analysis, the reader might reasonably expect to hear a different story as we turn to review the Colombian situation. What is fascinating, however, is how strikingly *similar* the story sounds. Again we may legitimately query who, if anyone, actually plans public investment. The system in Colombia begins in the Ministry of Finance, which estimates the amount of money available for the year for investment – as a residual after current needs. This budget is passed to Planeación, which decides its allocation, in principle working with the different Ministries and the various decentralised agencies such as ISA (Interconección Eléctrica SA). It is finally approved in COMPES. However, in practice the institutional weaknesses of the system are not so dissimilar from the Peruvian study. The Planning Department is considered by many 'to have only really planned under Lleras'. Appointing heads who either did not believe in planning or who were ineffective has been an easy way to neutralise the institution. Typically the Department is considered to be too involved in short-term issues and too concentrated in construction projects – least so under Betancur. Meanwhile the Ministries have *never* had good planning machinery. The lack of qualified people and coherent direction is marked throughout, and notably in the Ministries of Development, Agriculture, and Education.

It would take a far stronger system than this to overcome the structural forces undermining the autonomy of the planning process, here as in Peru. In regard to inertia, in the words of an ex-planning official, this makes planning of the investment budget 'a mockery'. First, a large chunk must be allocated to foreign debt, then come existing commitments: in his experience this typically used up the entire budget leaving very little margin for the plans any administration wanted to carry out.

Further, the limits on freedom of choice, when there *is* choice, are serious. The Colombian analysis varies interestingly from the Peruvian: whereas in Peru the stress was principally on the role of outside agencies, the Colombian view combines this with the strength of regional pressures. Although in principle, the central agencies are meant to plan, evaluate and direct, in practice proposals come from the regions with a political head of steam already behind them. A particular project will then be taken up by a funding agency – the World Bank or the IADB – which then plays a huge role in developing it and further building the head of steam. Vested interests are created, with commissions in prospect. Against all this, central planning institutions or the Ministry of Finance have little say. Feasibility studies tend to be formal justifications of projects already rolling in political terms.[17] The bias introduced by the international agencies is huge: they typically have thought in terms of a fixed budget, and within that have strong preferences for projects easy to monitor: thus 'social' or 'small' projects suffer.

The rules of these agencies on tendering also affect local suppliers, as in Peru. The difference is that Colombia has had since Lleras Restrepo an institution with a clear mandate to ensure that local suppliers are protected in government procurement: INCOMEX. But it is interesting to observe the reasons for the ineffectiveness of the policy. Basically, there is little or no comprehension elsewhere in the system of the rationality of such protection. It implies both cost and difficulty, since if local firms win contracts, local financing must be sought and delays are known to be inevitable. As a result, the regional or sectoral development agencies, for example, do all they can to achieve 'turnkey projects' and *avoid* local participation. One foreign ambassador complained bitterly when INCOMEX refused an import permit for his country's project, on the grounds that the regional development agency involved had specifically requested that the tender require entirely imported components.

The incomprehension extends also to other organs of Central Government – the Banco de la República and even Planeación – and certainly also to politicians who see their pet projects threatened when import permits are refused. Given lack of good will, it is always possible to evade control – e.g. by an accommodating definition of 'local supplier'.[18] And important projects are outside the control of INCOMEX – for example, government-to-government deals and World Bank or IADB contracts where Colombian firms find it difficult to tender. This is usually because of the size of the tender, with the funding agency being unwilling to break the project into smaller units, or because of technological requirements, which insist on the latest technology, not always with good reason, which may put the project beyond the capacity of local supplies.

There are attempts to fight the pressures, of course – and more examples of such attempts than can be found in Peru, until the recent across-the-board effort under García. The most recent example in Colombia is interesting as the first of its kind in terms of the extent and source of the pressure brought to bear. It concerned electric cable for an electricity project. The private sector had studied ISA plans for the sector and estimated a demand for certain types of cables; on this basis investment in a plant had been carried out. When the tenders finally appeared, however, they specified other technology and other cables, not made in Colombia. Interestingly, it was the *union* which began the fight (as yet unresolved), and convinced the producer associations to join. The pressure was to disaggregate the tenders, so that local firms might bid.[19]

In conclusion then, the points we are making here are first, that the earlier judgment on 'good management' is relative: that Colombian institutions are also deficient in important ways, nowhere better exemplified than in this field of public investment planning. Second, variations in the quality of institutions may well be 'noise' compared with the structural problems faced: we have taken the striking example of the role of pressures from international agencies plus domestic political interests, plus the basic fact of inertia, to show that while 'prudent fiscal policy' is one thing, coherent and independent management of public sector investment is quite another.

Distribution, welfare and the basic needs record

The previous chapters have argued that one of the outstanding differences between the two experiences is Colombia's much greater ability to 'manage' the short term. In this chapter we have argued that this 'good management' comprises not greater adherence to the rules of the game in terms of free market policies, but rather flexible and pragmatic use of interventionist policies combined with conservative spending policies. This final section takes up the obvious corollary: 'so what'? How much does all this good management actually achieve for Colombia compared to Peru, in terms of welfare, distribution and basic needs?

A basic contrast between the two countries is clearly that in the one case – Peru – populist experiments have at times provided the political basis for quite radical redistributionist policies, at least in intent, notably under Velasco with the modern sector and García, while Colombia has been conspicuous for its lack of populist governments. An obvious question therefore is whether populist experiments and subsequent crises actually benefit the poor more or less at the end of the day than incrementalist policies pursued with more consistency and less chaos.

The record and the policies

We established in Chapter 3 that the distributional and basic needs records of our two countries were remarkably similar at the beginning of the 1970s. While several of Colombia's indicators were distinctly better than Peru's (particularly infant mortality and illiteracy), the personal income distribution was rather similar, and extremely unequal, and certain *urban* indicators suggested more poverty for Colombia (urban men were more illiterate than Peruvian men, urban income distribution was slightly more unequal, more urban households were unable to meet minimum consumption needs).

We have now seen that through the following seventeen years Colombia experienced far more growth in income per capita, achieved by *consistency* rather than by notably high rates in particular years. How far was this spread through the population? Throughout these years there was considerable official *concern* for welfare and poverty issues. We first look briefly at welfare policies, before attempting to evaluate results.

The data on public sector spending in the social sectors are given in Table 10.1. Colombia has consistently spent more than Peru, despite her smaller state, though in education alone Peru has spent more. The level of spending has varied with the administration, the López government spending least, though figures are not yet available to see the effect of recession on the Betancur record. The Colombian 'style' has typically taken the form of a strong personal commitment of the President to a poverty programme, with the emphasis varying since each administration must have its distinctive mark. The Lleras period was the exception in not having a programme, though the administrative reforms carried out did much to make possible what came later.[20] Pastrana chose construction and employment as the foci of his policy, but also expanded education and health.[21] The López presidency saw two important initiatives with the Integrated Rural Development Plan (DRI) and the Food Nutrition Programme (PAN). With the ending of some foreign-funded programmes, fresh expenditure took time to get

Table 10.1a
Colombia and Peru: Public Investment in Social Sectors[a] as Percentage GDP
1970–86

	Colombia	Peru
1970	0.85	n.a.
1975	0.87	0.4
1980	1.1	0.5
1983	0.89	0.4
1984	n.a.	0.3
1985	n.a.	0.4
1986	n.a.	0.5

Table 10.1b
Colombia and Peru: Total[b] Government Spending in Social Sectors[a] 1970–84
(as percentage of government spending)

	Colombia	Peru
1970	6.6	4.6
1975	6.9	5.0
1980	7.7	4.7
1983	7.5	3.9
1984	7.5	3.5

[a] Social sectors = education, health, housing and labour.
[b] The Peruvian data are for Central Government only, but local government spending up to 1986 was very small indeed. This could not account for the difference.
Sources: Peru: Banco de la Republica, *Memoria*
Colombia: DANE, *El Sector Publico Colombiano*, 1940–81.

going and some of the benefit was only felt in the Turbay period. The latter's policy was strongly infrastructure-based, using the rather abundant resources of those years and with much participation of the World Bank. The Betancur programme, 'Change with Equity', focused on housing; an extraordinary quantity of houses was built but social organisation was neglected. The Barco administration saw the most sophisticated programme, his 'fight against absolute poverty', the problems of which we return to in the concluding section.

While all these (except possibly the last) were paternalistic in nature, the other actor on the scene was not. The Coffee Federation had through all this period an active programme of schools and health care and in the case of schools required local participation. The agreement with the state was that the latter would staff schools or supply equipment to hospitals once constructed, so there has been also a 'leverage' effect (recently, fiscal problems have in fact meant hospitals going unused).[22]

The 'coffee factor' immediately highlights the difficulty of making sense of a comparative analysis in this area, since we have repeatedly argued that Peru has no equivalent social or economic force. In other words not only is policy different, but it is different in part precisely because the underlying parameters are different. In Peru, the Velasco regime provided a discontinuity in welfare and basic needs aspects as in so much else. As explained in Chapter 4, the extensive redistributionist policies were in fact limited in their direct effect – but the accompanying creation of 'agents of change' such as SINAMOS began a process of change the results of which are only slowly being felt today. Programmes and projects that were very progressive in terms of the concepts used, of social participation and organisation, had hardly had time to get going when with economic crisis and a new regime the context changed. The enthusiastic social reformers of the Velasco era typically moved out of the state to create one of the innumerable 'centros' or non-governmental organisations which exist today in Peru, with foreign funding and with varying levels of expenditure. Meanwhile both resources and increasingly commitment were lacking within the state. This changed radically with García to meet head-on the problem of how to execute good intentions faced with a technically impoverished state and highly clientelistic party. We return to the issue of the obstacles to 'better' basic needs policy in our final section below. First, let us consider the results of policy.

The basic needs record is shown in Table 10.2. Perhaps the most impressive aspect of the table is the similarity of the gains given the dissimilarity of the growth experience. The fall in infant mortality in Peru is 30 per cent and in illiteracy 40 per cent, while Colombia improved less in both indicators (reasonably enough given the room for improvement in the case of Peru). The regional figures for Peru show that the improvement was rather uniform across the country. The fall in the Colombian figures for access to piped water and sewerage is too great to be credible – but again the balance of this kind of evidence is that there is no case for concluding that Colombia's improvement was greater than Peru's. A study giving a world ranking of 'physical quality of life indicators' summarises the contrast by showing that between 1960 and 1980, Peru lost 12 places on GDP per capita but only 3 on the quality of life, while Colombia lost one place in GDP and held her own in quality of life.[23]

Another approach to basic needs is to consider the minimum income required to satisfy a basic basket of consumption needs and to estimate the number of families falling below this poverty line. A CEPAL study

Table 10.2
Colombia and Peru: Welfare Indicators 1970–80

	Around 1970	Around 1980–82
Relative availability of calories		
Peru	96% (1969–71)	93% (1979–81)
Colombia	92% (1969–71)	108% (1979–81)
Per cent illiterate		
Peru	28 (1972)	17 (1981)
Colombia	19 (1973)	15 (1981)
Enrolment rate ages 6–11		
Peru	79% (1970)	84% (1980)
Colombia	62% (1970)	70% (1980)
Infant mortality per 1 000 (0–1 years)		
Peru	133 (1965–70)	82 (1980–85)
Colombia	74 (1965–70)	53 (1980–85)
Life expectancy at birth		
Peru	52 (1965–70)	59 (1980–85)
Colombia	58 (1965–70)	64 (1980–85)
Urban population with sewers		
Peru	62 (1969)	55 (1979)
Colombia	72 (1969)	68 (1979)
Population with access to piped water		
Peru urban	69% (1969)	79% (1979)
Colombia urban	98% (1969)	86% (1979)
Peru rural	8% (1969)	13% (1979)
Colombia rural	48% (1969)	23% (1979)

Source: WHO, UNESCO, FAO Yearbooks, CEPAL, *Statistical Yearbook for Latin America and the Caribbean.*

gives us a comparison of 1970 with 1981: Peru, it is estimated, improved her figures by one percentage point, Colombia by two – and both remained below the continental average.[24]

Child malnutrition is a further indicator that should be helpful. Unfortunately we meet here problems of comparability, since as we explained in Chapter 3 different studies use different criteria. The strongest conclusion we can draw at present is that child malnutrition has fallen somewhat in Colombia, while it has probably risen in Peru. In Colombia the only comparable studies show a fall from 24 per cent of children malnourished in 1965–66 to 19 per cent in 1977–80.[25] In Peru the studies are not comparable, but whereas Peru's figure in the early 1970s was of the same order of magnitude as Colombia, by 1984 on the WHO

Table 10.3
Peru: Household Income Data

	DECILES					GINI
	1 &2	1 to 5	3 to 5	6 to 8	9 & 10	
PERU						
Lima Metropolitana						
1971–72[a]	5.5	21.1	15.6	29.1	49.9	0.43
1985–86[b]	3.8	20.7	16.9	30.1	49.2	0.49
Urban Areas						
1971–72[a]						
Major cities	3.7	18.6	14.9	33.4	48.0	0.46
Other urban	2.6	15.6	13.0	31.0	53.4	0.49
1985–86[b]	3.8	19.7	15.8	30.1	50.2	0.46
Rural Areas						
1971–72[a]	1.7	10.8	9.1	25.8	63.4	0.56
1985–86[b]	4.4	20.3	16.0	30.0	49.9	0.41
All Peru						
1971–72[a]	1.4	10.7	9.3	28.4	60.9	0.55
1985–86[b]	3.1	17.6	14.5	28.3	54.0	0.49

Notes
[a] Refers to households; data taken from Amat and Leon (1981).
[b] Refers to households; data taken from *Encuesta Nacional de Hogares Sobre Medición de Niveles de Vida* (1985–1986), INE, April 1988.

criterion Peru had 37 per cent while Colombia was less than 20 per cent. This is consistent with the significant fall in the birth rate in Colombia, which would tend to reduce the incidence of malnutrition among children.

The most difficult evidence of all to handle is the behaviour of global income distribution. The problems are the obvious ones which are discussed in Chapter 3: unreliable data, variable coverage, variations in the bias depending on how far elements such as income from capital and income in kind are guessed at or simply omitted. As we move now to compare trends over time we have the further problem of ephemeral or 'conjunctural' factors versus long-run trends. This is a problem for both countries but affects particularly Peru. As will be seen in Table 10.3, the only years for which we have solid household surveys of comparable national coverage are 1971/2 and 1985/6.[26] At first sight the results are rather striking. While income distribution in Lima seems to have worsened, in rural areas it improved and the global Gini fell six points. However, as Chapter 6 made clear the years 1985–86 are exceptional and

Table 10.4
Colombia and Peru: Real GDP and Apparent Food Consumption Per Capita
1950–84 Annual Averages
(Indices: 1965–69 = 100)

	PERU		COLOMBIA	
	Real GDP	Apparent Food Consumption (Per Capita)	Real GDP	Apparent Food Consumption (Per Capita)
1950–54	66.9	92.4	50.0	105.3
1955–59	75.0	84.4	62.6	103.0
1960–64	88.7	87.9	78.7	102.7
1965–69	100.0	100.0	100.0	100.0
1970–74	109.1	102.1	139.1	100.3
1975–79	112.3	98.0	178.6	111.7
1980–84	105.1	97.4	216.1	122.3

Source: Own estimates from national data.

likely to fall outside any long-run trend, since, particularly in 1986, there was a strong and probably short-lived redistribution to the rural population and to wages. It is therefore difficult to conclude anything from Table 10.3. Webb's preliminary evaluation, based in addition on earnings and data over time, is that 'the degree of inequality has not diminished to any significant degree and in fact, it may have increased'.[27]

Turning to Colombia, the conjunctural factors are less strong but still intervene. The data have been thoroughly analysed by the leading expert on Colombian income distribution, Miguel Urrutia, who published in 1985 his estimates for the 1970s (Urrutia, 1985). Briefly, he argues that income distribution did not worsen in the 1970s, and may even have improved, both the rich and the poor gaining at the expense of the middle strata (largely formal sector wage and salary earners). This was the product however of a *worsening* in the first half of the decade, followed by an improvement in the second half. But here we enter again into the question of what is trend. While Urrutia refers to the first years as an aberration,[28] unfortunately it is the forces leading to the improvement in the second half that would appear to be temporary and abnormal. The key factor was the coffee boom, aided by drugs. As I have shown in an earlier chapter, the degree to which the coffee boom was allowed to percolate through to the grassroots is now generally considered to have been an error, carefully not repeated in the following boom. Also, the intense demand for labour during the boom was related to the switch to 'caturra' coffee with the *transient* labour need implicit in new planting and land preparation: this was abnormal and a once-for-all effect. Further, the drugs boom of the late 1970s was in marijuana – grown in Colombia, with good employment effects. This has now been replaced by cocaine, not produced in Colombia and yielding a different and far more concentrated income structure. It would therefore be dangerous to conclude that the improvement of the late 1970s reflected a process that will be sustained so as to affect underlying trends in basic needs variables in a major way.

The overall picture that emerges is one of disappointing progress in the case of Colombia, while not all Peru's indicators are quite as weak as we might have expected. This is consistent with one final piece of evidence: the movement of food consumption over time compared to real income (shown in Table 10.4). A 'normal' income elasticity of demand for food at low levels of income being about 0.7, if relative prices do not change strongly one can expect food consumption per capita to rise at at least half the rate of GDP per capita, if the increase is evenly spread. The fact that the increase is negative in Peru and far below the increase in GDP for Colombia, again suggests that in *neither* case can we be sanguine about the degree to which the poor are benefitting proportionately. The Peruvian record is consistent with the decline in availability of calories shown in Table 10.2.

Two major contrasting causal factors have emerged from the analysis of the welfare record. The first is the outstanding one and emerges from the discussion of education in an earlier chapter: the relative desire and freedom of Colombian women to pursue schooling. We have seen that this one difference explains most of the better record of Colombia in education, and in its turn goes far to explain differences in population growth rates and infant mortality. The reasons for this contrast go far beyond the factors explored in this study and remain a challenge to research. The second and less important factor is the role of coffee, which did not produce better income distribution, contrary to the expectations of many analysts, but did lead to relatively better rural social infrastructure and thereby some further explanation of better basic needs indicators.[29]

Urban poverty however was worse than Peru's at the start of our period, and is not radically better today despite better growth. The *basic* conclusion is that neither country has yet gone very far in attacking its poverty problem. Unfortunately, once we reflect on the political economy of 'the fight against poverty', it is all too easy to understand why so little progress is observed.

Our discussion of 'policy competence' in the first half of this chapter led us to reflect that Colombia's notable success in management – the comparative factor the preceding chapters had put most weight on – was indeed important but was limited to those areas where the clear interests of the dominant groups dictated coherence and collaboration and where structural pressures did not undermine this. We took public investment as an example where structural pressures, inertia and the limited avail-ability of competent and committed technocrats did undermine coher-ence. Reflecting on the political economy of social policy simply deepens this point. At any moment forces parallel to those we have described in the broader field of public investment may curtail progress – *corto placismo* and inertia affect this type of project of course too. Social expenditure is clearly extremely vulnerable to sheer shortage of cash. An obvious and fundamental obstacle may be lack of political will and more subtly, of 'inappropriate' political will, so that paternalism and/or clientelism distort what is done. But both our case studies illustrate with their most recent experiences – in a remarkably parallel way – a further 'level' of obstacle. An expert closely involved in Barco's programme agrees, based on detailed personal experience, that the political will, the cash and even a healthy policy design were there.[30] But those in charge of the programme then faced the problem of 'inertia' in a further sense: bureaucrats who preferred not to be bothered with the difficult task of getting money through to poor municipalities without the capacity to cope with forms and regulations and administration of money. At the end of the day the quality of institutions, the inherited attitudes and levels of motivation are all fundamental. It would have taken an extraordinary degree of leadership to transform attitudes and control clientelism, by now a major problem.[31] Similarly, SENA was to be the vehicle which capacitated the community to organise itself – but SENA is a tripartite organisation of government, employers and workers, and neither of the two latter were willing to back the proposed shift of emphasis to a 'social' rather than 'technical' role.[32] Again, only very strong leadership could have won trust and conveyed the right message.

With García in Peru, suddenly the motivation and political will did seem to be present – and there was a conviction that financial constraints were for the time at least not binding. Yet the successes were not impressive, and the example illuminates still further the constraints. There was leadership, too – at one level – but what was required was the translation of that into a mass of small teams of motivated people – with enough training to consolidate their motivation. Instead, the minimum employment programme, for example, had to be suspended after nine months because the clientelism had become so blatant. No one could even begin to imagine how to put together teams to implement an integrated rural development effort – with the result that the ample supply of rural credit often failed in its purpose.

Conclusion

The findings of this final chapter have radically shifted the balance of our appraisal of our two case studies. At the end of the previous chapter we were already beginning to modify the rather optimistic view of Colombia emerging from our initial concentration on short-term management. This good management, we have argued, has been tightly related to coffee and to the extensive institutional development around it, and the shifting composition of exports will require deliberate institutional development. The new pressures on food supplies, the need to move against drugs in a way that must affect drug income and the pressures for regional development and autonomy must all greatly complicate the macro management problems for the 1990s.

This chapter has added two fundamental themes, if in a speculative fashion, since each requires several research projects to generate firm conclusions.

First, it has attempted to explore what lies behind relative 'good' and 'bad' management. The significance of the historical and structural roots of the functioning of the two political economies cannot be overstressed. It is this which makes clear the importance of the inverted commas around 'good' and 'bad': we are not talking here of relative virtue, but of the way in which long-run trends emerging from factors such as geography, resource endowment, and political and social structure result in institutions and the articulation of interests so as to lead, or fail to lead, to coherent policy.

This has led us to a conclusion that is important in terms of current debates in Peru on the relative roles of the market and the state: what we observe in Colombia is successful intervention in and manipulation of the market, not in any sense the success of pure market forces.

The second strong conclusion of this chapter has been that whatever the relative efficacy of short-term policy management, the same efficacy has not extended to the area of welfare and basic needs. Although it would be hard to claim that Colombia's record has been as bad as Peru's, it is equally hard to prove it has been substantially better – and this is not surprising, given the lack of strong political backing for such a project. Ironically, Peru's greater development of popular organisations could in principle in the long run provide a better basis for such a project. This would require political and institutional development, however – for it is one of the most basic messages of this comparative case study that development policies require effective institutions as well as political will.

Notes

1. Interview, Gabriel Seminario, Lima, May 1987.
2. See Durand (1982), ch. 3.
3. Interview, Flavio Gerbolini, Lima, May 1987.
4. The contrast with Colombia is identified by a Peruvian businessman with the following story: – He went to Colombia on business in the late 1960s. He happened to turn on the radio, in the middle of someone talking on the problems of industry in Colombia. The speech showed remarkable insight into the sector's situation: he decided it must be the president of the Society of Industrialists speaking. It was of course the country's President. 'Never in Peru would you have that experience', is his conclusion. (Interview, Flavio Gerbolini, Lima, May 1987.)
5. Interview with a leading industrialist, Juan Francisco Raffo, Lima, May 1987.
6. Interview with Fabio Echeverri, President of ANDI, Bogotá, July 1987.
7. 'Everyone in Colombia – except possibly Carlos Lleras Restrepo – has a foreign bank account' is a typical response on the issue of capital export. But this is on the whole a means of keeping the freedom to do what one wants to do – e.g. educate one's children abroad – rather than a speculative activity or a response to lack of confidence in internal conditions.
8. Rodrigo Llorente tells how a Frenchman looking at his CV exclaimed in horror at the number of moves. When he recounted the story to President Alberto Lleras, Lleras explained 'the bottle theory'. In most countries, one can think of a particular career as a bottle, with many insiders fighting to make it to the top of the narrow neck and few succeeding. Colombia has discovered that one advances much better by jumping from bottle to bottle. (Interview, Rodrigo Llorente, Bogotá, 1987).
9. This interpretation is that of José Antonio Ocampo, the Colombian scholar who has most closely studied both the history of the coffee sector and the contemporary policy-making process.
10. The material for this section comes from interviews conducted in Lima in May and in Bogotá in July 1987, and from my own experience as an advisor in the Institute of Planning in Lima.
11. The figure in the National Plan 1985–90 is 75 per cent.
12. A controversial report of the World Bank on public investment in Peru has risked having its valuable points ignored because of the anger it aroused. One of its most valuable criticisms was to point out the lack of maintenance. Maintenance has been 'cut to the point where the ultimate project benefits have often been sacrificed' (IBRD, 1987).
13. A classic example of the system at its most perverse is the Tinajones irrigation project in the 1970s. The increased supply of water with the reservoir, plus the coincidence of several years of good rains 1970–76, led to the abandonment of maintenance and good conservation practices – with the result that waste and salinity had recreated a water shortage by the 1980s – and today there is pressure for the second stage of the project, to accommodate this need.
14. Such agencies are under understandable pressure to spend their budget, and their bureaucracies make it extraordinarily difficult to spend fast or flexibly. There is also no doubt an instinct to have confidence in international suppliers and known technology.

15. Interview with Carlos Otero, Lima, May 1987.
16. A review of all World Bank and IADB projects was concluded in early 1987. It recommended the outright cancellation of only one project – Pichis. It is illuminating that political pressures appear to have secured the continuance of the project. (Interview with Alejandro Seminario, Lima, May 1987.)
17. This was the general view – and explicitly the view of the Head of one of the organisations responsible for a large portion of public investment.
18. To obtain an import permit, you must show there is no local supplier. But of what? For example, one application showed no local production of electric trains, when what they wanted to import were not trains but components for assembly – some of which of course were locally available.
19. Interview, Gabriel Turbay, Director of FEN, Bogotá, July 1987.
20. For example, giving substance to institutions like SENA and ICBF. The most negative, long-run aspect of the Lleras period from the point of view of welfare was probably the erosion of regional autonomy.
21. Desertion rates fell strongly during the Pastrana years to stay rather steady thereafter (data from DANE bulletins and UNESCO). (The desertion ratio compares those who drop out during the school year to the initial enrollment.)
22. Interview with Alvaro Rodriguez and Gonzalo Paredes, Federación Nacional de Cafeteros Colombianos, March 1988.
23. Nissan and Caveney (1988).
24. Molina (1982).
25. Pavillon *et al.* (1987), DANE (1988).
26. A study is at present under way which is making an in-depth evaluation of the degree of technical comparability. This will be extremely important in taking this analysis forward. The study is being carried out by Richard Webb with a team from the World Bank.
27. Webb, unpublished ms., Lima 1988. I am extremely grateful for his generous sharing of this work.
28. '... poverty increased temporarily ...' (p. 114).
29. Unfortunately the relatively great regional autonomy to which coffee historically gave rise was steadily eroded through the period we are considering here (though recent reforms are trying to reverse it). As violence and social conflict erode 'quality of life' indicators in both countries, *regional* policy incorporating rather fundamental attention to distribution should be at the centre of the policy agenda.
30. This section is based on a thought provoking interview with Ulpiano Ayala, who was an advisor in Barco's poverty programme.
31. At least the National Front kept a measure of control on clientelism – and Betancur's leadership was stronger than Barco's.
32. The workers feared co-optation.

References

Actualidad Económica, Lima, monthly.
AGUILAR, LUIS I., and PERFETTI, J., (1987), "Distribución del Ingreso y sus Determinantes en el Sector Rural Colombiano" in Fedesarrollo, *Coyuntura Económica*, Vol. XVII, No. 1, April.
ALARCO, German (1984), "Es Inflacionario el Déficit Fiscal?", Universidad del Pacifico, Serie Discusiones Programáticas, Documento No. 7, Lima.
—— (1987), "Elementos Críticos de la Nueva Política Económica", in *Reactivación y Política Económica Heterodoxa 1985–1986*, Lima.
Alerta Económica, Ministerio de Economía y Finanzas, Lima, monthly.
AMAT Y LEON, C. (1981a), *La Desigualdad Interior en el Perú*, Centro de Investigaciones de la Universidad del Pacifico, Lima.
—— (1981b), *Distribución del Ingreso Familiar en el Perú*, Centro de Investigaciones de la Universidad del Pacifico, Lima.
—— and LEON, H. (1983), "Niveles de Vida y Grupos Sociales en el Perú", Lima, Fundación F. Ebert – CIUP.
Andean Report, monthly, Lima.
ANGELL, A. and THORP, R. (1980), "Inflation, Stabilization and Attempted Democratization in Peru, 1975–1979", *World Development*, Vol. 8, No. 11, November.
ARANGO, Mariano (1977), *Café e Industria 1850–1930*, Carlos Valencia, ed., Bogotá.
—— (1982), *El Café en Colombia 1930–1958: producción, acumulación y politica*, Carlos Valencia, ed., Bogotá.
AYALA, M. and UGARTECHE, O. (1975), "International Comparative Analysis of Financial Markets in Colombia and Peru", MS, London, Graduate School of Business Studies, London.
BCRP, (Banco Central de la Reserva del Peru), *Boletin*, Lima, monthly.
——, *Cuentas Nacionales de Perú*, Lima, Annual.
——, *Memoria*, Lima, annual.
——, *Nota Semanal*, Lima.
——, *Reseña Económica*, Lima, monthly.
—— (1983), *El Proceso de Liberación de las Importaciones: Perú 1979–82*, Lima, May, 1983.
Banco de la República, *Revista*, monthly, Bogotá.
——, *Informe del Gerente*, annual, Bogotá.
—— (1987), *Colombia: 20 anos del Regimen de Cambios y de Comercio Exterior*, Bogotá.
BELL, P. L. (1921), *Colombia: A Commercial and Industrial Handbook*, Washington, D.C.
BERGQUIST, C. (1973), *Coffee and Conflict in Colombia 1886–1904*, Stanford University Press, Stanford.
—— (1986), *Labor in Latin America: Comparative Essays on Chile, Argentina, Venezuela and Colombia*, Stanford University Press, Stanford.
BERRY, A. and THOUMI, F. (1985), "Colombian Economic Growth and Policies 1970–1984", mimeo.

BERTRAM, G. (1974), "Development Problems in an Export Economy: A Study of Domestic Capitalist, Foreign Firms and Government in Peru 1919–1930", D.Phil. thesis, Oxford University, Oxford.

—— (1974a), "Entry of the Cerro de Pasco Mining Company to Peru", Oxford University MS, Oxford.

BEYER, Robert (1947), "The Colombian Coffee Industry: Origins and Major Trends 1740–1940," thesis, University of Minnesota.

BIRD, R. and WIESNER, E. (1982), "Finanzas Intergubernamentales en Colombia", Informe Final de la Misión de Finanzas Intergubernamentales, DNP, Bogotá.

BLEJER, Mario and GARCÍA, Jorge (1985), "The Timing and Sequencing of a Trade Liberalisation Policy: Colombia", World Bank Working Papers, Washington, D.C.

Boletín de Agricultura, Colombia, Ministerio de Industrias, Bogotá, 1927–1945.

Boletín de Comercio e Industria, Colombia, Ministerio de Industrias, Bogotá.

BOLLINGER, W. A. (1971), "The Rise of US Influence in the Peruvian Economy 1869–1921", M.A. thesis, UCLA.

BOLOÑA, C. (1980), "Free trade and protection in Peru, 1840–1980", D.Phil thesis, Bodleian Library, Oxford University, Oxford.

BOURRICAUT, F. (1970), *Power and Society in Contemporary Peru*, Faber and Faber, London.

CABALLERO, J. M. (1976), "Agrarian Reform and the Transformation of the Peruvian Countryside", MS, Cambridge University, Cambridge.

CÁCERES, A. (1989), *El Ajuste Forzado: La economía Peruana durante 1988*, Fundación F. Ebert, Lima.

CAPUÑAY, M. (1951), *Leguía: Vida y Obra del Coustructor del Gran Perú*, Imprenta Bustamante, Lima.

CARRIZOSA, Mauricio (1985), "Las Tasas de Interés y el Ahorro Financiero en Colombia", in *Revista Banca y Finanzas*, No. 189, ASOBANCARIA, Bogotá.

CEPAL (1957), *Analisis y Proyecciones del Desarrollo Económico: El Desarrollo Económico de Colombia*, Anexo, Mexico.

—— (1983), *El Financiamiento de la Exportaciones en América Latina*, Santiago.

CHU, David (1972), "The Great Depression and Industrialization in Latin America: Response to Relative Price Incentives in Argentina and Colombia, 1930–1945", Ph.D. thesis, Yale University, New Haven.

—— (1977), "The Great Depression and Industrialisation in Colombia", The Rand Paper Series, Santa Monica.

CHUDNOVSKY, Daniel (1974), *Empresas Multinacionales y Ganancias Monopólicas en una Economía Latinoamericana*, Siglo XXI, Editores, Buenos Aires.

COLLINS, C. D. (1987), "Local Government and its Reform in Colombia between 1974 and 1986", D. Phil. thesis, Birmingham University, Birmingham.

—— (1989), "The Rise and Fall of the National Decentralized Agencies in Colombia", in *Public Administration and Development*, Vol. 9.

CONASEV (1982–84), *Indicadores Financieros Empresariales*, annual, Lima.

Contraloría General de la República, *Boletín de la Contraloría*, monthly, Bogotá.

COTLEAR, D. (1986), "Technological and Institutional Change among the Peruvian Peasantry", D. Phil. thesis, University of Oxford, Oxford.

COTLER, Julio (1978), *Clase, Estado y Nación en el Perú*, IEP, Lima.

DANE, (Departamento Administrativo Nacional de Estadística), *Boletín Mensual de Estadística* (BME), monthly, Bogotá.

———, "Situación Nutricional de los Niños Colombianos de 3 a 35 meses", in BME No. 424, July 1988.

———, *Colombia Estadística*, annual, Bogotá.

———, *El Sector Público Colombiano 1970–1981*, Bogotá.

—— (1985), *Cuentas Nacionales de Colombia 1970–1983*, Bogotá.

—— (1988), *Cuentas Nacionales de Colombia 1965–1986*, Bogotá.

D.N.P. (Departamento Nacional de Planeación), *Revista de Planeación y Desarrollo*, Bogotá.

DE SOTO, Hernando (1986), *El Otro Sendero: La Revolución Informal*, Editorial el Barranco, Lima.

DEVLIN, R. (1980), "Los Bancos Transnacionales y el Financiamiento Externo de América Latina: La experiencia del Peru 1965–1976", CEPAL, Santiago de Chile.

DIAZ-ALEJANDRO, Carlos (1976), *Foreign Trade Regimes and Economic Development: Colombia*, Columbia University Press, New York.

Dirección Nacional de Estadística, *Extracto Estadístico del Perú*, 1918–1943; subsequently *Anuario Estadístico de Perú*, Lima.

DUNKERLEY, H. (1968), "Exchange Rate Systems in Conditions of Continuing Inflation. Lessons from the Colombian experience", in G. Papanek (ed.), *Development Policy: Theory and Practice*, Harvard University Press, Cambridge, Mass.

DURAND, F. (1982), *La Década Frustrada: Los Industriales y el Poder 1970–1980*, DESCO, Lima.

Equus, Lima, weekly.

ECHAVARRIA, Juan J. (1981), "The History of Colombian Foreign Debt", unpublished MS, Oxford.

—— (1987), "Colombia 1970–1985": Management and Consequences of Two Large External Shocks", Working Paper No. 20, Overseas Development Institute, London.

Economía (1989), "Opciones de Politica Económica en el Perú Actual", special issue, June 1989, Universidad Católica, Lima.

Econometría LTDA (1985), *Plataforma Metalmecánica*, Fedemetal, Bogotá.

ECLA, (Economic Commission for Latin America), *Statistical Yearbook for Latin America and the Caribbean*, Santiago de Chile, annual.

ENCA (Encuesta Nacional de Consumo Alimenticio) (1984), Instituto Nacional de Estadística y Ministerio de Agricultura, Lima.

ESPINOSA, Abdon (1970), *Memorias de Hacienda 1966–1970*, Bogotá, Ministerio de Hacienda, Bogotá.

FALCONI, C. (1983), "Efectos de la Apertura al Exterior sobre el Sector Industrial del Perú 1978–1981", mimeo, Universidad del Pacífico, Lima.

FAO, *Production and Trade Yearbook*, Rome.

Federación Nacional de Cafeteros de Colombia (FNCC) (1987), *Los Propósitos de la Industria Cafetera Colombiana, 1850–1986*, Bogotá.

—— (1979), *Economía Cafetera Colombiana*, Fondo Cultural Cafetero, Bogotá.

Fedesarrollo (1987), "Finanzas Públicas, 1950–1984: Tendencias y sensibilidad al Ciclo Externo", mimeo, Bogotá.
——, *Coyuntura Económica*, quarterly, Bogotá.
FERNANDEZ, H. (1985), *Aspectos Sociales y Económicos de la Educación en el Perú*, AMIDEP, Lima, July.
FERNER, A. (1975), "The Evolution of the Peruvian Industrial Bourgeoisie", MS, ESAN, Lima.
—— (1983), "The Industrialists and the Peruvian Development Model", in S. Booth and B. Sorj (eds) *Military Reformism and Social Classes: The Peruvian Experience*, Macmillan, London.
FERRERO, R. (1946), *La Política Fiscal y la Economía Nacional*, editorial Lumen, Lima.
FIGUEROA, A. (1981), *La Economía Campesina de la Sierra del Perú*, Lima.
Financial Times, London.
FITZGERALD, E. V. K. (1976), "The State and Economic Development: Peru Since 1968," Department of Applied Economics, Occasional Paper No. 49, Cambridge University Press, Cambridge.
—— (1976a), "Some Aspects of Industrialisation in Peru, 1965–75, Cambridge University, Latin American Center, Working Paper No. 22, Cambridge.
—— (1979), The Political Economy of Peru, 1956–78: Economic Development and the Restructuring of Capital, Cambridge University Press, Cambridge.
Foreign Office (FO), UK government papers available in Public Records Office, London.
GARAY, L. J. (1984), "El Proceso de Endeudamiento Externo Colombiano" in *Controversía*, October 1984, Bogotá.
GARCÍA, Antonio (1937), *Geografía Económica de Caldas*, Contraloría General de la República, Bogotá.
GARCÍA García, Jorge (1987), "Macroeconomic Policies and Growth in the Long Run: the Case of Colombia", mimeo, Bogotá, May 1987.
—— (1986), The Timing and Sequency of a Trade Liberalization Policy: Colombia 1967–1982", mimeo, World Bank.
GARLAND Duponte, A. (n.d.), *Lo que el Oncenio hizó por el Perú bajo el mando del Presidente Leguia*, Imprenta Gil, Lima.
GÓMEZ, Hernando J. (1988), "La Economía Ilegal en Colombia: Tamaño, Evolución, Características e Impacto Económico", in Fedeserrallo, *Coyuntura Económica*, Vol. XVIII, No. 3, September.
GRIFFITH-JONES, S. and SUNKEL, O. (1986), *Debt and Development: The End of an Illusion*, Oxford University Press, Oxford.
HARDING, C. (1975), "Land Reform and Social Conflict in Peru", in A. Lowenthal (ed.), *The Peruvian Experiment: Continuity and Change under Military Rule*, Princeton University Press, Princeton, NJ.
HIRSCHMAN, A. O. (1968), *Journeys Toward Progress*, Greenwood Press, New York.
HOPKINS, R., Ph.D. thesis in progress, Queen Mary College, London (to be completed in 1992).
HORTON, D. (1974), "Land Reform and Reform Enterprises in Peru", Report submitted to the Land Tenure Centre and the IBRD, Wisconsin, Land Tenure Centre.

HUNT, S. J. (1973), *Price and Quantum Estimates of Peruvian Exports, 1830–1962* (Princeton University: Woodrow Wilson School Research Program in Economic Development, Discussion Paper No. 33).

INE (Instituto Nacional de Estadística), *Compendio Estadístico*, Lima, annual.

——, *Boletin de Estadística Peruana*, Lima.

INE/PNUD (1988), *Pobreza Crítica en el Perú*, Lima.

Instituto Nacional de Planificación (1971), *Plan del Perú: Plan Nacional de Desarrollo para 1971–1975*, Vol. I, Plan Global, Presidencia de la República, Lima.

Instituto Peruano de Administración de Empresas (1988), *Estadísticas para CADE '88*, Cuanto, Lima.

IBRD (International Bank for Reconstruction and Development) (1987), "Policy and the Public Sector in Peru", mimeo, Washington, D.C.

IMF (International Monetary Fund) (1984), *Request for a Standby Arrangement*, Western Hemisphere Department IMF, Washington, D.C.

—— (1982), "Report on the Economy of Peru", mimeo, Washington, D.C.

—— (1977), "Peru – Recent Economic Developments", mimeo, Washington, D.C.

——, *International Financial Statistics* (IFS), Washington, D.C., monthly.

JARAMILLO, J. C. (1982), "La Liberación del Mercado Financiero", in *Ensayos sobre Política Económica*, March.

JARAMILLO, OCAMPO, H. (1980), *1946–1950: de la Unidad Nacional a la Hegemonía Conservadora*, Editorial Pluma, Bogotá.

JIMENEZ, F. (1989), *Economía Peruana: Limites Internos y Externos al Crecimiento*, Fundación F. Ebert, Lima.

JUNGUITO, R. and CABALLERO, C. (1982), "Illegal Trade Transactions and the Underground Economy in Colombia", in V. Tanzi (ed.), *The Underground Economy in the United States and Abroad*, Lexington Books.

—— (1986), *Memoria del Ministro de Hacienda 1984–85*, Banco de la República, Bogotá.

—— (1980), "Precios Agricolas, Producción y Asignación de Recursos: La Experiencia Colombiana", in Fedeserrallo, *Coyuntura Económica*, Vol. X, No. 1, March.

KAMAS, Linda (1986), "Dutch Disease Economics and the Colombian Export Boom", in *World Development*, Vol. 14, No. 9.

KLINE, H. F. (1987), *The Coal of El Correjón*, Penn State Press, University Park and London.

KOFFMAN, Bennett E. (1969), "The National Federation of Coffee Growers of Colombia", Ph.D. thesis, University of Virginia.

LABARTHE, P. A. (1933), *La Política de Obras Públicas del Gobierno de Leguia*, Imprenta Americana, Lima.

LAJO, M. (1983), *Alternativa Agraria y Alimentaria: Diagnóstico y Propuesta para el Perú*, CIPCA, Lima.

Latin America Bureau (LAB) (1984), *Peru: Paths to Poverty*, London.

Latin America Economic Report, London, weekly.

Latin America Political Report, London, weekly.

Latin America Regional Report (LARR), Andean Group Report (several issues a year).

LEDGARD, Carlos (1932), in *West Coast Leader* 26–I–32, Lima, Imprenta Americana.

LLERAS RESTREPO, Carlos (1970), *Mensaje Presidencial*, Tomo IV, Bogotá.

—— (1981). *Economía Internacional y Regimen Cambiario*, Bogotá.

LÓPEZ, Hugo (1973), *Estudio sobre la Inflación en Colombia en el periodo de los años 20*, Universidad de Antioquia, Medellín.

LÓPEZ MEJÍA, Alejandro, "Las minidevaluaciones en Colombia: un largo período de busqueda de una tasa de cambio libre pero intervenida", in Banco de la República (ed.), *Colombia: 20 años del regimen de cambios y de comercio exterior*, Vol. 2, Bogotá, 1987.

LORA, Eduardo (1989), "Coffee and Oil Shocks in the Short and Long Run: An Application of Alternative CGE Models for Colombia", mimeo, Fedesarrollo.

LOVE, J. and JACOBSEN, N. (1988), *Guiding the Invisible Hand: Economic Liberalism and the State in Latin American History*, New York.

MACARIO, S. (1964), "Protectionism and Industrialisation in Latin America", in *Economic Bulletin for Latin America*, Vol. IX, No. 1.

MARTÍNEZ ORTIZ, A. (1986), *La Estructura Arancelaria las Estrategias de Industrialización en Colombia 1950–1982*, Universidad Nacional, Bogotá.

MAULLIN, Richard (1967), "The Colombia–IMF Disagreement of November–December 1966: An Interpretation of its Place in Colombian Politics", The Rand Corporation, Santa Monica, June 1967.

McGREEVEY, William P. (1971), *An Economic History of Colombia 1845–1930*, Cambridge University Press, Cambridge.

Ministerio de Economía y Finanzas (MEF) (1978), *El problema de Caja de Petro–Peru en 1978*, Lima.

MOHAN, R. and SABOT, R. (1985), "Educational Expansion and the Inequality of Pay: Colombia 1973–1978", World Bank and Williams College.

MOLINA, Sergio (1982), "La Pobreza. Descripción y Analisis de Política para Superarla", in *Revista de la CEPAL*, No. 18, Santiago de Chile, December.

MONTENEGRO, Armando (1983), "La Crisis del Sector Financiero Colombiano", in *Ensayos Sobre Política Económica*, December 1983, Bogotá.

MONTENEGRO, Santiago (1989), "External Shocks and Macroeconomic Policy in a Small Open Economy", D.Phil. thesis, University of Oxford, Oxford.

MUSGRAVE, R. and GILLIS, M. (1971), *Fiscal Reform for Colombia*, International Tax Program, Harvard University Press, Cambridge, Mass.

NISSAN, E. and CAVENEY, R. (1988), "Relative Welfare Improvements of Low Income versus High Income Countries", *World Development*, May 1988.

NORMANO, A. (1931), *The Struggle for South America*, Boston.

OCAMPO, Jose A. and MONTENEGRO, S. (1984), Crisis mundial, protección u industrialización, *Ensayos sobre Historia Económica de Colombia*, CEREC, Bogotá.

—— (1984), *Colombia y la Economía Mundial 1830–1910*, Fedesarrollo, Siglo XXI editores, Bogotá.

—— (1984), "The Colombian Economy in the 1930s", in R. Thorp (ed.), *Latin America in the 1930s: The Role of the Periphery in the World Crisis*, Macmillan and St. Antony's College (UK), London, and St. Martins Press (USA).

OCAMPO, Jose A. and MONTENEGRO, S. (ed.) (1977), *Historia Económica de Colombia*, Fedesarrollo, Siglo XXI Editores, Bogotá.
—— (1987), "Crisis mundial y cambio estructural 1929–1945", in Ocampo (ed.), *Historia Económica de Colombia*, Fedesarrollo, Siglo XXI Editores, Bogotá.
—— (1987a), "Crisis and Economic Policy in Colombia, 1980–1985", in R. Thorp and L. Whitehead, *Latin American Debt and the Adjustment Crisis*, The Macmillan Press and St. Antony's College, London; Pittsburgh University Press, USA.
—— (1988), "Foreign Assistance and Economic Development in Colombia", mimeo, Fedesarrollo, Bogotá.
—— (1989), "Efectos de la liberación y del control de importaciones sobre la industria manufacturera", in Fedeserrallo, *Coyuntura Económica*, Vol. XIX, No. 1, March.
—— (1990), "The Transition from Primary Exports to Industrial Development in Colombia", paper prepared for the IDB project on the Comparative Economic Development of Latin America and Scandinavia, mimeo, Bogotá.
—— and LORA, E. (1987), *Colombia*, World Institute for Development Economics Research of the United Nations University (Stabilisation and Adjustment Policies and Programs: Country Studies).
—— (1988), *Colombia y la Deuda Externa*, Fedesarrollo–Tercer Mundo Editores, Bogotá.
—— and RAMIREZ, M. (ed.) (1987), *El Problema Laboral Colombiano: Informes de la Misión Chenery*, Contraloria General de la República, Bogotá.
OCHOA, Mario (1986), "Hambre y Desnutrición en Colombia", in A. Machado (ed.), *Problemas Agrarios Colombianos*, Siglo XXI Editores, Bogotá.
OQUIST, Paul (1980), *Violence, Conflict and Politics in Colombia*, Academic Press, New York.
OSPINA VÁSQUEZ, L. (1955), *Industria y Protección en Colombia*, Editorial Santa Fé, Bogotá (1974). Second edition, Editorial Oveja Negra, Bogotá.
PALACIOS, Hugo (1986), "Un Programa para Sembrar la Bonanza", Ministerio de Hacienda, Bogotá.
PALACIOS, Marco (1979), *El Café en Colombia 1850–1970*, Editorial Presencia, Bogotá.
PARRA, Rodrigo (1980), "La Educación en la Zona Cafetera Colombiana", in E. Reveiz (ed.), *La Cuestión Cafetera*, Universidad de los Andes, CEDE, Bogotá.
PAVILLÓN, C., DELGADO, E. KOOP-TOLEDO, J. B., LEONARD, F., ARAUJO, M., HARREL, M. and FRANKLIN, D. (1983), *Un Analisis de la Situación Alimentaria – Nutricional en el Perú*, Sigma-One Corporation, Raleigh, N. Carolina.
——, HARRELL, M., and FRANKLIN, R. L. (1987), *Nutritional Functional Classification Study of Peru: Who and Where are the Poor?*, Sigma-One Corporation, Raleigh, N. Carolina.
PECAUT, Daniel (1989), *Crónica de dos décadas de Política Colombiana 1968–1988*, Siglo XXI Editores, Bogotá.
PERRY, G. "Las Reformas Tributarias de 1974 y 1975", in Fedeserrallo, *Coyuntura Económica*, November 1977.

Perú Económico, monthly, Lima.
The Peru Report, Lima, monthly.
Peruvian Times, Lima.
PHILIP, G. D. E. (1975), "Policy-making in the Peruvian Oil Industry with Special Reference to the Period since 1968", D.Phil. thesis, Oxford University, Oxford.
—— (1978), *The Rise and Fall of the Peruvian Military Radicals 1968–1976*, University of London, Institute of Latin American Studies, Monograph No. 9, Athlone Press, London.
PIRANI (1977), "La Demanda por Importaciones", unpublished study, Banco Central, Lima.
PLATA, R. (1979), "Fading Out of Foreign Investment in the Colombian Economy", M.Phil. thesis, Oxford University, Oxford.
PUYANA, A. (1988), "El Narcotráfico y la Sociedad Colombiana", mimeo, CRESET, Bogotá.
QUIROZ, A. (1989), "Banqueros en Conflicto", CIUP, Universidad del Pacífico, Lima.
RANIS, G. and FEI, J. (1990), "The Political Economy of Development Policy Change", in G. Meier (ed.), *The New Political Economy and Development Policy-Making*, International Centre for Economic Growth, San Francisco.
REM, *Macroconsult*, Lima, quarterly.
REYES POSADA, A. (1986), "Tendencias del Empleo y la Distribución del Ingreso", Informe Final presentado a la Misión de Empleo, CCRP, May 1986, Bogotá.
REYNOLDS, C. (1977), "Social Reform and Foreign Debt: The Peruvian Dilemma", mimeo, memo to Wells Fargo Bank.
ROBERTS, B. (1978), "The Basis of Industrial Cooperation in Huancayo", in B. Roberts and N. Long, *Peasant Cooperation and Capitalist Expansion in Central Perú*, Austin, Texas.
ROSSINI, R. and THOMAS, J. J. (1987), "The Statistical Foundations of *El Otro Sendero*", World Development, February 1990. Published in Spanish by Fundación Ebert, Lima, 1988.
RUIZ, Hernando (1979), "Implicaciones Sociales y Económicas de la Producción de marihuana en Colombia", in *Marihuana: Legalización o Represión?*, Asociación Nacional de Instituciones Financieras "ANIF", Bogotá.
RUIZ, Hernando and LOPEZ, José Fernando (1981), Exportaciones Clandestinas, Economía Subterranea y las Perspectivas del Sector Externo", ANIF, *Carta Financiera*, No. 48, Enero–Marzo, pp. 15–53, Bogotá.
SAFFORD, Frank (1977), *Aspectos del siglo XIX en Colombia*, Ediciones Hombre Nuevo, Medellin.
SANDILANDS, R. (1976), "Indexing in Colombia, Brazil and Chile with Special Reference to Housing Finance", Ph.D. thesis, University of Strathclyde, Glasgow.
SARMIENTO, E. (1982), "Estabilización de la Economía Colombiana, Diciembre de 1976–Junio de 1978", in *Inflación, Producción y Comercio Internacional*, Procultura–Fedesarrollo, Bogotá.
SCHULDT, J. (1987), "Desinflación Selectiva y Reactivación Generalizada en el Perú 1985–1986", paper presented at a seminar on "Anti-inflationary Policies in Argentina, Bolivia, Brazil and Peru", *Trimestre Económico*, Vol. LIV, September.

SCOTT, C. (1986), "Cycles, Crises and Classes: the State and Capital Accumulation in Peru, 1963–1983", in C. Anglade and C. Fortin (eds), *The State and Capital Accumulation in Latin America*, Vol. II, Macmillan, London.

Sociedad de Agricultores, *Revista Nacional de Agricultura de Colombia* (SAC), Bogotá.

SOJO, Jose R. (1955), *Barranquilla: Una Economía en Expansión*, Corporación Civica de Barranquilla, Barranquilla.

South American Journal, London.

SPITZER, E. (1969), *The International Monetary Fund 1945–65*, Ch. 20, Vol. III, M. de Vries, IMF, Washington, D.C.

STALLINGS, B. (1978), "Peru and the US Banks: Who has the Upper Hand", University of Wisconsin, Madison, mimeo.

TAYLOR, L. (1983), "Maoism in the Andes: Sendero Luminoso and the Contemporary Guerrilla Movement in Peru", Working Paper No. 2, University of Liverpool, Centre for Latin American Studies, Liverpool.

THOMAS, Vinod (1985), *Linking Macroeconomic and Agricultural Policies for Adjustment with Growth: the Colombian Experience*, World Bank, Washington D.C.

THORNE, A. (1985), "Savings Determinants in a Developing Economy: the Case of Peru", manuscript, Oxford University, Oxford.

—— (1986), "The Determinants of Saving in a Developing Country: the Case of Peru 1960–1984", D.Phil. thesis, Oxford University, Oxford.

THORP, Rosemary (1972), "La Función Desempeñada por las Instituciones Financieras en el Proceso de Ahorro Peruano: 1960–1969", Comisión Nacional de Valores, Lima.

—— (1976), "Valuation Problems in Peruvian Trade Data 1895–1930", mimeo, Oxford.

—— and BERTRAM, G. (1978), *Peru 1890–1977. Growth and Policy in an Open Economy*, Macmillan, London.

—— (1984), *Latin America in the 1930's: The Role of the Periphery in the World Crisis*, (ed.) Macmillan and St. Antony's College (UK), St. Martin's Press (USA).

—— and LONDOÑO, C. (1984), "The Effect of the 1929 Depression on Peru and Colombia", in Thorp (ed.), *Latin America in the 1930's: The Role of the Periphery in the World Crisis*, Macmillan and St. Antony's College (UK), St. Martin's Press (USA).

TORO, Jorge (1987), "Tasa de Interes y Variaciones en el Grado de Apertura de la Economía Colombiana durante el Periodo 1967–1985", in *Desarrollo y Sociedad*, U. de los Andes, Bogotá, September.

TRIFFIN, R. (1944), "La Moneda y las Instituciones Bancarias en Colombia", *Revista Banco de la República*, August, Bogotá.

UGARTECHE, O. (1986), *El Estado Deudor. Economía Política de la Deuda: Perú y Bolivia 1968–1984*, Instituto de Estudios Peruanos, Lima.

UNESCO, *Statistical Digest*, Paris.

United Nations, *Foreign Trade Yearbooks*, New York.

URIBE CAMPUZANO, T. (1954), *Brown Gold: The Amazing Story of Coffee*, Random House, New York.

URRUTIA, Miguel and ARRUBLA, M. (1970), *Compendio de Estadísticas Históricas de Colombia*, Universidad Nacional, Bogotá.

—— (1985), *Winners and Losers in Colombia's Economic Growth of the 1970s*, Oxford University Press.

VAITSOS, C. V. (1970), *Transference of Resources and Preservation of Monopoly Rents*, Harvard University Press, Economic Development Report No. 168, Cambridge, Mass.

VELASCO ALVARADO, Juan (1972), *Velasco, La Voz de la Revolución*, Editorial Participación, Lima.

VILLANUEVA, V. (1972), *EL CAEM y la Revolución de las Fuerzas Armadas*, Instituto de Estudios Peruanos, Lima.

WEBB, Robert (1974), "Government Policy and the Distribution of Income in Peru, 1963–1973", Princeton University, Woodrow Wilson School Research Program in Economic Development, Discussion Paper No. 39.

—— (1974a), "Trends in Real Income in Peru 1950–66", Princeton University, Woodrow Wilson School Research Program in Economic Development, Discussion Paper No. 41.

—— (1987), "The Political Economy of Poverty, Equity and Growth, Peru 1948–1985", mimeo, April.

WILKIE, I. W. (1974), "Statistics and National Policy", *Statistical Abstract of Latin America, Supplement 3*, UCLA International Center, Los Angeles.

YEPES, del C. E. (1972), *Peru 1820–1920: un Siglo de Desarrollo Capitalista*, IEP, Campodónico Ediciones, Lima.

ZIMMERMAN, Zavala A. (1975), *El Plan Inca. Objetivo: Revolución Peruana*, Editorial Grijalbo, Barcelona.

Index